Harold Orlans

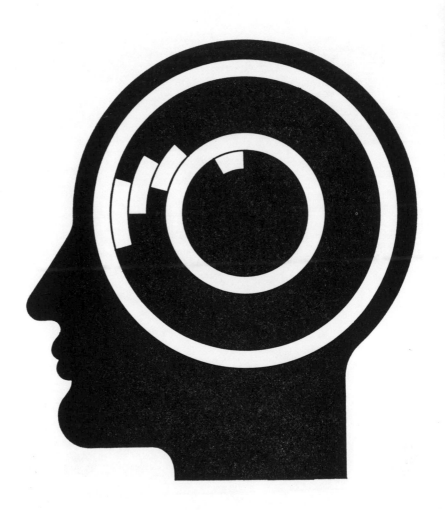

CONTRACTING
FOR
KNOWLEDGE

Jossey-Bass Publishers
San Francisco • Washington • London • 1973

CONTRACTING FOR KNOWLEDGE
Values and Limitations of Social Science Research
by Harold Orlans

Library of Congress Catalogue Card Number LC 72-11626

International Standard Book Number ISBN 0-87589-158-6

Manufactured in the United States of America

JACKET DESIGN BY WILLI BAUM

FIRST EDITION

Code 7301

The Jossey-Bass
Behavioral Science Series

General Editors

WILLIAM E. HENRY
University of Chicago

NEVITT SANFORD
Wright Institute, Berkeley

Preface

Objectivity is a quintessential objective of social science or, to be more exact, of those scientific and behavioral approaches to social knowledge which have exercised great influence in recent decades. Objectivity is a goal to which social scientists have aspired, while recognizing that their colleagues lack it in some measure and their fellow citizens in greater measure. Objectivity or dispassion, say the philosophers of social science, is the key to the portals of truth, as passion opens the portals of pleasure and vanity, politics and action.

Commendable as is the search for truth, there is something unconvincing about social scientists' position. If objectivity can be acquired with a few graduate courses, it cannot be rare and difficult; many humble citizens must have as much or more of it than many social scientists have. If subjectivity and self-interest are so prevalent in others, can they be absent among social scientists?

My answer to that question, which is discussed in the first chapter, is "no." I agree with Gunnar Myrdal that bias cannot be eliminated from social science; it can only be acknowledged or detected. In fact, I am more pessimistic than Myrdal, who does not give adequate weight to the bias which goes unrecognized for years because it is shared by all members of a profession, a nation, or a generation. The elements of bias, self-interest, and salesmanship in the public proclamations of social scientists are noted repeatedly in *Contracting for Knowledge*.

Social scientists speak with many voices, quiet and loud, precise and slovenly, modest and brash, unemotional and passionate. An innocent bystander who paid equal attention to everything they said might conclude that theirs was a tower not of learning but of babel. The experienced sponsor of research and the experienced spokesman for the professions are not that innocent, but their sophistication can render them discreet— which is to say, silent— about certain troublesome matters that occupy professional circles. In this respect, the spokesman acts not as a scholar, who is supposed to present all the significant facts bearing on the question at hand, but as an advocate, who presents facts which serve his cause and overlooks those which do not.

My interest in the bias and advocacy of social scientists—or, to put it more abstractly, in the sociology, psychology, and politics of their knowledge—grew during a staff inquiry which I conducted for a House subcommittee. The purpose of the inquiry was to put on record testimony and opinion of informed scholars and administrators about the adequacy and usefulness of government social research programs, preparatory to possible hearings by the Research and Technical Programs Subcommittee of the Committee on Government Operations, chaired by Representative Henry S. Reuss of Wisconsin. This testimony, related information, and documentary material were published in four volumes titled *The Use of Social Research in Federal Domestic Programs* (Reuss, 1967, cited henceforth by Roman numeral and page, thus: II, 122). As it happened, hearings were never held, and in 1969 the subcommittee itself was disbanded.

Since Senator Fred Harris (1967a) and Representative Dante Fascell (1965) held hearings on government social research in foreign areas just prior to the Reuss inquiry, we concentrated on social research dealing with domestic problems. We examined extramural research, which is conducted for the government under contracts and grants, because it is easier to identify than intramural research by government staff, which frequently merges with, and is indistinguishable from, program planning, evaluation, and statistical and administrative activities. As it turned out, some three-quarters of identifiable social research expenditures were allocated extramurally. The inquiry consisted of questions circulated to two groups of social scientists and administrators, who will shortly be described, and ad hoc queries to government officials, leading scientists, university business officers, foundation officials, and others.

Contracting for Knowledge does not repeat or summarize all the information obtained in the Reuss inquiry or the conclusions that may be drawn from it. Some of that summarizing has already been done in the introductions to the published volumes, and another summary appears elsewhere (Orlans, 1968b). Rather, I discuss a number of the broad issues which are posed by government-sponsored social research but which could not be dealt with adequately in the report, drawing freely upon other sources, on selected portions of the inquiry, and on subsequent work.

Some explanation should be given of the terms I use. I use the term *social research* because it is noncommittal about the verifiable general laws implied by social "science" research. "Behavioral" science is too limited and modish; if the government were confined to behavioral research, which excludes products and unique events, it would receive a far thinner gruel of information than it needs.

In the Reuss inquiry, social research was defined to include research in what the National Science Foundation (NSF) calls social science and in social psychology, which NSF classifies with physiological psychology under the separate rubric *psychology:* "*Social research* includes research in the social and behavioral sciences, including economics, sociology, political science, cultural anthropology, archeology, economic and social geography, history, social psychology (including educational, personnel, and developmental psychology, and research on personality, group processes, interpersonal relations, opinions, and attitudes), and other social sciences. Social sciences are directed toward an understanding of the behavior of social institutions and groups and of individuals as members of a group. In addition to work in disciplines or subjects traditionally considered social science, it is intended that this field should also include work in other disciplines or subjects in which the work is undertaken primarily for the purpose of understanding group behavior" (I, 20–21). In other contexts, social research includes forms of empirical inquiry into social phenomena that NSF might not deem sufficiently "scientific" to support.

In reporting their research expenditures for the NSF statistical series, agencies have been more liberal about their interpretation of social science and research than NSF has been in its grants programs. Nonetheless, the NSF definition of research provides the ostensible basis for the most widely cited statistics of government expenditures, and it was necessarily accepted in the Reuss inquiry: "Research is systematic, intensive study directed toward fuller scientific knowledge of the subject studied. Such study covers both basic and applied research. *Basic research* is research that is directed toward increase of knowledge in science. It is research in which the primary aim of the investigator is a fuller knowledge or understanding of the subject under study, rather than a practical application, as is the case with *applied research*. Research does *not* include programs of demonstration, training or education, routine data collection; the construction of buildings and facilities; or the development of equipment, materials, devices, systems, methods, prototypes, and processes" (I, 20).

The central purpose of *Contracting for Knowledge* is to assess the value and limitations of the knowledge yielded by applied social research, and my conclusion is that such research has considerable value but, because of the irremediable uncertainties of social knowledge, not as much as many social scientists have claimed. An additional purpose is to subject the claims of social scientists to the same critical scrutiny which they are accustomed to apply to others.

The three chapters of Part One present three bodies of fact that are often overlooked by protagonists of the social sciences: the political views of social scientists, the political and social positions which the major social science associations have adopted, and the generally unimpressive and politicized efforts of these associations to develop ethical codes. Facts of this kind are, I submit, manifestly important in assessing the practical uses of social research and the confidence that can be placed in it. Most derive from the open literature, especially from the journals devoted to public issues of concern to each profession. That these facts have been neglected in discussions of the value of social research may be because they are embarrassing: they disturb the posture of political neutrality, social responsibility, and personal moderateness which leading social scientists assume in their role as experts, in their appearances before Congress, and in their appeals for an influential role in public policy-making. In truth, the problems posed by the politics of social scientists and by the public policies and ethical standards of their associations are extremely troublesome politically and intellectually. They plague each association and distress many members who see themselves both as dispassionate scholars and as politically responsible citizens, as professional men who can and must observe society objectively and as moral men who, living in that society, can and must assume their share of responsibility for what transpires there.

I do not know any solution to these problems that will satisfy all factions among the professions and the laity, and I doubt that one exists. A number of feasible alternative solutions will set the professions off on different courses, to the satisfaction or dismay of different factions. The two main alternatives are a putative apoliticism no longer credible or tolerable to many activists and rebels, humanists and inhumanists, professional men and laymen, and a more open politicization that can tear the associations apart and cannot forever be concealed from, or financially indulged by, the political professionals in Congress and the Administration. The middle course seems to be one in which leading professionals condone and temper many expressions and actions that they cannot stop, hoping for tolerance from government officials, who are not without comparable problems of their own.

In Part Two, I turn from the painful spectacle of the fratricidal professions to consider what use social scientists may be to the government, taking as my point of departure the views expressed by respondents to the Reuss inquiry. Chapter Four discusses what responsibility the scholar may have to government agencies which are not the incarnate image of his desire but carnal instruments of our collective needs and contradictions. As will be seen, most scholars evidently believe that they have little responsibility, or no more than they wish to assume. When they do assume some and undertake research for the government, what is the product? What kinds of knowledge do they believe they can provide and, examining the matter critically, what kinds should the government prudently expect and sponsor? Chapter Five addresses these highly academic and highly practical questions, and Chapter Six considers the difficulties of government program evaluation, a type of research that has promised more than it has delivered.

As these chapters and certain other sections rely heavily on statements submitted to the Reuss inquiry, something more should be said about how they were obtained. A set of twenty-one questions (III, 4–8) was sent to prominent social scientists and officers of independent research organizations. The questions were, for the most part, broad and difficult. They raised such enduring issues as the contributions that social scientists can make to the resolution of social problems, the degree to which an investigator's bias may influence his findings, the best institutional location for different kinds of research, and who should be responsible for the maintenance of ethical standards in research; several dealt with administrative issues such as government restraints on the release of research and the desirability of establishing an Office of Social Sciences in the Executive Office of the President.

The men to whom these questions were sent were respected in their professions as well as knowledgeable about federal programs, employed by both academic and nonacademic organizations, located in different regions, and engaged in both pure and applied research. They were chosen with the advice of numerous authorities, including the secretaries of five professional associations, who were, however, in no way responsible for the final selection. They included roughly two dozen economists, political scientists, psychologists, and sociologists; seven to ten persons each from anthropology, history, and operations research or survey research; and smaller numbers from geography, law, management consulting, psychiatry, and other fields. Of the 146 persons addressed, 53, or 36 percent, replied. That rate may be considered poor by normal survey standards or adequate in this instance in view of the number and difficulty of the questions and the fact that only a few weeks could be allowed for the reply. In any event, these replies are presented not as statistically representative but as informed and thoughtful and worthy of attention.

Neither the initial population nor the final group of respondents was statistically representative of all social scientists and especially of younger men and those less well informed about and more hostile to government programs. However, an effort was made to obtain dissident as well as "respectable" opinion, and a reading of the replies demonstrates the seriousness with which many leading scholars took the inquiry. Their views (found in Reuss, III) merit attention, and that is the only claim I make for them.

A second set of twelve questions (II, 26–27) about the adequacy and quality of federally sponsored research was sent to more than thirty social scientists and administrators of research and operating programs in each of six domestic areas: crime and law enforcement, education, poverty, social aspects of medicine and health, social welfare, and urban problems. (Their responses are in Reuss, II.) The substantive judgments about the quality and adequacy of research in these six areas are summarized in the Reuss report (II, 1–23) and are repeated here only where they are most germane to the broad issues with which I am concerned. (All told, 199 persons were asked to reply to one or the other set of questions. Sixty-two, or 31 percent, responded.)

Having discussed the main kinds of knowledge that the government can expect to receive from social research, I turn in Part Three to certain institutional aspects of this research. Chapter Seven examines allocations to academic and nonacademic organizations and the work which respondents believed each sector was best qualified to conduct, while Chapter Eight reports on the controls exercised by different agencies over the release of research findings. These two issues are related, for the location of research is often determined by the control exercised over the resultant report: usually, academic research can be released freely whereas nonacademic research requires prior governmental review. Chapter Nine considers the quality of sponsored research, which often leaves something to be desired.

The last section, Part Four, discusses not only the overt but the implicit uses of social research. There has been much talk of late about how to improve the "utilization" of social research. That word is discussed in Chapter Ten, which reaches the irreverent but, I believe, accurate conclusion that what is meant by "utilization" is the adoption of (usually liberal) changes espoused by social scientists. Administrative measures to enlarge social scientists' influence in government and the intractable problem of searching and seizing the right knowledge at the right time are discussed in Chapter Eleven. The concluding chapter argues that a fundamental function of social science is not to attain an unattainable certainty but rather to foster a sense of confidence in the midst of uncertainty. Thus, some of the essential uses of social research are subjective and, in a real sense, religious.

I want to thank Kathleen Archibald, Edna Gass, William E. Henry, Eugene M. Lyons, Jesse Orlansky, Gilbert Y. Steiner, and seven anonymous readers for their frank (and the more anonymous, the more caustic) comments which helped me to revise and, I hope, improve this manuscript. I also want to thank Edna Gass and Congressman Henry S. Reuss for sanctioning the congressional staff inquiry upon which much of *Contracting for Knowledge* is based and some 150 prominent social scientists and research administrators for their thoughtful responses to that inquiry. To subject their views to critical examination is to take them seriously, and to share their interest in the truth.

Washington, D.C.   HAROLD ORLANS
January 1973

Contents

THREE : LOCATION AND CONTROL OF
SPONSORED RESEARCH

FOUR : USES OF SOCIAL KNOWLEDGE

Contracting for Knowledge

Values and Limitations of Social Science Research

1

Social Scientists' Politics

What are the political views of social scientists? The more readily accessible information yielded by national surveys is summarized in Table 1. The methodological weaknesses of many surveys are evident: some are based on large numbers whose representativeness is uncertain; others, on small samples whose recollections of their votes in earlier elections are not necessarily representative of the votes of their professional colleagues in those years. A more serious distortion may arise from excluding nonvoters, political independents, Socialists, supporters of other third parties, and those whose political views were not ascertained. And much of the information is surprisingly dated. Until April 1970, when preliminary results of an important national survey conducted by Seymour Lipset, Martin Trow, and Everett Ladd were reported (Scully, 1970), the timeless horizon of academic scholarship apparently contained only one published finding about the presidential votes of a national sample of social scientists for any election after

1956. However, the additional information about political predilections presented in Table 1, Part B, and in the reports of the
studies summarized therein, is so remarkably consistent, and consistent, too, with a large body of opinion, that the following generalizations can be made.

Since at least 1948 and, more likely, the 1932 election of
Franklin Delano Roosevelt, a large majority of social scientists have
preferred Democratic to Republican national candidates and
policies. During the last two decades, if not over a longer period,
social scientists also appear to have undergone an increased "De-
mocratization," which may be attributable to a marked concomitant
reduction in their support for Socialist and third party candidates.
For example, Socialist candidate Norman Thomas drew 5 to 18
percent of sociologists' votes in each presidential election from 1928
to 1948, after which he ceased to run; in 1948, 17 percent of sociologists, 14 percent of psychologists, and 11 percent of political scientists voted for third party candidate Henry Wallace, Norman
Thomas, or other minor candidates (Turner and others, 1963a,
1963b; McClintock and others, 1965).

The data suggest that the allegiance of most social scientists
to the Democratic Party has been shared by social workers, his-
torians, philosophers, and other humanists, in contrast to the Republican preferences of most faculty in business, engineering, and
agricultural schools. The political outlook of most academic scientists is not so clear from the data at hand. The prominent role
played by social scientists in academic petitions to change American
policy in Vietnam is demonstrated by Ladd (1968, 1970), and
other evidence suggests that they have played a similar role in supporting student protests (Somers, 1965; Langer, 1965; Ladd and
Lipset, 1971).

"The facts about the politics of American intellectuals are
fairly clear," Lipset writes (1959; and see also Lipset and Dobson,
1972). "During the twentieth century, the great majority of aca-
demics (particularly those in the social sciences), as well as most
significant literary figures and most leading journals of opinion,
have been opposed to conservative thought and action in political
and religious realms." The facts have not been lost to the Republican Party. "It was anomalous to many Republican leaders that

Table 1
PARTY PREFERENCES OF SOCIAL SCIENTISTS, 1948–1970

A. Percentage Voting for Democratic Presidential Candidate[a]

Professional Group	1970	1968	1967	1964	1962	1960	1959	1956	1955	1952	1948
Sociologists		90						79		80	80
Political scientists		86						75		71	66
Anthropologists		85									
Psychologists		82				80		68		64	69
Social scientists		80		90						66	69
Economists		77									

B. Percentage Favoring Democratic Party[b]

Professional Group	1970	1968	1967	1964	1962	1960	1959	1956	1955	1952	1948
Sociologists											
Political scientists	84		79			88–83	82–79				
Psychologists					80–77						
Social scientists									75		
Business economists		27									

[a] Among those voting for Democratic and Republican candidates; nonrespondents, nonvoters, and those voting for other candidates are excluded.

[b] Among those indicating a preference for Democrats and Republicans (usually in national elections); nonrespondents, independents, and those favoring other parties are excluded.
Sources: Fedor (1968), Ladd and Lipset (1972), Lazarsfeld and Thielens (1958), McClintock and others (1965), Scully (1970), Spaulding and Turner (1968), Turner and others (1963a, 1963b), Turner and Hetrick (1972), and, for the 1967 entry, tabulation of a membership survey provided by Earl Baker of the American Political Science Association.

virtually all studies showed that college-educated people voted Republican in substantially higher percentages than did grade school—or even high school—educated people. Yet this correlation seemed to be reversed at the Ph.D. level, at least in the social sciences, and among the intellectual opinion leaders in general" (Monsen and Cannon, 1965, p. 212). One outcome of this rankling observation was the establishment by the Republican National Committee of an Arts and Sciences Division in 1959 to identify faculty with Republican sympathies and to secure their help in Republican Party activities and particularly in national and local election campaigns. In 1966, one-third of the membership of several thousand professors and researchers were said to be natural scientists and the remainder, largely political scientists; but, without denigrating its achievements or other efforts to rally intellectuals to the Republicans, the Party cannot be said yet to have changed the dominant Democratic and liberal complexion of the intellectual and especially the social science communities.

Horn (1966) observes that "when the Republican Party was founded it was the party not only of the urban businessman . . . , the free farmer . . . , the free laborer . . . , but also of the intellectual." However, as he and other Republican liberals and intellectuals have regretted, that "also" is no longer true. "The great mistake of the Republican Party since the time of Theodore Roosevelt," Lippmann writes, "is that it quarreled with the intellectual community . . . and alienated them, and then under [Republican Senator] McCarthy's regime persecuted them, and they all went over to the Democrats and that gave the Democrats an intellectual capacity for dealing with issues that the Republicans simply don't have" (1965, p. 224).

Lipset suggests that intellectuals are liberal because "the size and decentralization of American intellectual life remove the individual intellectual from contact with other sections of the elite and give him a sense of deprivation" (1959, p. 472). Shils (1949) speaks of social scientists' "contemptuous and fearful alienation from the holders of power." And Parsons (1959) writes, "It is because of, not in spite of, a high and rising status that most intellectuals, being energetic and ambitious people, are dissatisfied with what they have." Friedrich Hayek believes that bright conservatives go into business and other profitable pursuits, while bright radicals, rejecting the profit system, are more inclined to intellectual activities (Lipset and Dobson, 1972, p. 165). Others have sought to construct a political demography of the professions in which older full professors with higher incomes, Protestants and religious men from small towns, educated and employed at smaller private institutions are more likely to be Republicans, and younger faculty of lower rank and income, non-Protestants or irreligious men from larger cities and larger public institutions, Democrats; over each profession a distinctive ideological veil descends in graduate school that colors the subsequent social and political views of its members (Spaulding and Turner, 1968). Glazer (1967) observes that "Sociologists are for the most part liberal Democrats, with a substantial minority further to the left. We may find Republican political scientists and economists; but if there are Republican sociologists, they are not the leaders of the field, and they are rather quiet." He then tries to explain this sociologically. "Sociology . . . is the newest and least secure of the social sciences and the one least connected with the traditional upper classes. Political science, economics, history, and even anthropology all do better: young Rockefellers may become anthropologists, but hardly sociologists. [But why not? Both Prince Peter Kropotkin and Count Leo Tolstoy tried their hand at sociology.] Sociology attracts students from marginal groups: Jews today, Negroes tomorrow. . . . The social groups from which sociologists are recruited are new groups, aspiring groups . . . , parvenu and *nouveau riche* groups."

The analysis is interesting, but—setting aside the small matter of evidence—too short sighted in its time perspective. The substantial representation of Jews in departments of sociology, particularly at leading universities, has occurred primarily since World War II. "Throughout the thirties and well into the forties, our major universities were still staffed almost entirely by old-stock Protestants. Except for a few fields like anthropology, it was almost impossible for a Jew to obtain a tenure position on the faculty . . . departments of sociology were among the worst offenders as far as anti-Semitic hiring policies were concerned" (Baltzell, 1966, p. 336).

That changes in the social composition, economic status, and type of employment of a profession should affect its political and social outlook is quite likely; but this has been intimated better than it has been demonstrated. However, for our present purpose, the origin of social scientists' politics and ideology is not as important as its nature and consequences in their work.

That political and personal conviction or bias affects this work—in the choice of problem, in the facts and theories which catch attention, and, thus, in the nature of conclusions—cannot, I believe, be denied without denying social scientists their humanity. However, the precise nature of these effects, and indeed of the biases which engender them, is debatable. They can be gross or subtle, deliberate or unconscious, manifest or covert. And the biases that divide social scientists are plainer than those that unite them, which become visible only after time renders them distant and strange. So, biases of a past (or, to the young, of an older) generation are easier to detect than those of the present, just as strange customs are easier to recognize than our own—only foreigners talk with an accent.

The Reuss inquiry asked: "Is there a danger—and, if so, how serious do you believe it is—that social scientists will allow their personal and political views to color, if not their research findings, then the way they report them? How can this danger be reduced?" (Reuss, 1967, vol. III, p. 6. Reuss citations are referred to hereafter only by volume and page number). All but one of the forty-five respondents who dealt with the question recognized the danger, though all did not regard it as serious. Bias, some suggested, was significant only for certain individuals; "that a number of social scientists have served with distinction . . . under both Republican and Democratic administrations is evidence that many can work objectively without letting their work be unduly colored by personal views," Dael Wolfle reasoned (III, 212). Others saw the roots of frailty not in social scientists but in humanity: "responsible social scientists [do not] intentionally allow their personal or political views to color their findings. . . . As human beings there is always a danger that unconsciously such coloring may occur" (III, 22).

Several respondents took quite the opposite position that, at any rate in the choice of problems, strong personal views should not be suppressed since they were an asset in or a necessity for good social science. It is "important that social scientists worthy of the appellation be allowed to let their personal and political views dictate which problems deserve their attention and how solutions to those problems may be derived," Robert Krueger, head of the Planning Research Corporation, declared (III, 118). Anatol Rapoport doubted that a person without strong personal and political opinions on matters of social importance would make a good social scientist: "the motivation would be lacking" (III, 163). Herbert Simon observed, "We expect an applied scientist to respond to values—an engineer to the value of good roads, and a doctor to the value of good health"; controversy arises only when values conflict (III, 186). Others agreed that problems of bias arose also among natural scientists, whose "political views can readily be camouflaged as technical judgments and . . . [who] can masquerade as experts on social science and political affairs" (III, 144).

The predominant view was that the problem of bias is most serious in the realm of action or policy formation, when the social scientist forsakes his more neutral role of factual analysis. However, bias could not be eradicated even in the technical heartland of professional work since it could derive from either intellectual obliviousness or consciousness. The effects of experimenter attitudes and expectations upon subjects' responses, which Rosenthal (1966), Friedman (1967), and other psychologists have described, afford a striking example of what may be called the bias of obliviousness. Stuart Rice astutely noted the equally widespread bias of consciousness. "Because of the vast range and complexity of social life and of the interactions within it, the relative importance of a particular social problem is automatically exaggerated when it is singled out for research. This in itself may produce the effect of bias in the research findings" (III, 169).

How should bias be dealt with by social scientists and public officials? The most common response was that truth is winnowed from the chaff of bias by the normal processes of scientific research, whose most important features are full publication of the data and the methods upon which conclusions are based, so that they can be subjected to critical scrutiny and replication by professional colleagues. The sponsorship of such replication and of independent studies of the same problem by different agencies and social scientists representing a spectrum of opinion would help to isolate objective facts from diverse personal and social biases. One significant spectrum of views is that between the generations; accordingly, the government should "support the research of younger social scientists, often in less conspicuous universities, whose reputation does not depend on the perpetuation of a particular point of view" (III, 106). An alternative to multiple studies by persons with divergent views is the choice of "persons who do not have strong positions . . . on the topic at hand" (III, 56). Another is the review of manuscripts prior to publication by scholars of diverse viewpoints. The counterpart procedure for a government agency is the use of diverse consultants to review and evaluate important research. This procedure can be particularly helpful in maintaining the quality of classified and confidential research not subject to public professional scrutiny.

Prime responsibility for guarding against bias was placed on the social scientist himself, who has an obligation to be alert to the possibility of bias, "to be rigorous in his work and to label personal views as personal" (III, 141). Some called for "an explicit statement of relevant personal values from the researcher" (III, 33). Thus, two contrasting (or, perhaps, parallel) approaches to the personal control of bias were advocated: rigorous restraint and open avowal.

The practical measures advocated to mitigate bias included an emphasis on what Simon termed "the 'is-ought' distinction" (III, 186) and Arthur Burns called the distinction between "fact" and "policy . . . objectivity in research can be more surely achieved if there is a clear demarcation between the results of research, which tend to concentrate on findings of fact, and policy recommendations, which are nearly always bound to be affected by value judgments" (III, 53). James Coleman even suggested that statisticians be employed more often in lieu of social scientists: "the use of statisticians rather than social scientists . . . will insure less biased results. Their greater use of quantitative techniques, their greater dedication to the method and the integrity of the method, means that they are more likely to let the chips fall where they may" (III, 56).

In a lengthy appendix to *An American Dilemma,* Myrdal (1944) examined and rejected this idea that bias can be mitigated by an emphasis on statistics and the strict separation of "facts" from "recommendations" (pp. 1038, 1041–1044, his italics):

> . . . biases in social science cannot be erased simply by "keeping to the facts" and by refined methods of statistical treatment of the data. *Facts, and the handling of data, sometimes show themselves even more pervious to tendencies toward bias than does "pure thought."* . . . *When, in an attempt to be factual, the statements of theory are reduced to a minimum, biases are left a freer leeway than if they were more explicitly set forth and discussed.*
>
> *Neither can biases be avoided by the scientists' stopping short of drawing practical conclusions.* . . . [*Biases*] *are not valuations* attached *to research but rather they* permeate *research. They are the unfortunate results of* concealed *valuations that insinuate themselves into research in all stages, from its planning to its final presentation.*
>
> . . . There is no other device for excluding biases in social sciences than to face the valuations and to introduce them as explicitly stated, specific, and sufficiently concretized value premises. *If this is done, it will be possible to determine in a rational way, and openly to account for, the direction of theoretical research. It will further be possible to cleanse the scientific workshop from concealed, but ever resurgent, distorting valuations.*

Some respondents indicated that those who seriously breach normal standards of objectivity will suffer professionally for it. However, cases are not unknown in which those who flouted the standards of their profession—such as Sigmund Freud, Wilhelm Reich, C. Wright Mills, or, in their own way, Margaret Mead and Marshall McLuhan—went on first to public and later to professional recognition. Surely, in the present national mood, passionate forms of expression may be rewarded in professional as well as political circles.

Communicating, like quarreling, takes two people. To interpret research findings and to cope with their defects and biases requires a considerable degree of experience and sophistication. Sophisticated consumers are as important to maintaining the standards of intellectual merchandise as of other products. Accordingly—as Davis Bobrow rightly observed—to make proper use of social research, administrators must learn to detect its biases and their own, "so that they do not only recognize as biases views different from their own" (III, 33). In this process of interpreting and using research, there is no real substitute for "broad public discussion—among scientists, and with laymen—of scientific findings that lead to policy recommendations, with a view to laying bare the value assumptions" (III, 186). It is hard to disagree with Arthur Brayfield's observation that "Social and behavioral scientists who become directly involved in public policy issues expect to be confronted with searching questions from policy and decision makers. They wear no cloak of special privilege. Their judgments as well as their facts are open to question. This is a normal process in science itself as well as in public affairs" (III, 44).

It is often contended that social science is necessarily radical in its intellectual and political implications because any dispassionate examination of existing institutions must be critical, and any public exposure of their defects, disenchanting. Thus the anthropologist Francis Ianni, who was for some years responsible for the research programs of the Office of Education, stated that "by admitting the necessity of the search for new knowledge we implicate our present practices . . . research is fundamentally revolutionary" (II, 124). A similar line of thought can be found in the report of the Organization for Economic Cooperation and Development (1966), which asserts, "Any social science research cannot help being a critical enterprise, capable of (at times forced to) questioning the grounds of political decisions, the prevailing concept of power and the modes of its exercise, the goals of a given society and the techniques used to achieve them" (p. 48). But why does the criticism of a part imply or require criticism of the whole: Do we reject those we love because of their imperfections? And why must new knowledge necessarily revolutionize existing practice instead of entrenching it by indicating how weaknesses and flaws can be remedied or removed? That is precisely the radical's complaint against liberal social science: that by ministering to the ailments of society it serves to perpetuate existing institutions instead of overthrowing them.

Freud's profound pessimism about the limitations of human character and the irreconcilable conflict between man and society affords little hope for a socialist utopia—but with a few revisions in his doctrine, Reich and Erich Fromm could readily envisage one. The sociology of Herbert Spencer and Emile Durkheim, William Sumner and Talcott Parsons was an instrument to preserve and extol their society; indeed, the founder of sociology, Auguste Comte, believed that a truly scientific sociology would necessarily have conservative consequences, for what was the point of rebelling against a scientific law?

> . . . the positive spirit tends to consolidate order, by the rational development of a wise resignation to incurable political evils. . . . Human nature suffers in its relations with the astronomical world, and the physical, chemical, and biological, as well as the political. How is it that we turbulently resist in the last case, while, in the others, we are calm and resigned, under pain as signal, and as repugnant to our nature? Surely it is because the positive philosophy has as yet developed our our sense of the natural laws only in regard to the simpler phenomena; and when the same sense shall have been awakened with regard to the more complex phenomena of social life, it will fortify us with a similar resignation . . . in the case of political suffering [Comte, 1896, p. 186].

Spencer (1896) reasoned similarly that a science of society "will dissipate the current illusion that social evils admit of radical cures. . . . [Social] evils are not removed [by social action], but at best only redistributed" (pp. 19–21).

But anarchists, populists, and radicals of all persuasions rebel against the laws of man, not nature, and *their* sociologists— Friedrich Engels and Kropotkin, Mills and Herbert Marcuse—explain why it is necessary to do so. "Necessity" is the mother of revolution and reaction, of change and stability, and the reasoned call for one or the other must, therefore, be an expression of conviction, not knowledge—or, rather, a marshaling of that knowledge which serves one or the other conviction. There are good social scientists within and without every major church, army, and social cause; their work is not less good for serving a cause nor is the cause any less political for their service.

To summarize, all available evidence indicates that, for several decades, a decided majority of academic social scientists have preferred the Democratic Party to the Republican in national elections. A substantial minority have also been political independents or, especially before 1952, have supported third party and Socialist candidates. Of late, there has been a resurgence of radical opinion, 9 percent of academic psychologists and economists, 14 percent of political scientists, and 19 percent of sociologists characterizing themselves as politically "left" in one survey (Scully, 1970). Islands of Republicanism have survived in schools of business, the National Association of Business Economists, and, doubtless, other special preserves.

The dominant Democratic sympathies of social scientists have resulted from their liberal political and social disposition—or (to use their own language) ideology and bias. Respondents had varied, and in part contradictory, suggestions for reducing the effects of such bias in social research. Some suggested that the utmost scrupulousness, concentration on quantitative methods, and careful separation of facts from opinions and recommendations should eliminate or diminish bias. That has been the general hope, belief, and teaching of the large central schools of academic and applied social science. Other respondents argued to the contrary, as has Myrdal, that subjectivity can no more be eliminated from the selection of data than from their interpretation; that bias, being human, is ineradicable from the work of human investigators; and that political views inevitably influence research conclusions.

A great deal of attention has been devoted to the problem in the professional literature. Both optimistic and pessimistic conclusions abound, and different conclusions appear warranted in dealing with different data, for a count of heads or railroad cars does not present the same problems as an assessment of attitude, intelligence, or achievement or the analysis of almost any contentious social and economic issue.

The pragmatic test of objectivity—that some staff have satisfactorily served both Democrats and Republicans—is good but insufficient. It may simply be a test of adaptability and may demonstrate nothing more than the large area of shared values, or common bias, which identifies the middle range of our politics and distinguishes one political system, nation, and generation from another.

The following remarks should be labeled plainly as opinion because, though facts can be adduced to support them, they are unlikely to convince readers who disagree (and can cite another set of facts).

Myrdal's view that political bias can be declared but not eliminated embarrasses the claim of social scientists to conduct strictly apolitical analyses of public problems. Many who represent the social sciences in governmental affairs would like to mute political discord by confining the activities of their profession to the (preferably undefined and inexplicit) sphere of centrist political ideology. But they too have had their troubles and have been attacked by young and radical colleagues as an establishment which, precisely because of its apolitical stance, courts the powers-that-be rather than those that might be.

To my mind, the "establishment" is right on the practical strategy for getting research funds and strengthening the social science professions, for in union there is strength; but the radical critics are right in their fundamental intellectual point that a man, even an academic man, has to stand somewhere, and that social scientists can no more escape their political and ideological functions than they can escape the time into which they are born. As things stand, success for the critics would represent an intellectual victory but a political defeat, for the social science professions would be broken into fragments associated openly with every major political cause. The supposed neutrality of social scientists is already threatened by their overwhelmingly liberal and Democratic allegiance, which raises serious doubt about the capacity of many to serve without bias either a Democratic or a Republican administration and to seek the truth on public issues and nothing but the truth, without fear or favoritism.

If (as I believe) Myrdal's position is correct, then the liberal social changes often recommended by social scientists are not the only changes compatible with all the available data, for the recommendations and the selection of data upon which they are based must also be compatible with the investigator's personal and political biases. This correspondence between recommendations and personal preferences is, of course, equally true of research that reaches centrist or conservative political conclusions.

There is nothing wrong with social reform, but it gives a distinctly protagonist flavor to much of the social sciences. And while there is also nothing wrong with protagonism, it is unrealistic to expect political antagonists to finance their opponent's work or to stand silent with awe and admiration at its scientific pretensions. The *Origin of Species* was a great work of science not only because Charles Darwin gathered evidence for his theory for more than twenty-eight years but because he devoted those years in equal measure to an examination of the evidence that might disprove it.[1] When social scientists become as assiduous in their attention to negative evidence as to that which confirms their predilections, they will merit the status of scientists more than they now do.

---

[1] See especially Chapter VI, "Difficulties of the Theory"; Chapter VII, "Miscellaneous Objections to the Theory"; and the first part of Chapter VIII, on "Instinct." In the final chapter, Darwin writes: "That many and serious objections may be advanced against the theory of descent with modification through variation and natural selection, I do not deny. I have endeavored to give them their full force." How many social scientists treat their own theories this way?

2

Public Policy
and Professional
Associations

"Who speaks for science?" Sayre (1961) once asked. "No one really can, but almost everyone does" might summarize his answer. And if that is true for the natural sciences, is it not more true for the social sciences, in which any honest and intelligent person, speaking at least with the authority of an object to whom their laws should apply, can provide evidence to bolster or discredit many a grand theory? How fortunate are entomologists that insects do not talk back to them!

Sayre was concerned primarily with the question of who can speak in the public arena for the interests of scientists, rather than for the truths of science. But the two points are related, because the public is interested in scientists for their access to certain truths; and, though a truth may initially be discerned only by one man, it must be recognized and certified as true by a number of

15

reputable scientists before a public agency is likely to do much with it. To be sure, the truth is not usually determined by the majority vote of experts. But public agencies may naturally turn for advice—on both what is good policy and what is true—to the principal associations, which should combine a broad enough membership and a serious enough interest in the truth to be able to speak with competence on both points. Yet the five major social science associations (with the periodic exception of the American Psychological Association) have seldom been able to speak effectively for their professions. The responsibilities they have failed to discharge have, perforce, been assumed by ad hoc groups and individuals.

This is not the place to recite the history of the social science associations, but clearly they have been dominated by the academic sector of each profession and particularly by faculty engaged in research at leading universities. Members engaged primarily in undergraduate teaching, academic administration, or nonacademic work have seldom exerted influence in their association commensurate with their numbers. Partial exceptions are the important (but, to them, inadequate) roles of clinical psychologists in the American Psychological Association[1] and of museum-based anthropologists during the early years of the American Anthropological Association. More characteristic are the abstention of potential members who are simply not interested in what interests university faculty (most secondary-school teachers of government have abstained from membership in the American Political Science Association); the withdrawal of members who fail to obtain significant recognition and their occasional establishment of independent associations (as, dissatisfied with their status in the American Economic Association, business economists established in 1959 the

---

[1] Bugental (1967) complained that: "The APA now numbers about 25,000 members. A very small proportion of these (Spence . . . estimates 1,000) is committed to and actively engaged in narrow, laboratory experimentation and publication of their findings. This 4% or less of APA seems to the professional [that is, the clinical psychologist, among others] to want to demand that the whole of psychology be made in its image. They want to preempt the PhD, the title 'Psychologist' and the government of APA. The great bulk of APA does not publish research. The bulk of APA is concerned with other than the narrow parochial issues of the psychonomes."

National Association of Business Economists) ;[2] conscious measures to maintain faculty control by relegating other members to subordinate status; and acceptance of the rule of scholars by members whose interests are largely served by receipt of the association's journal. In exchange, ordinary members enlarge the association's influence—and budget, as Ogg observed four decades ago:

> *It is characteristic of American learned societies (in contrast with the typical European academy) that they embrace in their membership not only scholars but laymen. . . . The latter maintain a more or less passive relationship, which, however, in any event includes payment of yearly dues. . . . The typical American learned journal is, therefore, the organ of a society dominated by scholars but numbering among its members and supporters people who are not equipped either by training or disposition, to do research. . . . This is true of the American Historical Review, the American Economic Review, the American Journal of Sociology . . . the American Political Science Review [1930, pp. 187–8].*

Ogg went on to say that the learned journal must not, therefore, "be so technical, in manner and substance, as to repel the intelligent but non-specialist reader." That this could hardly be said

[2] "Of 71 presidents of the American Economic Association, every one has been an academic. So have virtually all the other officers in the AEA, despite the fact that about one-third of all economists are business economists. Without exception, every medal the profession has given has gone to the academic economist" (Silk, 1969).

At the April 1949 meeting of the AEA executive committee, "A protest was communicated . . . complaining that business economists were not adequately represented in the organization and activities of the A.E.A. . . . The plea was . . . for a recognition of these members in the consideration of candidates for office, participants in the annual program, contributors to the Review, and other activities. It was suggested [in reply] that no professional lines are being drawn in the selection of personnel but that each member stands on his own merits" (Bell, 1950).

The National Association of Business Economists' charter declares that "To be eligible for membership, a person must have an active interest in business economics and be associated with private business either as a proprietor, employee, or consultant . . . full-time government, academic, or trade union economists are not eligible for membership."

today of the last three journals cited reflects significant changes in the character and composition of the associations. As their size has grown and their beachhead in the graduate schools has expanded, affiliations with neighboring disciplines, represented by the common departmental titles of earlier years (such as philosophy and psychology, history and political science, or economics and sociology), have been attenuated and the specialized modern disciplines have emerged, each with its own concepts and methods and a special language spoken by its own corps of Ph.D.'s. "True learning," a wit has remarked, "is being killed in the Universities slowly, by *degrees.*" Perhaps the social sciences have grown so academic because, maturing in a period when the entire higher education enterprise expanded so vastly, the largest proportion of their Ph.D.s have been taught not to work in the outside world (like medical and law students, for example) but to teach others; and upon graduation, most have remained in academia.

Lindsey Harmon's studies show that at every period examined from 1935 through 1965, from 60 to 80 percent of new social science Ph.D.s remained in academic employment. In 1962–1966, psychology was the only social science in which teaching was not the first job taken by a majority of fresh Ph.D.s (National Academy of Sciences, 1968, p. 5; 1967, p. 87). In 1970, more than 80 percent of Ph.D. sociologists, political scientists, and anthropologists, 75 percent of Ph.D. economists, and 59 percent of Ph.D. psychologists were employed by educational institutions (Table 2). However, most professional associations remain hospitable to laymen and students. Non-Ph.D.s outnumber Ph.D.s two to one in the political science and sociology associations, and in the anthropology association, almost four to one; only in the American Psychological Association were half the members Ph.D.s.

Evidently, dominance by academic specialists is maintained not by numbers but by a natural alliance of intellectual interests. In the psychological, sociological, and anthropological associations, this has been bolstered by the assignment of non-Ph.D.s and graduate students to inferior membership categories, though students have recently won voting rights in the latter two associations (with results which have shaken the outlook particularly of the anthropological association) and those with master's degrees may soon receive full

Table 2
Numbers in Various Social Sciences, 1970

Field	Professional association members	Number in NSF register	Ph.D.s in NSF register	Ph.D.s on campus	Percent of Ph.D.s on campus
Psychology	30,839	26,271	17,593	10,465	59
Economics	18,908	13,386	7,225	5,449	75
Sociology	13,928	7,658	3,690	3,229	83
Political science	13,663	6,493	3,996	3,421	86
Anthropology	5,857	1,325	1,260	1,043	83

Source: National Science Foundation (1971) and association publications.

membership in the psychological association. The political science and economics associations continue the tradition of one-class membership, open to all and with equal rights to all, that characterized the five associations at the outset.

The establishment of two or more classes of members is not, of course, merely a device whereby a few self-qualified fellows can rule a larger number of members who are thereby pronounced to be professionally unqualified. It is part of a trend toward professionalization that has progressed furthest in psychology—where diplomates are issued by the association to certify fellows' competence in specialized fields and where, as of June 1972, legal licensure was required for clinical practice in forty-six states—and least far, or hardly at all, in economics and political science. This trend is of concern to the public and particularly to the government, since some kind of professional certification might ease the burden of identifying those who are really qualified to perform the increasing number of services being requested of social scientists.

However, except for the American Psychological Association, with a five-million-dollar annual budget, substantial real estate and publication properties, a staff of 160 and relatively sophisticated management, the social science associations are, by any normal test of organizational performance, frail and inefficient enterprises, barely capable of running their present affairs let alone assuming major new public obligations. With a part-time secretary and part-time editor to serve more than twenty-six thousand members and subscribers, the American Economic Association has issued a journal and held annual meetings but for most other purposes has been virtually nonexistent; the many significant activities which have made economists influential and powerful in Washington and Wall Street have been conducted through every other conceivable channel. The American Anthropological Association, evacuated in 1967 from the Carnegie Institution of Washington to quarters in an apartment house that had seen better days, was literally, not figuratively, on the verge of bankruptcy, and the June 1968 issue of its journal did not appear until November. Though influential members have sought to convert the former American Sociological Society into a more professional association, changing its name to the American Sociological Association, establishing categories of membership, raising the dues for fully certified members, and moving from New York to Washington in 1963 (to more modern quarters than those of the AAA), the August 1968 issue of *their* journal was not distributed until December. The American Political Science Association has accumulated assets totaling $2.7 million in 1968; as its members and friends include key figures in the Executive and Congress, it is potentially a highly influential association; but during the 1960s, internal discord and distrust of at least some of its officers grew. It took six months to elicit a response from the executive secretary during the Reuss inquiry.

If association staff have often been unable publicly to present either their own views or those of their association, this has been due to the difficulty of representing members who are divided about, and not organized to facilitate, the adoption of policy positions or their effective implementation. Thus, the secretaries of several associations have declined recent congressional invitations to testify, suggesting that the association president, or members representing diverse views on the issue at hand, be called. Rarely have they had the authority given in 1967 by the council of the American Historical Association to its executive secretary, Paul Ward, to testify on the proposed National Foundation for the Social Sciences at his discretion, either as an individual or on behalf of the association. The governing council of most associations meets infrequently; authority to act during the interval may or may not be delegated to a smaller executive committee, and executive secretaries have experienced frustration in attempts to contact busy committee members whose service is unpaid and often unappreciated. "[The secretary of another association] may get six answers to twenty-five special delivery letters; I may get three, to eight," one secretary remarked in a 1968 interview.

Several factors operate to perpetuate this situation. Money is one, since more frequent and effective meetings and communications might require an increase in dues. The turnover of officers elected for short terms, the ignorance of many scholars about the most elementary facts of Washington, and their disinclination to assume administrative responsibilities or to appear before congressional committees are further handicaps.[3]

---

[3] The secretary of one association tried ten members before one agreed to testify at the sympathetic hearings on establishing a National Foun-

It is difficult for a mass-membership scholarly association to delegate authority to a committee or staff and to ensure that their work will not later be rejected by the membership. Many members firmly oppose any increase in the size and influence of the association bureaucracy. Some regard association officers and staff as a clique or establishment that serves its own interests or, still worse, those of insidious forces headquartered in the Pentagon, big business, the multiversity, and the Ford Foundation. They may object even to the acceptance of National Science Foundation grants to improve the curriculum in their field or to include members in the National Register. Association supporters are not slow to defend its activities or to attack the rebels' introduction of "political" issues as a threat to the scientific standing of the profession. Battles are fought between those who favor public service activities and those who would confine the association to scholarly and scientific concerns and between those who desire rigorous standards for graduate departments and association members and those who regard such measures of professionalization as incompatible with the independence of intellectuals and the shaky status of knowledge in their field. Ensnared in these conflicts, overworked, and suspect from many sides, it is not surprising that the poor association secretary is often rendered immobile.

Sensible Psychologists

The American Psychological Association should be neither misrepresented nor glorified. The magnitude and variety of its activities and the sophistication of its management contrast so markedly with the more faltering operations of its fraternal associations in the social sciences that it seems the only professional one while the others appear amateurish. Psychologists can be as foolish in their public utterances as anyone else; and the association has been rent by serious dissension between scientific and clinical psychologists. "This has been a turbulent year in the APA organiza-

dation for the Social Sciences held in 1967 by the rising liberal Democratic Oklahoma Senator, Fred Harris. The staff of several congressional committees and of private agencies seeking to enlarge the public influence of social scientists, and several episodes in the Reuss inquiry, confirmed the typicality of this experience.

tion," the chairman of the APA Board of Professional Affairs declared in 1965. "Charges of professionalism and scientism have been traded, calls for crusades have been broadcast, and threats of secession have been hurled" (Bordin, 1965). "Some members feel that the association has not acted with sufficient speed and force on either social issues or professional concerns, e.g., insurance reimbursement and legislation affecting the relationship of psychology to other professions. Other members feel that too much attention is given to such concerns and urge concentration on the scientific and scholarly roles of the APA" (Eichorn, 1968).

More than two decades ago, a group of members who felt that the APA was too little concerned with social problems formed the Society for the Psychological Study of Social Issues, now an affiliated section of APA. In 1971, a group of activists organized CAPPS, the Council for the Advancement of the Psychological Professions and Sciences, to lobby for fuller recognition of psychology in such legislation as the health professions manpower and national health insurance measures. The APA can be as torpid as other bureaucracies. The chairman of its board of professional affairs laments that "it can take at least two years for committee reports to be approved and action taken. If a report or policy recommendation is sent back . . . for revision . . . a minimum of another year is added" (Schultz, 1972). Nonetheless, the APA has enough established programs and interests to keep its large staff busy, and it has managed to function in the public arena without confronting daily and on every issue the kind of harassment and fierce ideological disputation that has beset political scientists, sociologists, and anthropologists, though it has hardly upset the wondrous repose of economists.

Among the objectives of the APA, its bylaws state, are "to advance psychology as a science *and as a means of promoting human welfare* . . . [and] to advance . . . *the application of research findings to the promotion of the public welfare*" (my italics). The 1953 APA code of ethics states forthrightly that "the welfare of the profession and of the individual psychologist are clearly subordinate to the welfare of the public."

The APA executive secretary undoubtedly holds the record among the five association secretaries for testifying before congressional committees and, probably, for informal consultation with government officials. However, only infrequently has the association taken policy positions on public issues not plainly related to psychology, though that may be changing under the pressure of events (and, broadly interpreted, psychology, like the other social sciences, can embrace most things human). Thus, the council declined, in 1961, to oppose a resumption of nuclear testing, stating that the "Association should speak for the psychological profession on social and political issues only when psychologists have a professional expertise which is clearly relevant to the issues involved." Nonetheless, it supported University of California faculty who refused to sign a loyalty oath in 1950; it has opposed racially segregated convention facilities; and it has recently required evidence of nondiscriminatory employment from all organizations doing more than a ten-thousand-dollar-a-year business with the association.

In 1958, the board authorized the appointment of a committee to examine "the role of psychologists in the maintenance of peace," which was succeeded the following year by a committee on psychology and national and international affairs. Committee members, competent and outstanding, have pondered some of the great problems of our time and every time; they have issued reports—often recognizing the need for additional research—and somehow the foundations of the association have not crumbled. In 1971, a new department of social and ethical responsibility was formed to deal with the association's ethical standards and public policies. And in 1972, in what executive officer Kenneth Little termed "an extraordinary and unusual action," the board expressed "its profound distress with the continuation of the killing and uprooting of the Indochinese population. . . . We find it morally repugnant for any government to exact such heavy costs in human suffering for the sake of abstract conceptions of national pride or honor. . . . As students of human behavior, we have a special obligation to speak out against such wanton destruction of human life and celebration of violence and killing" (APA Board, 1972).

It may be that the secret of the APA success, relative to other social science associations, in dealing with public issues lies in the greater adulteration of its academic elements by members with practical interests in clinical practice, education, industry, and government; in the greater segmentation of its members into sections with special interests so that, being thus recognized, they are more tolerant of the special interests of others; and in the overall vigorous promotion of bread and butter issues, while it hews, in a moderate way, to the central liberal doctrines of American life. However, sheer size has encumbered its action and bred frustration among its several constituencies. Believing that unity now imparts less strength than federation might, the Policy and Planning Board (1972) has proposed that the APA become a federation of constituent societies: "the heritage of high scientific and academic aspirations can no longer be protected through the forcing of all psychologists into a common mold."

Somnolent Economists

The charter of the American Economic Association, the most somnolent large assemblage of social scientists, states that it "will take no partisan attitude, nor will it commit its members to any position on practical economic questions." But charters can be changed or disregarded; another provision, that the AEA shall encourage "especially the historical study of the actual conditions of industrial life," has been disregarded since the ascendancy of econometric and quantitative approaches. After World War I, great debates developed in the AEA about the tariff and other economic policies. After World War II, a committee on public issues was appointed "(1) to arrange for the preparation of statements on issues of public policy and (2) to formulate questions on which the entire membership . . . , or specialized groups therein, would be circularized, and to report the results of such circularization to the President, who shall have the authority to decide whether or not to give the results publicity and at what time. The Executive Committee suggests consultations with an expert on the formulation of questions for opinion polls and the presentation of the results." Several polls of specialists were undertaken but apparently none of the general membership, and when Sumner Slichter, chairman of the public issues committee, submitted a brief report on economic stability to the AEA executive committee in 1949, the executive committee noted that the "responsibility for content of the reports is solely that of members signing."[4] In any event, the committee was designed to analyze alternative policies, not to agree on the desirability of any one.

The postwar policy activities of the AEA may have crested at that point. Recognizing the native divergence between conservatives and liberals on major economic issues, and between scholars and activists on the adequacy of economic knowledge to guide policy, leading economists evidently reached a tacit accord that the AEA should remain a forum for scholarly discourse while the potentially divisive issues of policy would be pursued and debated elsewhere. That course seems to have succeeded in preventing serious disruption—or vitality—in the association's affairs. The AEA has resisted all pressures to enlarge its staff (it is the only social science association without a full-time professional secretary), to move to Washington (it is the only association still in the political hinterland), and to engage in uncountable activities. In 1960, the AEA gave glancing attention to the problems of preserving economic data and making them more accessible to the profession; but somehow Richard Ruggles, deputized to explore this question, ended up doing so under the aegis of the Social Science Research Council; and the work of his committee and that of a subsequent committee chaired by Carl Kaysen which lead to the proposal for a national data center and to extensive congressional hearings on the dangers such a center posed to privacy, were thus disassociated from the AEA. To Senator Harris' proposal that a National Social Science Foundation be established the AEA executive council responded that "it would be inappropriate for the Association to adopt an official position."

Programs to inform the public about the status of knowledge in their field or to improve curriculum, particularly in secondary schools, have been undertaken by associations reluctant to embark on other public activities. When the Committee for Economic Development offered to finance a national task force on economic education "if the President of the American Economic Association would appoint the members," President George Schultz did so

---

[4] See *American Economic Review,* May 1948, p. 530 and May 1950, p. 593).

early in 1960; but G. L. Bach (1961), chairman of the task force, made clear immediately that his committee "is a completely independent unit . . . responsible neither to the Committee for Economic Development nor to the American Economic Association for its recommendations." This position was adopted to protect everyone concerned; it may nonetheless appear that there is an ambivalence in seeking AEA sponsorship only to disown it. If so, it is an ambivalence frequently encountered among the sponsors of policy research.

The subsequent activities of the task force and its successor, the committee on economic education, proved so successful that they have pushed the AEA toward a greater show of life. "During the past two years," Bach (1967) wrote, "members of this Committee have been increasingly involved in attempts to represent the profession in contacts with government agencies, especially the United States Office of Education and the National Science Foundation. . . . Unless economics is represented in such discussions, as a practical matter the funds tend to go elsewhere, for teacher workshops, for research undertakings, for teaching experiments, and the like." Similar arguments made for many causes of interest to many AEA members have been met by arguments to maintain the association at a level where life is preserved but not pronounced. So far as can be judged by the price that new Ph.D.'s bring and the influence of economists in business and government, the moribundity of the AEA has not harmed, and may possibly have enhanced, the rewards and power of economists. That result in itself is a significant lesson for anyone inclined to exaggerate the importance of social science associations to their members.

Both proponents and opponents of greater association activity could draw support for their position from two episodes that threatened to flare up into major battles within the AEA as within other associations; but in the deoxygenized environment that enables the profession to tolerate all the data it ingests, the flames soon flickered out.

At the 1967 annual meeting, many members felt that the association should take a position on the Vietnam war. Informed about the constitutional prohibition of policy statements, they responded that the constitution should be changed and that the AEA should survey membership opinion on the matter, which was not prohibited by the constitution. The executive committee stated that it was not inclined to sponsor such a survey, because of the difficulty of stating the issues accurately, and reaffirmed its opposition to political statements.

In 1968, the hot issue was whether the AEA should cancel its Chicago meetings, as the four other social science associations had done, either to protest police actions against demonstrators at the August Democratic National Convention or (as the Council of the American Psychological Association phrased it) because such a meeting place would be poorly attended. When the executive committee split five to five on the issue, President Kenneth Boulding cast the deciding vote to meet in Chicago. In a letter of explanation to AEA members, he wrote, "I believe that the meeting can be used, more effectively, in Chicago, as a fulcrum to help move the future rather than as a stick to belabor the past. I propose that we devote time . . . to a searching discussion of the agonizing discontents of our world." The Chicago meeting was, indeed, poorly attended. As promised, a special discussion was held, though how searching it was, and how much it may move the AEA to anything but additional discussions, is moot.

The following December, in New York, some twenty-five members of a group of radical economists interrupted the annual business meeting and eventually succeeded in having their spokesman read a statement denouncing the association and the profession: "Economists are the priests and prophets of an unjust society. They preach the gospel of rational efficiency, justifying the reduction of man and nature to marketable commodities. . . . The economists have chosen to serve the status quo. We have chosen to fight it" (MacEwan, 1970). Political discontent with the association and intellectual discontent with its journal—"a quaint periodical containing mathematical models understandable to but a portion of the economic profession and totally incomprehensible to almost everyone else" (Sackrey, 1971)—have led to the recent formation of new associations and the issuance of new journals by institutional economists, welfare economists, black economists, radical economists, and other groups. But the AEA marches on with accustomed obliviousness.

Apolitical or Political Scientists?

In 1972, the American Political Science Association appeared a few short steps ahead of the AEA in corporate activity, but it had paid a price in internal discontent for many steps that it took. To dip into the pages of the *American Political Science Review* and recall a few episodes noted there affords no balanced picture of the association's varying detachment from and involvement in public affairs. But it does indicate the perennial character of the choices which the association has faced and suggests that the consequences are likely to be less momentous than seems to be the case at the moment of decision.

Until 1968, the APSA constitution stated that the "Association as such is non-partisan. . . . It will not commit its members on questions of public policy nor take positions not immediately concerned with its direct purpose." That, however, was a declaration of relative and not absolute principle, within which it remained possible for the association and its governing council to do what they really wished.

Even a glance at the past demonstrates that the APSA has not been quite so pure in its avoidance of policy recommendations and actions as some members seem to think. During the 1940s, an association committee chaired by George Galloway devoted four years to preparing a report on *The Reorganization of Congress* which contributed to the establishment in 1945 of a Joint Committee on the Organization of Congress that subsequently agreed with all but one of the Galloway committee's recommendations.

The explosion of atomic bombs in 1945 led APSA president John Gaus to appoint a committee to follow nuclear developments. When it reported to the executive committee, one member offered a resolution endorsing civilian control of a U.S. atomic energy agency and U.S. cooperation with United Nations efforts to promote international control of atomic energy. Though several council members observed that such a resolution would be contrary to the provisions of the constitution, it was adopted, six votes to five. At the same astonishing 1946 meeting the executive council also endorsed the inclusion of the social sciences in a proposed National Science Foundation.

The 1954 annual business meeting adopted an outspoken resolution to the effect that APSA should "advise all members of the Special Committee of the House of Representatives to Investigate Tax-Exempt Foundations, Reece Committee, that it objects to the false statements of fact and conclusion contained in the staff reports of that Committee and to the haste with which its public hearings were closed and rebuttal testimony cut off." The resolution authorized the executive committee to initiate "as soon as possible" discussions with the American Civil Liberties Union "and other appropriate organizations" about ways they might work together to promote "academic and civic freedom."

And in 1961, an APSA committee chaired by Millett (1962) issued a scorching indictment of political science instruction at many higher education institutions which, had it been taken seriously, could only have led to some form of accreditation of at least graduate departments. The committee annulled the union of history and political science: "Today, this particular combination of scholarship serves no useful academic purpose." It professed that political science instruction should be discontinued unless a college "has the resources to meet acceptable standards of quality," which apparently demanded a requisite number of political science Ph.D.s teaching a requisite number of courses for no more than a requisite number of hours at an institution whose library had a requisite number of political science volumes. "We have given some thought to establishing a procedure for the accreditation of departments of political science," the committee wrote; but having worked itself up to that point, it drew back, aware that the association would not follow.

In the latter 1960s events took the lead and the association followed. In February 1967, the press disclosed that the executive director of APSA, Evron Kirkpatrick, and its unpaid, part-time treasurer and counsel, Max Kampelman, were also officers of a non-profit organization, Operations and Policy Research, Inc. (OPR), which had received funds "from foundations said to have received funds from Central Intelligence Agency sources." A committee of four past APSA presidents was appointed by APSA president Robert Dahl to look into the episode and "the broader and extremely complex problem of standards of behavior for all political scientists in their relationships with government agencies." The threat to the composure of the association was evident in the speed with which the committee reported to the executive committee and the latter, in turn, to all members in an April 6 letter stating that the association "has received no funds directly from any intelligence agency of the government, nor has it carried on any activities for any intelligence agency." However, APSA had received grants from the Asia Foundation, an acknowledged conduit for the Central Intelligence Agency, to finance memberships, travel grants, and fellowships for a few Asian political scientists. OPR had indeed received funds "from foundations reported to have received money from CIA," but for "unclassified research completely under OPR control."

The four ex-presidents concluded, "Nothing that has come to our attention lends the slightest credence to concern that any use might have been made of the APSA for intelligence purposes. . . . We think it appropriate to acknowledge, on behalf of the membership of our organization, the great service which both Kirkpatrick and Kampelman have rendered to the American Political Science Association" (Dahl and others, 1967). To commend the services of two officers surely lay within the competence of former presidents; but to speak for a membership whose opinions had not been ascertained was an assumption of authority to represent the unrepresented that recurs often enough in the pronouncements of scholars.

To look into "the broader . . . problem of standards of behavior for all political scientists," Dahl appointed a new committee chaired by Marver Bernstein, whose work will be discussed in the next chapter.

In a 1963 survey of APSA members, Somit and Tanenhaus found 42 percent agreeing and only 12 percent disagreeing (46 percent were undecided) that "There has developed an inner group in the American Political Science Association which, in large part, controls the key panel assignments at the annual Association meetings" (1964, pp. 16–17). The discontent latent in that opinion was fueled by the Kirkpatrick-Kampelman episode and fanned by rebels against the apolitical posture—or imposture, they would say—of APSA. Thus Christian Bay (1967) protested the lack of genuine discussion of genuine issues at the annual business meeting in 1967 (the only regular occasion when association activities and policies can be discussed and voted on by all members present):

> *Next year I trust time will be set aside for meaningful discussion of issues affecting our roles and responsibilities as professional political scientists. And I trust we will find a way to defeat or rise above the ban on the expression of political principle by the APSA. . . . If the APSA cannot be moved to place concern for politics above a more convenient concern with public and governmental relations, then surely we need a new Society for the Study of Political Problems for those of us who want to get out from under the wings of our own establishment.*

Bay's proposed society moved closer to realization immediately after the meeting, which so distressed him and a goodly number of his colleagues that they organized a Caucus for a New Political Science. To Caucus members, APSA was not just an association to promote the "scientific" study of politics but one "to preclude . . . study and discussion of all of the great social and political dilemmas facing American democracy today" and especially "searching, critical examination of the weaknesses of American's democratic institutions" (Caucus, 1968).

By the September 1968 business meeting, it was plain how much progress the dissidents had made. To the "nonpartisan" clause of the constitution that meeting added the exact sentence requested by the Caucus: "But the Association nonetheless actively encourages in its membership and its journals, research in and concern for significant contemporary political and social problems and policies, however controversial and subject to partisan discourse in the community at large these may be." The meeting also adopted one constitutional amendment, endorsed both by Caucus spokesmen and their abhorred establishment, to the effect that "The Association shall not be debarred . . . from adopting resolutions or taking

. . . other action . . . in support of academic freedom."[5] and another enjoining "Officers and employees . . . from engaging in intelligence and other covert activities."

So many sessions of the program were turned over to the Caucus that some opponents began to demand equal time at the annual meeting for their own panels. Another line of attack was directed at the palpably undemocratic procedure under which association policies were determined by the vote of the 2 to 6 percent of members who might be present at an annual business meeting. These critics very reasonably requested that any contested elections for association office, any proposed amendments to the constitution, and any proposed resolutions contested by at least 20 percent of the members voting at a business meeting be resolved by mail ballot of the membership.[6] It takes no great discernment to forecast that the vote of the normally silent majority of members might dampen fires that a small number of activists could stoke at a business meeting. From election and resolution voting, one Caucus officer subsequently deduced that "the 'establishment' position seems, at present, to have the support of approximately two-thirds of the membership whereas the Caucus position is supported roughly by one-third" (Fox, 1971).

Sociological Carnival

Developments within both the sociological and anthropological associations resembled those within APSA. The former associations have a "fellow" category that puts them further on the road to professionalization than is APSA and may make it somewhat easier for their ruling councils to control student dissidents;

[5] At the annual business meeting of September 1967, President Dahl had ruled unconstitutional a resolution in defense of academic freedom, a ruling that epitomized the separation—indeed, the decapitation—of the academic mind from its corporal body. Evidently a cry of pain at an arrow piercing the body did not befit the dispassionate objectivity of political "science."

[6] Letter by twenty-one APSA members, including Donald Herzberg, Stephen Bailey, Sebastian de Grazia, Charles Jones, and James McCamy. P.S., Fall 1968, 44–45.

however, relatively more of their fellows appear to be radically critical of American society.

The same complaint that the association has been run by a clique or an establishment is encountered among sociologists, and it has been charged also that the hold of that establishment was strengthened by the association's move to Washington and by the adoption, in 1963, of a new constitution enlarging the powers of the governing council. If so, it is a peculiar establishment, for two recent ASA presidents, Moore and Rose, alerted members to the danger of its existence,[7] and a third, Sorokin (1965), openly criticized the growing power of the ASA executive office and the trend toward professionalization—the "deflection of the Association from . . . the pursuit of scientific knowledge . . . [to the] pursuit of the professional interests of sociologists." Former ASA president Parsons (1966) did not so much dispute this analysis as welcome what his Harvard colleague resisted. "We have to develop an organized Executive Office in place of . . . purely voluntary services . . . and we have now elevated that Office to a major position of power and influence, necessarily so if our functions as a professional group were to be effectively performed."

While Sorokin berated him for wielding too much power, the poor ASA executive officer stood immersed in the association's affairs and, like Dr. Dolittle's pushmi-pullyu, often could not know which way to move. The world, he pointed out patiently, affected sociologists at many points, and while the association waited to make up its mind on these points, there was no assurance that the world would wait for it. Should the issues involved in government financing and use of social research, he asked, "be left to individual con-

---

[7] "I have heard some talk to the effect that this report [proposing revisions in the ASA constitution] is a method of consolidating the control of a clique or cabal or establishment. Read the proposals, please, with care, and then ask what bearing they have on such a suggestion," Moore advised members (1965). Rose, who was subsequently elected ASA president (although death prevented him from assuming office), warned that "the Secretary has . . . enough power to run everything in ASA between Council meetings except the nominations committee . . . he can greatly influence the professional lives of the members of the Association, and I know of instances when this has been done arbitrarily. . . . I believe that there should be as much dispersion of power in a scientific society as is possible without damaging efficiency seriously" (1965).

sciences and preferences, or should the Association, after sufficient study and debate, adopt official positions? . . . If not, external events may affect . . . sociologists and their research in significant ways, and ultimate decisions may be made without their advice and consent" (Volkart, 1967).

Taking as his point of departure the desirability of changing the government's Vietnam policy, one ASA member envisaged the establishment of a national academic lobby staffed by full-time lobbyists; as a start, the ASA should form a committee on public policy to develop "coherent and imaginative alternatives to present government policy" (Scheff, 1968). The cost in labor and money of developing serious alternatives to the government's well-financed program and policy development activities was a matter he did not go into. An ASA committee appointed in the spring of 1966 was discontinued the following year on its chairman's recommendation because funds were not available for even one meeting (Coser, 1967). Another committee, able to meet frequently because its three members all lived in Washington, for two years conducted a considerable investigation on behalf of the association and nonetheless reached a pessimistic conclusion about the usefulness of such committees in representing the interests of the profession. Its experience is worth relating.

The following resolution was adopted at the 1966 annual ASA business meeting: "Whereas, Social scientists who accept U.S. Government grants must now submit their questionnaires to the Bureau of the Budget for approval if the project is conducted in this country, and the project itself must be approved by the State Department if it is cross-national in scope. . . . Resolved, That the Executive Office be asked to cooperate with a committee whose task will be . . . to recommend to the council appropriate action toward restoring freedom of social research under governmental grants." Plainly, these issues were important to the profession. But, as the committee that was appointed pursuant to the resolution later noted (Biderman, 1967), the Budget Bureau review which the ASA deplored had been initiated in response to earlier protestations by social scientists, including the ASA itself; indeed, committee member Stuart Rice had played an important part in instituting the Bureau's review procedure in 1942. Was the ASA to fly from pillar to post, ignorant of the past and ill-informed about the present? The resolution contained significant factual errors, for most social scientists conducting research on government grants (as distinct from contracts) were *not* subject to Budget Bureau or State Department review.

In its final report, the committee noted that the measures that had been singled out for criticism and investigation could not satisfactorily be considered in isolation from important related issues such as the protection of individual privacy and the disclosure of the sponsorship and findings of research. But beyond that, just because it had worked diligently at its task, the committee despaired of accomplishing anything significant. Merely to explain adequately the situation that had led to the Budget Bureau and State Department controls would require a lengthy report; but that would be of doubtful value because the situation was not static—for example, the Budget Bureau had made significant changes in its review procedures, which were too recent to assess. And why recommend further ASA action and the monitoring of the government's response if ASA was not set up to provide such monitoring or authorized to act upon it? Accordingly, the committee concluded that "the question assigned it will only be adequately approached if the Association establishes permanent and continuing mechanisms for taking account of the broad range of problems involving the relationships between sociology and the government, and more generally, the public." As a final thrust, the committee observed that "both sets of governmental review procedures that have been our subject operate under explicit injunctions to maintain working relationships with the relevant professional associations. However sincere governmental interests in such relationships [may be], it does not appear that ASA is adequately organized for them" (Biderman, 1968).

For the ASA, as for other professional groups, the special hangup in recent years has been U.S. policy in Vietnam, which may safely be regarded as both public and political, but professional "only" in the sense that the lives of many, if not all, members of the profession were affected by it to a greater or lesser extent. At the 1967 ASA meeting in San Francisco, this issue obtruded in the form of a telephone call from the hotel management to the council reporting "that a demonstration was in progress and that some confusion existed"; which generated from the council the unanimous response that "(1) The Council need take no action on the demonstration; (2) the Association is not responsible for the behavior of its individual members; (3) if legal action is necessary it should be taken by the hotel" (Williams, 1967, p. 225). While thus disowning any responsibility for the behavior of its members, the association assumed some responsiblity for that of its government. In what former president Moore (1967) termed an "unseemly hubbub" and all but "mob rule," the August 1967 business meeting approved by voice vote a resolution demanding "an immediate end to the bombing of Vietnam and the immediate withdrawal of American troops from South Vietnam."

Under the terms of the ASA constitution, this resolution comprised an expression of "sentiment" to be conveyed to the council, rather than an official ASA statement; and should the council disapprove—which in this case it did—both the resolution and any alternative resolution proposed by the council would be put to all voting members by mail ballot. In due course, ballots were thus mailed to the 4,429 voting members. Following a brief explanation that the council felt that the ASA should not take a stand on political issues, members were asked the following two questions:

This Resolution concerns a matter on which the American Sociological Association, as a scientific and professional body, should [should not] take an official position
Regardless of above answer check one of the following:
[   ] *I favor the Members' Resolution*
[   ] *I am opposed to the Members' Resolution.*

The result was that 65 percent of respondents agreed with the council that ASA should not take an official position on this issue, but 54 percent nonetheless favored the members' resolution; which was a good way to have their cake and eat it too (Results . . . , May 1968, p. 164).

The political storms thus weathered in San Francisco burst all over the 1968 annual meeting in Boston. William Gamson (1968) analyzed well the reasons why many, especially younger, activists rejected the apolitical stance of professional objectivity. To

them, the conflicts in Vietnam and in American cities were not just
two among thousands of "political" issues but critical moral issues
of the time "on a par with [those] . . . faced by German intellectuals during the 1930's." They believed it impossible to be both
apolitical and alive. They saw "the sociological guild" adopting
innumerable (implicit, if not explicit) political positions that served
the powers that be; why, then, ban contrary positions? To activists,
apoliticism was a pose that perpetuated existing institutions; they
wanted not merely to understand society but to change it.

In Boston, the association encountered threats that a com-
motion might occur at the plenary session to be addressed by
Health, Education and Welfare secretary Wilbur Cohen. Secretary
Cohen spoke about the gap between social knowledge and social
policy, and described the work being done to develop statistical
"indicators" of the nation's social condition. While he spoke, protesters circulated leaflets among the audience, and when he had
finished, Martin Nicolaus (1969), speaking for the protesters by
agreement with ASA officers, took the rostrum to charge that the
sociologist is "a kind of spy. . . . The professional eyes of the
sociologist are on the down people, and the professional palm of the
sociologist is stretched toward the up people. . . . What if that
machinery were reversed? What if the habits, problems, actions,
and decisions of the wealthy and powerful were daily scrutinized by
a thousand systematic researchers?"

The following night, the protesters—variously estimated to
number from fifty to three hundred persons, mainly graduate students and young faculty—gained support from Whitney Young
(1968), executive director of the National Urban League, who
excoriated sociologists for their "scientific" outlook. "Historically,"
he declared, ". . . sociology in this country was deeply concerned
with the problems of ethnic minority groups, including black people.
. . . from the late 20's to the late 30's, sociology was almost synony-
mous with social reform. . . . But by the 40's . . . sociology took
a disastrous turn toward irrelevance. . . . 'Scientific Sociology'
meant an allegedly scientific study of man divorced from programs
of action. . . . Sociologists of the period, and it has continued
. . . right up to the present day, said they were building a science
of society. People became digits."

At the business meeting next morning, members defeated a resolution calling for "an end to American imperialism" and support of "the just objectives of national liberation movements . . . whether or not they may be influenced by communism." They were then confronted with a resolution presented by The Caucus of Black Sociologists calling for black participation on the ASA council and committees, in professional sessions with "major relevance to the Black community," and as referees of papers submitted to ASA journals. The resolution—was it "professional" or "political"?— was approved by the meeting and the ASA council, and President Ralph Turner "solicited copies of a list of black sociologists so that the names might be available to Council and other ASA Committees considering Committee appointments."

There was then presented to the meeting a resolution that, lacing passion and error with a trace of fact, moved from events at the Chicago Democratic Convention to epic historical judgments. The concluding passages may convey the tenor:

> . . . *almost all the violence this spring and summer . . . has come from those who are against freedom and justice from the people in power. We cannot direct our outrage exclusively against Mayor Daley and the City of Chicago. Humphrey lives in Washington, his sidekick lives in Texas. Both of these men could have vetoed police violence. Neither did. Sociology must focus on cracked skulls, maced lungs, and burned corneas.*
>
> THEREFORE, *the American Sociological Association resolves to express outrage at Gestapo-like suppression and brutalization of demonstrators everywhere, both in Chicago and Prague, in Saigon and Warsaw—wherever people struggle for freedom and justice.*

This final heroic declaration, commencing with "Therefore," was adopted by the members and approved by the council with little substantive change.

Two more happenings at this sociological carnival are worth mentioning. Besides the Sociology Liberation Movement and the Caucus of Black Sociologists, there emerged in Boston an ASA

Radical Caucus which presented the following resolution to the convention:

> *1. Sociologists should do no research in which they are not permitted to publicize all findings, adverse or favorable.*
>
> *2. Sociologists should regularly communicate their findings to those who are affected by them in a language, in a medium, and at a price accessible to those affected.*
>
> *3. Any limitations imposed by the funding organization, such as questionnaire rights or rights of prepublication review, should be clearly stated in any resulting publications.*
>
> *4. University researchers whose research funds come from sources outside the university should clearly label themselves as researchers for the funding organizations, not as members of the university.*
>
> *5. Sociologists should devote an equitable portion of their energies to the solution of "problems" as defined by those who cannot pay for research.*
>
> *6. Finally, we demand that sociologists who participated in the Camelot project [the Army-financed, American University Study of Counterinsurgency in Chile] be censured by the A.S.A.*

Voting separately on each section, members rejected points 4 and 6; the remainder were approved and endorsed also by the ASA council.[8]

It is difficult to follow accurately what has been happening subsequently in the ASA—and also in the anthropology association. Both have extended the vote to certain categories of graduate students; yet they have withdrawn powers formerly lodged in the annual business meeting, so that resolutions passed there must be submitted again to the governing board and the entire membership before becoming official policy. The effect is to disperse the record of action in three or more places, each of which alone (and sometimes all together) is insufficient to explain what has transpired. The

---

[8] Unless otherwise noted, the foregoing account of the Boston meeting is drawn from the *American Sociologist,* November 1968; the *Chronicle of Higher Education,* September 2, 1968; and *Science News,* September 7, 1968,

entire procedure is a poor model of either democracy or reporting.

A cleavage between younger, nonvoting participants and voting members emerges repeatedly in the minutes of annual business meetings. (During the 1972 political science meeting, nonmembers were for the first time excluded from the annual business session; how long will it be before other associations adopt similar controls?) Thus, nonvoting participants have approved and voting members disapproved resolutions that sociologists study the corporate, military, and bureaucratic "oppressors" of "oppressed peoples"; that all research funds "should be controlled by a collective forum of faculty and students in each institution"; that sociologists should refuse government and foundation funds; that all members should have the right to vote and hold office; that the association should meet in nonprofit rather than in commercial facilities; and that "the ten thousand dollars now allocated to the committee on public policy for the purpose of creating more ties to the government shall be used instead for legal defense of sociology faculty and students suffering arrests and university reprisals for their activities with respect to public policy" (Rossi, 1970).

Both nonvoters and voters have approved resolutions stating that all members should have the right to vote and hold office (in 1970, a year after voting members had rejected the same resolution); that a drug control bill should be based on a "rational" rather than a "punitive" approach; that the association should give one thousand dollars to Operation Black Camille in aid of hurricane victims; that ASA "urge our colleagues in the Soviet Union . . . and in all other places where anti-Semitism exists . . . to take the initiative in fighting anti-Semitism"; that ASA cease distributing the government's National Register questionnaires; and that ASA "castigates and excoriates the management" of the Washington Sheraton-Park Hotel for tolerating pay toilets and "resolves never again to meet in a hotel where such an indignity is inflicted on its members" (Rossi, 1970; 1971).

It only takes a vote to establish a majority and, thereby, a position on any issue. Although sociologists have adopted countless positions, they have had difficulty founding them on the systematic or rational methods they espouse. After devoting two all-day meetings to considering the association's involvement in issues of public

policy, the governing council concluded that "the only contributions of ASA to areas of public policy will be . . . by facilitating
the work of . . . sociologists, rather than by acting directly as an
Association" (Statement of Concern . . . , 1969). At first, the
committee on public policy appointed to implement this policy
decided that its charge—to be "austerely scientific . . . *and* reflec-
tive of political and moral commitments of the membership"—was
not viable (Grimshaw, 1970). Persevering, the committee eventually recommended an essay competition and a study of sociologists
and public policy. The council was so uninspired by this return on
its ten-thousand-dollar investment in committee expenses that it discharged the committee.

Anthropological Fissions

Smallest of the five associations we have considered, the
American Anthropological Association acquired its first full-time
professional staff director upon moving in 1959 from the Logan
Museum in Beloit, Wisconsin, to free quarters at the Carnegie Institution of Washington. In 1967, the association was rescued from
danger of bankruptcy, attributed to poor management, by a ten-
dollar emergency assessment paid by 1050 of its 1157 fellows and
additional contributions volunteered by 105 fellows.

Until World War II, anthropology was more like a clan
than a profession, since leading men knew personally all active
Ph.D.s. Thereafter, growth weakened the old familial bonds, and
the recent influx of youthful members and graduate students not
entirely devout about their elders' scholarly interests or adequately
represented in AAA affairs has been one source of disturbance.
Another has been the U. S. government. Anthropology benefited
from its connections with biology (which made it and psychology
for long the only social sciences represented in the National Academy of Sciences) and exotic character (which made it politically
less vulnerable) by receiving more research funds from the National Science Foundation than did any other social science but
psychology. But as the profession most dependent for its data on
access to overseas peoples, anthropology has also been most affected
by fluctuations in the esteem of Americans overseas. Following the

demise of Project Camelot and President Johnson's August 2, 1965, directive to Secretary of State Rusk "that no Government sponsorship of foreign area research should be undertaken which in the judgment of the Secretary of State would adversely affect United States foreign relations," anthropology also became the social science whose freedom to function is most critically dependent upon the sanction of government, a painful fact with which the profession continues to grapple.

The Camelot fiasco halted or embarrassed the work of so many anthropologists, particularly in Latin America, that the AAA executive office advised Defense Department representatives "to postpone further negotiations with anthropologists until the whole matter could be discussed at the [November] 1965 Annual Meeting of the Association." At that meeting, AAA fellows directed the executive board to explore and make recommendations on "the widely ramified issues involving the relationship between anthropologists and the agencies . . . that sponsor their research." Former AAA president Ralph Beals and executive secretary Stephen Boggs thereupon undertook, on behalf of the board, an extensive inquiry among anthropologists and agencies sponsoring their research.

In May 1966, the board, "speaking only for itself," released a statement that "the involvement of some universities and individual social scientists in 'counter-insurgency' research threaten[s] the integrity of the social sciences and trust in the disinterested scholarship and good faith of academic institutions." The statement was issued partly in response to queries by foreign (especially Latin American) anthropologists about the position of their American colleagues on the Camelot imbroglio and anthropologists' involvement with military and intelligence agencies.[9] Testifying before Senator Harris (1967b) the following month, Boggs observed that the suspicion of serving outside powers, under which anthropologists had long labored, was now exacerbated by revelations about their sponsorship by military and intelligence agencies. He stated that "an absolutely impassable barrier must be established between the

[9] The foregoing account of developments in the American Anthropological Association is taken from the AAA *Fellow Newsletter*, December 1965, March and September 1966, and January 1967.

intelligence agencies of the U. S. Government and the universities, private foundations, and international voluntary organizations engaged in research"—in short, that the government must deprive government intelligence agencies of significant sources of intelligence. Beals and Boggs also noted jointly that "a number of government decisions important to social science research have been made without consultation with professional organizations" and called for establishment of an office of social science advisor to ensure that such advice would be provided.

The Beals inquiry was rebuffed by some anthropologists but received the cooperation of an unusual number in an association whose sense of common purpose was so shaken that, in 1968, the president had to phone nine fellows before finding three who would consent to become candidates for president-elect (Rouse, 1969).

Beal's report to the November 1966 AAA meeting[10] was informative, reasonable, and moderate. It recognized that if Camelot had not arisen, "the internal situation and conflicts in Chile . . . might have produced very similar reactions at that particular time." However, the report was highly critical of the quality of certain expensive research projects undertaken overseas by independent organizations competing with and embarrassing the work of academic scholars. It expressed concern about the delay and "the potentiality of censorship" involved in State Department clearance and the additional controls exercised by some U. S. embassies in Africa. Lending credence to stories of CIA agents posing as anthropologists and anthropologists also serving as, or assisting, CIA agents, it nonetheless criticized "loose, completely unsubstantiated, and often scarcely credible allegations of spying or intelligence activities made by a few anthropologists against their colleagues."

Debate on this report and on a Vietnam war resolution turned the meeting into "the most turbulent annual gathering of the association in the memory of its senior members" (Raymont, 1966). Some months later, 93 percent of the 788 fellows who responded to a referendum endorsed a twelve-hundred-word statement on ethics which declared that:

[10] Beals gave an oral presentation at the meeting. Our account and the subsequent quotations in this paragraph are drawn from his written report (Beals and Executive Board, 1967).

*Except in the event of a declaration of war . . . aca-
demic institutions should not undertake activities or accept
contracts in anthropology that are not related to their normal
functions of teaching, research, and public service. . . . The
review procedures [of the] . . . Department of State . . .
offer a dangerous potential for censorship of research. Additional demands by some United States agencies for clearance
. . . are contrary to assurances given by Mr. Thomas L.
Hughes, Director of the Bureau of Intelligence and Research,
Department of State, to the President of the American Anthropological Association. . . . Academic institutions and individual members of the academic community, including students,
should scrupulously avoid both involvement in clandestine intelligence activities and the use of the name of anthropology,
or the title of anthropologist, as a cover for intelligence activities [American Anthropological Association, 1967].*

This statement elicited from Hughes (1968) the response that
"When foreign area research is funded, and even formulated in
considerable detail, by agencies centrally involved in foreign affairs,
it may transcend its character as a scientific enterprise and take on
political overtones. Under the circumstances, review by the [State]
Department is necessitated."

It may appear that *some* political issues were involved in this
exchange. But the propriety of AAA "political" statements was
posed more acutely by a resolution adopted at the 1966 meeting:
"we condemn the use of napalm, chemical defoliants, harmful
gases, bombing, the torture and killing of prisoners of war and
political prisoners, and the intentional or deliberate policies of
genocide or forced transportation of populations for the purpose of
terminating their cultural and/or genetic heritages by anyone anywhere. These methods of warfare deeply offend human nature. We
ask that all governments put an end to their use at once and proceed as rapidly as possible to a peaceful settlement of the war in
Vietnam." Kathleen Gough (1967), who, together with her husband, David Aberle, introduced the resolution in a stronger form,
has provided the following account of that meeting: "The chairman felt obliged to judge the resolution political, and hence out of

order. . . . A hubbub ensued . . . one member suddenly proclaimed, 'Genocide is not in the professional interests of anthropologists!' This allowed the proponent to cite previous political resolutions passed by anthropologists. . . . A motion to overrule the chair then passed. . . . The amended resolution was passed by a large majority, some of whom later said it was the strongest, and others the weakest, that they could hope for." According to *New York Times* reporter Raymont (1966), "An attempt by a group of younger members . . . to pass a resolution sharply condemning the Johnson Administration's Vietnam policy was thwarted . . . by several moderates. . . . Nevertheless, the Administration critics scored an unexpected victory when the meeting voted down the council's president . . . who had ruled the resolution out of order. It was at this point that Dr. Mead . . . was instrumental in securing the adoption of a toned-down resolution . . . [omitting] the implied attack on President Johnson."

During ensuing months, the *Fellow Newsletter* and the correspondence section of *Science* printed letters discussing the wisdom of this resolution.[11] Three former AAA presidents were "deeply disturbed by an apparent disposition among the Fellows . . . to involve the Association in political controversy" which "will in the end force the withdrawal of sections of the . . . membership and lead to ruinous dissension." Ultimately, they warned, the AAA could lose its tax-exempt status and mailing privileges and become ineligible for grants from tax-exempt foundations. One member denied that " 'These methods of warfare deeply offend human nature'. . . . Does eating human flesh deeply offend the human nature of a cannibal? Did the ritual killing offend the human nature of an Aztec? . . . We can condemn forms of warfare . . . as much as we like, but we must do . . . this as middle-class American liberals or as humanitarians . . . not as anthropologists."

A cogent response to these criticisms was offered by David Aberle, a proponent of the original resolution:

The question is not whether the Association should be political; it has made itself political. The only question is what

---

[11] The subsequent discussion is drawn from the *Fellow Newsletter*, February, May, and June 1967 and September and October 1968.

kind of political positions it should adopt. . . . We serve as a clearing house for recruiting personnel for the Peace Corps . . . and the Executive Board . . . encourages us to become Education Officers for the Department of State. These are actions that tie the Association unreflectively to the purposes of the U. S. Government. . . . those who now urge an apolitical course of action on us mean that we should be "apolitical" for the U. S. Government, not against it. . . . The Association is a body that takes political action; it must now decide what its politics are [Aberle, 1967].

Others supporting the resolution recalled again the "apolitical" scientists of Nazi Germany and affirmed the moral responsibility of scientists to address openly the human problems of their times. "To speak is to shoulder the burdens of Archimedes, Galileo, Darwin, and Oppenheimer." And Kathleen Aberle suggested that the AAA bylaws be changed so that the association's purpose would be "to advance the science of anthropology and its application to human welfare" (which would be similar to the "public welfare" provision in the charter of the American Psychological Association).

Subsequent developments suggested that, at least for a while, the AAA would broaden its conception of legitimate professional activity. Candidates for election to AAA office in the fall of 1968 set forth, in addition to their academic qualifications and experience, a brief statement of their platform, which was distributed to all members. Thus, David Aberle was elected to the executive board on this platform: "At present, the Executive Board . . . seems to regard activities in support of U. S. Government policies as service and activities in opposition to those policies as politics. One of my chief concerns is for the Association to rethink this indefensible position. . . . A second concern is for more power for graduate student members. . . . A third is for more scope in our journal for openly value-committed articles." In 1968, a special committee on organization recommended measures to increase the number of association officers and staff; to include two graduate students on a governing board of eleven; and to broaden association activities ("The distinction between professional interests and political issues was deemed frequently indistinguishable").

After graduate students were granted the vote in 1970, AAA resolutions became too voluminous to chronicle fully. On many issues, the younger and more activist members now dominated policy. The ethical and political issues associated with overseas research are recounted in the next chapter. Other issues which have concerned the association include an academic freedom controversy at Simon Fraser University; the status of minorities and women in the profession; the treatment of natives in Alaska, Brazil, and elsewhere; opposition to assertions of racial differences in intelligence; U. S. policies in Latin America and Asia; and the legalization of all consensual sexual acts. The association's changing outlook was characterized by Berreman (1971) as "The Greening of the American Anthropological Association." In the past, he wrote, "anthropologists saw the world as their laboratory. Now we find that the world is a community, of sorts, in which anthropologists are members rather than disinterested observers. Its other inhabitants talk back to us . . . all of them question us and our motives."

The new mood of open and abundant politicization, replacing the traditionally more discreet and limited political action of professional associations, has posed new problems. A Canadian member resigned from the executive board so as not to be implicated in positions based upon national, rather than international, grounds, and Canadians are now granted a choice between full or foreign membership. President Foster (1971a) observed that there was within the association "growing dissension with respect to purposes and goals. Put simply, the question is whether professional or political ends will take precedence (or what the proper 'mix' should be)."

That mix may ultimately be determined by budgetary considerations. One member has suggested that all resolutions be accompanied by a twenty-five-dollar filing fee. Foster noted that serious committee work and investigations are costly. "Before major recurrent investigating becomes a routine part of the Association's functions we must make sure this is the will of the majority . . . and that we are willing to shoulder the burden of much higher dues that will be essential."

That the increased politicization attendant on increased student involvement would not be happily received by many senior fellows was suggested by an outgoing president's address. Traditionally, this has been a scholarly address, but President Rouse (1969) devoted himself to the internal problems of the association. As he saw it, the scholarly functions of the association had been assumed by specialized societies in physical anthropology, ethnology, archeology, and other fields. In consequence, the AAA "had ceased to be an organization devoted primarily to the advancement of knowledge. . . . Instead, it has become a trade organization. . . . Its main function . . . is to promote the professional interest of . . . anthropologists. . . . We now have a bureaucracy, and must continue to have one whether we like it or not. . . . If I had a choice I would prefer to drop my subscription to the *American Anthropologist* and substitute one of the journals in my field of speciality."

Summary

The social science associations have generally been dominated by academic scholars and have primarily served their interests rather than those of social scientists engaged in undergraduate teaching, graduate study, applied research, private practice, or public service.

The two largest associations have pursued diametrically opposite courses with respect to the growth of professionalization and the advocacy of association interests. The American Psychological Association resembles (for good and ill) a classical professional association, with defined standards for membership and practice, a code of ethics, high dues, a substantial central staff, and machinery for following public affairs of concern to the profession and for determining and expressing the association's position on them. By contrast, the American Economic Association has hewed to the model of the traditional scholarly association, membership in which is open to all; whether by chance or design, the association has remained remarkably oblivious of policy questions, the many influential policy activities of economists being conducted through other channels; thus, by fighting elsewhere, economists have maintained comparative peace at home.

Despite having open membership rolls and scholarly traditions and aspirations like those of economists, the American Political

Science Association has been less successful at eschewing policy questions and in the last few years has been in the midst of considerable political turmoil. But its politicization is as nought compared to that which the anthropological and sociological associations have undergone. The anthropologists have pronounced confidential research for the government, and especially for the government's armed forces, an act of professional treason. The sociologists have adopted untold resolutions but have had great difficulty in acting effectively on any.

3

Professional Ethics
and Associations

If, as Sir Patrick Cullen remarks in *The Doctor's Dilemma*, "All professions are conspiracies against the laity," a function of professional ethics is to mitigate that conspiracy and to proclaim a profession's obligations to the public. And if the social sciences were indeed professions, they would be unrestrained conspiracies, for, as of 1972, the American Psychological Association was the only major social science association which had adopted a comprehensive code of ethics *and* taken serious steps to enforce it. However, as I argued in the preceding chapter, the social sciences can more accurately be regarded as disciplines—formerly scholarly and humanistic—in the throes of professionalization or, rather, of specialization into humanistic, scientistic, and professional elements; the five leading social science associations remain conglomerates harboring (real or putative) scholars, scientists, and professional men, in varying proportions.

The nature of these associations and their ability to enunciate

51

and enforce ethical standards governing their members' conduct is of growing practical significance. As the volume of government-financed research rises, *someone* must be held responsible for the proper and effective use of these public funds and for the professional performance of investigators. Of the principal parties who may be held morally or legally responsible—the investigator, his institution, his association, and his sponsoring agency—the association is now least accountable in any formal sense, although informally and indirectly its influence and responsibility may be great. Association membership remains voluntary; it is not necessary to the successful practice of social science research. Many poorly qualified persons do, and some prominent scholars do not, belong to the association in their field.

As has been noted, the recent interest in ethical questions, particularly by the anthropological and political science associations, has been aroused by threats to the conduct and integrity of academic research posed by the (real or presumed) ties of investigators to military or intelligence agencies. In contrast, the government's recent interest in ethical questions has been aroused by threats to the integrity of citizens posed by social science research. These threats have been investigated by several congressional committees and have led to corrective measures by the two agencies financing the largest volume of social research, the Office of Education and the Public Health Service.

In 1964, a congressional subcommittee held hearings on government use of polygraphs or "lie detectors." In 1965 and 1966, other subcommittees investigated the use of personality tests containing questions on religious, sexual, and other personal beliefs and attitudes as a condition of employment by government agencies or contractors; the administration of such tests to schoolchildren in government-financed research without their parents' consent; and the proposal to establish a central computer data bank to collate information about individuals and firms obtained in response to many separate government surveys and reporting requirements.

At the September 23, 1965, hearing of the House Special Subcommittee on Invasion of Privacy chaired by Representative Cornelius Gallagher, Francis Ianni, acting director of research for the Office of Education, stated: "the Office of Education will carefully review all questionnaires submitted to it, to prevent injuring public sensitivities in such matters as the challenging of established morals, the invasion of privacy, and the extraction of self-demeaning or self-incriminating disclosures, and the unnecessary or offensive intrusion of inquiries regarding religion, sex, politics, et cetera." In February 1966, Surgeon General William Stewart informed the heads of all institutions conducting research with Public Health Service funds that: "No new, renewal, or continuation research or research training grant in support of clinical research and investigation involving human beings shall be awarded . . . unless . . . the grantee institution will provide prior review of the judgment of the principal investigator or program director by a committee of his institutional associates. This review should assure an independent determination: (1) of the rights and welfare of the individual or individuals involved, (2) of the appropriateness of the methods used to secure informed consent, and (3) of the risks and potential medical benefits of the investigation" (IV, 223).

This policy, which applied to social as well as biomedical research, represented an attempt to deal with ethical problems that gravely concerned responsible scientists and administrators. Some problems had been brought to public attention by the 1964 episode at a Brooklyn hospital in which live cancer cells were injected into aged patients without their informed consent in research financed by the Public Health Service. In 1966, the New York Board of Regents suspended for one year the licenses of two physicians responsible for that research, finding them guilty of "fraud and deceit" (Langer, 1966). That many scientists were neglecting the rights and welfare of their subjects was the conclusion of a disturbing paper by Beecher (1966), who detailed twenty-two cases of apparently unethical research (reduced from fifty for reasons of space) and stated that 12 percent of the work reported in 1964 "in an excellent journal . . . seemed to be unethical."

Reuss Questions on Ethics

The following questions on ethics were therefore posed in the Reuss inquiry:

Of late, several ethical issues such as the individual's

*right to privacy and his right to consent or to abstain from
serving as a subject of inquiry and/or manipulation have posed
troubling questions in social research. One action that has
brought some of these issues to the fore is the Surgeon General's ruling requiring that each institution receiving funds
from the Public Health Service establish procedures to ensure
that the rights of individuals used as the subjects of research
(including psychological and sociological research) are safe-
guarded. What do you believe is the responsibility of federal
officials, professional associations, and research institutions, re-
spectively, to ensure that ethical standards are maintained in
the conduct of social research? Have each of these groups adequately discharged their responsibilities? What additional steps
should they take to do so? [III, 7].*

Half the respondents ignored the question or dismissed it with a
few inconsequential words. Among the more responsive, a number
declared that the government, professional associations, and research institutions were all responsible for maintaining ethical standards; but there was a noticeable reluctance to assign too firm or
detailed authority to government agencies, for fear that they would
become overbearing or tiresomely bureaucratic. The strongest support for government action came from two psychologists familiar
with the protection of subjects afforded by Defense Department
regulations. In their view, those regulations have protected the
rights of subjects as well as or better than have the practices often
prevailing in private research.

However, most respondents feared the restrictive consequences of government standards more than they welcomed the
possible protection these might afford to subjects. Accordingly, they
preferred to see standards voluntarily set and enforced by private
institutions and associations. They questioned the efficiency, competence, and independence of government officials and feared that
their enforcement of ethical standards might impose unreasonable
restraints on research, produce needless delays and paperwork, and
be used for bureaucratic and political purposes that could injure
rather than protect individual rights. Although many endorsed the
Surgeon General's delegation of responsibility for protecting these

rights to review committees at educational and research institutions, some, such as Alvin Gouldner, opposed even that approach as being government interference with scientific freedom. "I certainly do not believe that federal officials have a responsibility to insure that ethical standards are maintained in the conduct of social research. I believe that this responsibility is best fulfilled . . . by professional associations" (III, 103).

Others voiced similar pleas on behalf of the associations. "The most important safeguard will depend finally on the ethical sense of the professions," said one (III, 149). "Ethical standards are a prerequisite to professional status and they should be established and enforced by the profession. A professional without an ethical code is inconceivable," said another (III, 119). If that were true, then anthropology, economics, sociology, and political science—and, indeed, most natural sciences—would not have been professions, because no major association in these fields had yet adopted an ethical code.

These respondents were not alone in thrusting on the social science associations a responsibility that most have not assumed. A 1967 report of the Office of Science and Technology, *Privacy and Behavioral Research* (which may be regarded as the reply of the Executive Office of the President—or of an experienced group of private social scientists impaneled by that office—to congressional and public criticism), stated:

> *The scientific associations in the behavioral sciences are custodians of and spokesmen for the values of their scientific disciplines. The current mores of these groups are reflected both in the setting of ethical standards and in their requirements for the admission of new members and for retention of membership. . . . It is . . . logical to expect that these professional associations . . . will accept responsibility for establishing ethical principles and guidelines for conduct of research as one of their major purposes. . . . No mechanism within the behavioral sciences is as well equipped to carry out these essential functions as that which can be offered by the professional societies themselves [pp. 28–29].*

Since this panel was too well-informed to be ignorant of the facts, this passage is best viewed as a piece of wishful thinking about how the associations should develop; and certainly many responsible and influential social scientists are trying to move the associations in that direction (while other equally responsible and influential colleagues oppose any such movement). And perhaps the associations were painted this unrecognizably rosy color in order to quiet public concern and to discourage further governmental inquiry and possible regulation.

The Behavioral and Social Sciences Survey Committee (1969) painted a similar picture, asserting that "Professional organizations of behavioral and social scientists . . . bring effective force to bear to assure that . . . [ethical propositions] are observed" (p. 130). As will be seen, that statement is false and misleading with respect to the economic, political science, anthropological, and sociological associations—a fact which provides additional evidence, if any were needed, that when social scientists are defending their interests in public, their claims must be examined as skeptically as are those of other lobbyists. Let us see exactly what the associations have done about ethical codes.

American Economic Association

Although I have not made a complete search of all AEA transactions in recent years, the only formal action I have noted on an ethical issue occurred at the 1959 business meeting when a three-man committee chaired by Robert Calkins was appointed to investigate a charge of plagiarism. The committee was alloted five hundred dollars for its expenses and eventually dismissed the complaint.

Many of the differences in outlook between academic social scientists and those working for business or government arise because the latter are committed to designated goals and policies of their enterprise. They assume a posture of advocacy that can strike their academic colleagues as one-sided or partisan. The degree to which such advocacy can be reconciled with the objective facts, as academic scholars see them, is a test of the integrity of the social scientists involved. This often delicate task of reconciling professional judgment with political reality has been faced by many economists, but none is subject to closer scrutiny by his colleagues than the chairman of the Council of Economic Advisers.

The first chairman, Edwin Nourse, sought to solve this problem by keeping his recommendations private so that he would not have publicly to endorse presidential policies with which he disagreed. "There is no occasion for the Council to become involved in any way in the advocacy of particular measures," Nourse (1953) wrote President Truman in a 1946 letter setting forth his conception of the council's role "as a scientific agency" (p. 107). The consistency with which Nourse held to this view contributed to his ultimate resignation, as he indicated in a 1948 letter to Truman: "I am suited to my present position only if it is intended to make the Council a strictly professional agency. . . . If it is in any way to be assigned a political role . . . you would want an entirely different kind of chairman" (p. 273).

Subsequent chairman adopted a less rigorously academic position well expressed by Walter Heller (1966), CEA chairman under President Kennedy: "Advocacy poses no insoluble problems of integrity and few of objectivity (though silence may occasionally be golden). . . . Of course, the adviser will not always get his way. . . . The ideal solution may have to yield to 'second best.' To explain and defend a *good* policy measure under circumstances where the *best* is beyond the political pale need not offend the conscience of the economist." Heller predicated this position on the assumption that council members were "in harmony with the general aims and direction of the President. . . . A member . . . who felt otherwise would resign" (pp. 21–22). However, the opinion of some other economists about the professional performance of such a politicized council has been less charitable, and it may just be that an economist's politics has something to do with his opinion. Thus, speaking in 1967, when Gardner Ackley chaired President Johnson's council (and not during his own chairmanship of President Eisenhower's council), Arthur Burns declared: "No matter how excellent this or that report by the Council may be, it is by its very nature a political document. . . . Many citizens . . . have therefore come to feel the need for guidance in economic matters that is more objective." Burns suggested the formation of a bipartisan commission of economists to review council reports "in the spirit of science"—and of Nourse (Burns and Samuelson, 1967, p. 79).

Business economist Terborgh (1967) has argued for the legitimation of an advocacy role for economists in addition to their accepted role as objective scholars. He has observed that economists increasingly "appear in a   representative capacity, as . . . brief writers, organization spokesmen, expert witnesses. Yet the profession has not evolved a code of ethics appropriate to these new responsibilities." Terborgh suggested that "the academic code" was not thereby necessarily discredited, because "Nonacademic economists usually take employment with organizations whose broad philosophy and objectives are congenial." More ambiguous was the situation of the adventitious "expert," selected, like a lawyer, to make the best possible case for his client. Terborgh asked if the time had not come when a second code of advocacy should be added to the traditional academic code for economists. "The advocate is in duty bound to make the best possible case for his client regardless of his own views. Indeed, it is understood by all concerned that he is playing a game to which these views are irrelevant. For this reason, his character and integrity are not impaired by the assumption of positions in behalf of his own knowledge and beliefs."

Whereas Terborgh wished to legitimate advocacy, Rossant (1967) has denigrated it when the views advocated do not represent the independent conclusion of an economist qualified to reach that conclusion. Rossant's main target was not the staff expert who had done his homework but the partisan economist who had not. "It does not seem to me that the academic economists who signed the [1967] statement supporting the Administration's request for the tax surcharge were purely objective in their action. How many are professional forecasters? How many are experts on fiscal policy? How many have a relationship with the Administration? . . . I question whether economists who perform a public relations function . . . or a lobbyist's function . . . are living up to the ethical standards of the profession."

Surely, economists have their share of ethical problems— maintaining the confidentiality of data, maintaining the integrity of work undertaken for private clients and the government, avoiding conflicts of interest, and equitably discharging their obligations to students, clients, employers, and research sponsors. Yet so far they have prepared no formal statement of their obligations, they have established no machinery to review charges of misconduct, and their association has devoted less attention to ethical problems than has any other social science association. Leaders among social scientists in their public influence, economists remain laggards in confronting ethical problems.

American Political Science Association

One obstacle to the development of a code of ethics by the American Economic Association is the lack of any professional requirement for membership, since the application of a common standard of conduct to men with no common qualification is a dubious, if not futile, exercise. As the same obstacle exists for the American Political Science Association, it is interesting to see how that association has grappled with its ethical problems.

These problems were touched off by the Army-sponsored research project Camelot. Though that affair did not evoke as marked a response from APSA as it did from the anthropological association, members raised questions about the ethics of overseas research and how the integrity of academic scholars could best be maintained. Thus, Silvert (1967) questioned the integrity of academic social scientists conducting research on government contracts and even "whether social scientists under certain kinds of government contract should continue to have the protection of academic tenure." William Marvel urged "that any university, college, private body or organization in a position to do so [should] press upon the members of the academic community adherence to one simple rule, that of full disclosure" (Harris, 1967a, p. 164). In September 1965, the APSA council discussed the possibility of developing a code of ethics and machinery to enforce it but reached no conclusion. It also discussed and rejected proposals to establish any categories of association membership other than a distinction between members and mere subscribers to the *Review*.

Further action followed the February 1967 press accounts of the Kirkpatrick-Kampelman affair noted in the previous chapter.

After the issue of their conduct was dealt with by the special committee of four past presidents, the broader issue of standards of conduct of all political scientists in their relations with research sponsors was bestowed upon a new committee on professional standards and responsibilities, chaired by Marver Bernstein. Among the many questions put to the committee was: "Should the Association adopt a code of professional ethics? If so, what should the code contain? . . . Is a code of ethics enforceable?" The committee was authorized to inquire into any other relevant questions, to conduct studies, and to hold hearings. It was asked to make recommendations in time for the September 1967 annual meeting.

The committee's interim report (Bernstein, 1967) offered seven recommendations, all of which were endorsed by the council and the annual business meeting. Four were procedural: encouraging greater discussion of ethical questions; cooperating with other associations concerned with professional standards; obtaining staff assistance for the committee; and deferring action on other ethics resolutions until the committee could consider them. The substantive resolutions (1) enjoined APSA members and officers who speak out on policy issues to "make it as clear as possible that they are not speaking on behalf of the Association"; (2) sanctioned outside activities by APSA officers and employees "provided that such activities do not interfere with their duties and responsibilities to the Association"; and (3) affirmed that "openness concerning material support for research is a basic principle of scholarship. Accordingly each author should indicate in each of his publications (a) relevant sources of financial support; (b) any conditions imposed by his financial sponsors or others on his research; and (c) any constraints imposed or understandings reached with his sponsors concerning publication of his research materials, findings, analyses, or conclusions."

The final committee report (Bernstein, 1968) was a well-informed and thoughtful document. Four categories of members were identified: faculty, graduate students, research personnel at nonacademic institutions, and government personnel; the report was addressed mainly to faculty, although it contained perceptive comments about government employees. The committee had sensible things to say about faculty responsibilities to students and colleagues (full acknowledgment should be given to assistants; and a professor's views must not be imposed on others) and about faculty political activity (it is legitimate, but leave should be taken for full-time activity; political and policy endorsements should be individual, not departmental). But the bulk of the report dwelt on how to maintain the integrity of government-sponsored research. Some thirteen of the twenty ethical rules proposed by the committee dealt with the problem, as did the additional fourteen *Foreign Area Research Guidelines* issued by the government in December 1967, which were endorsed and incorporated in the committee report.

The common academic position that federal funds should be provided without federal "control" or detailed review of their use had been amply propounded to the committee. Some forceful advocates of that position were the members of the University of Oregon department of political science. (Did they thereby violate an ethical rule the committee later advanced—that public policies be espoused on an individual and not a departmental basis—or is such a rule inapplicable to any policy that acquires the status of an ethical principle to which all members of a profession must adhere? If the latter, it could be said that "policy" represents a realm of professional tolerance and "principle," of intolerance.) They declared that:

> *It should be solely the responsibility of the researcher to determine whether the findings of his research may have unwanted consequences, and it should be his responsibility alone to determine whether . . . he should report them or not. . . . at no time should his travel to a . . . foreign area be prevented on the grounds that it is incompatible with a given "national interest" as interpreted by a government agency. His scholarly interest, his right to pursue knowledge to the best of his ability, entails his right to unrestricted international travel—and he alone is capable of judging its advisability [Agger and others, 1967].*

(It would seem that a scholar who does not recognize any governmental responsibility for his activity or travel cannot with any consistency demand any governmental service or protection for them; ideally he should travel on an international passport and be financed by international sources.)

In accepting the FAR guidelines, the committee allowed

that: some government contract research may have to be classified; "no assurances can be given" that uses other than those initially stated will not be made of research; the government should at times ascertain whether research is acceptable to a foreign government; and staffs of government agencies or nonacademic institutions should undertake "specialized" or sensitive research that might embarrass the academy. In short, an effort was to be made to preserve the university as an island of neutrality in the seas of politics. With respect to disclosure, it stated, "Openness concerning material support of research is a basic principle of scholarship. . . . Political science research supported by government grants [but not necessarily contracts?] should be unclassified." The committee also acceded to the Oregon faculty view that "the dominant threat emerging in recent years lies in governmental influence over and control of research."

In its discussion, the committee showed awareness of the complexities and delicacies of research. In overseas research, "a political scientist . . . may be faced with the excruciating dilemma of retaining academic integrity at the price of the national interest or of denying to himself and his professional peers a continuing access to documents and interviews." In the interim report, there then followed a trenchant truth deleted from the final report: "There is no inherent right to know. There may be a compulsion to know. . . . The scholar must report the truth as he perceives it, but truth has consequences. A fearless exposition of corruption in . . . a friendly . . . nation, might have local as well as international consequences of the most serious nature." In dealing with domestic research, the committee stressed the contrary and more popular position that the social scientist's first duty is to the truth regardless of its consequences, asserting that a professor does not even have the right to withhold a truth: "his discoveries are not his private possessions, but must be made publicly available. . . . he may have been moved entirely by curiosity and without regard for social consequences. Still . . . he has an obligation to make his knowledge available."

Noting that members accused of unethical conduct had no avenue of recourse through the association, the committee recommended that APSA "provide an agency through which at least some of the charges of unprofessional conduct can be processed in a fair and judicious manner" by creating a standing committee on professional ethics authorized: to give and, at its discretion, to publish advisory opinions on—but *not* to adjudicate—significant ethical issues in response to the request of any APSA member or the officers of any American college, university, or learned society; to hear and judge charges of unethical conduct against any APSA member upon his appeal; and to deal with ethical charges against APSA officers. At the outset, the standing committee should issue only "advisory opinions" and not impose penalties because, unlike lawyers and doctors, political scientists were not licensed, their ethical and professional standards were less well developed, APSA authority over its members was "altogether tenuous," and its resources were inadequate to the full-scale enforcement of an ethics code.

The September 1968 annual business meeting in Washington accepted the committee report and a statement from the Oregon group and then referred both to the new standing committee on professional ethics "not as legislation binding all political scientists, but as expressions of principles to . . . serve as points of departure for the new Standing Committee's deliberations, and . . . [to] contribute to the possible eventual formation of a professional code of ethics."

By June 1971, the new committee had issued eleven advisory opinions dealing with such subjects as the multiple submission of manuscripts, reviewing manuscripts and books, permissions to reprint, a scholar's obligation to make his data available to critics, academic job offers and recommendations, fraudulent degree claims, and association electioneering. One opinion rebuked eight members for issuing a public statement on American foreign policy in which they were identified as present, past, or future presidents of the association; but the committee had not formally heard any charge of unethical conduct against an officer or member.

Thus, a crisis in confidence has engendered significant admonitory activity by a general-membership association with no mandatory code of ethics.

American Anthropological Association

At long intervals, one or another anthropological association has issued a statement of ethics, but there the matter has generally rested. The basic machinery for professional discipline did, however, exist, since fellows of the American Anthropological Association (who must normally possess a doctorate in anthropology) were admitted by majority vote and "For a just cause . . . may be deprived of their status by a two-thirds vote" of the executive board.

After two years of discussion and the circulation of two drafts, the Society for Applied Anthropology in 1948 unanimously adopted a ten-paragraph code prepared by a committee chaired by Margaret Mead. The code stated that "the applied anthropologist must take responsibility for the effects of his recommendations, never maintaining that he is merely a technician"; that "ends can never be used to justify means, and full responsibility must be taken for the ethical and social implications of both means and ends recommended"; that the applied anthropologist should attempt to prevent "irreversible losses of health or loss of life to individuals or groups or irreversible damage to natural productivity of the physical environment"; and that he "must take the greatest care to protect his informants, especially in those aspects of confidence which his informants may not be able to stipulate for themselves." Finally, he will seek "To advance . . . the integrity of the individual human being; to maintain scientific and professional integrity and responsibility . . . ; to respect both human personality and cultural values; [and] to publish and share new discoveries and methods with colleagues."

Beyond these vague goals—just what does integrity mean and just how does one advance it?—the code melded the anthropologist's holistic approach to culture and the theory of social equilibrium then fashionable among many members of the society into the curious moral imperative "That the specific area of responsibility of the applied anthropologist is to promote a state of dynamic equilibrium within the systems of human relationships" (Mead, 1949). The purpose of this rhetoric, Adams (1967) suggests, was "to discourage anthropologists from trying to change cultures or societies." Applied anthropologists "took the position that their major task was not to question the changes that were being demanded by the changing [American] technology and economy, but to find ways to adjust the society to them." Thereby, "they essentially played the role of agent for the controlling powers in the society."

In due course, as Adams sees it, some members of the society came to believe that the emphasis of the code on "not rocking the boat was misdirected and represented a general position that many did not subscribe to." In 1963, they obtained unanimous adoption of a new ethics statement which obliged the applied anthropologist to refuse any work whose results "will be used in a manner harmful to the interest of his fellowmen or of science." To science, the anthropologist had a commitment to make his findings available and "In the wake of his own studies . . . to leave a hospitable climate for future study." To his fellowmen he owed respect; he should not recommend any course of action "when the lives, well-being, dignity, and self-respect of others are likely to be adversely affected." To his clients "he must make no promises . . . that he cannot reasonably hope to fulfill" (Society for Applied Anthropology, 1963–1964).

In 1948, the AAA (1949) adopted the following resolution on freedom of publication: *"Be it resolved:* (1) that the . . . Association strongly urge[s] all sponsoring institutions to guarantee their research scientists complete freedom to interpret and publish their findings without censorship or interference; provided that (2) the interests of the persons and communities or other social groups studied are protected; and that (3) In the event that the sponsoring institution does not wish to publish the results nor be identified with the publication, it [shall] permit publication of the results, without use of its name as sponsoring agency, through other channels." Presumably, this resolution reflected the difficulty some anthropologists encountered in obtaining the release of reports based on information obtained while employed by the government during World War II. And, it should be noted, the association then espoused a principle of *not* disclosing the source of sponsorship contrary to that which it adopted in 1967.

I recounted in the preceding chapter how the American Anthropological Association responded to the Camelot episode with an inquiry that produced two formal statements on ethics. The first, by the executive board, declared that "Except in times of clear and present national emergency, universities should not undertake activities which are unrelated to their normal teaching, research, and public service functions" (American Anthropological Association, 1966). The second, adopted in 1967 by a 729 to 59 mail vote of AAA fellows, declared that anthropologists should willingly disclose "their sponsorship and source of funds, and the nature and objectives" of their research; that they should not work for or accept support from "organizations that permit misrepresentation of technical competence, excessive costs, or concealed sponsorship" an attack on research organizations operating overseas, sometimes covertly financed by intelligence agencies); and that universities, professors, and students "should scrupulously avoid . . . involvement in clandestine intelligence activities and the use of the name of anthropology, or the title of anthropologist, as a cover for intelligence activities." This last statement asserted, in effect, that intelligence agents might disguise themselves as businessmen, stevedores, poets, or librarians but never (like D. G. Hogarth, Leonard Woolley, T. E. Lawrence, or Jacques Soustelle) as anthropologists. Anthropologists in government employ "should recognize that they will be committed to agency missions and policies. They should seek in advance the clearest possible definition of their expected roles as well as the possibilities . . . for continuing to contribute to the profession through publication, and for . . . protecting the privacy of individuals and groups they may study" (American Anthropological Association, 1967). Plainly, the tone is more reproving than that of the APSA ethics committee, which takes a more sympathetic attitude toward government service.

The recent hostility of so many anthropologists toward government stems in part from the mood of radical protest but probably—because this attitude is held by a number of older and more conservative scholars—also from the fact that so many anthropologists are now employed on, and so few off, campus that they can be economically and ideologically more independent of the government than political scientists, psychologists, or economists. Adams (1967) has advanced just this explanation. Noting that the AAA fellows' statement "places the scholar's responsibility to other scholars above that to his government, except under specific conditions," he asks how such an attitude came to dominate the profession. His answer is that "anthropology . . . has passed from a status in which people were looking for jobs to one in which there is a high demand for trained people. . . . It is possible today to reject one employer and still expect to find another. Among the employers who can be so treated is the United States government."

In 1968, the AAA committee on organization urged the association to move toward a formal statement of ethics and professional standards. One of the first items of business acted on by the ad hoc ethics committee appointed that October to advance these recommendations was the publication in the August *American Anthropologist* of a Navy advertisement for a research anthropologist to assist in psychological warfare in Vietnam. The committee found the advertisement "not in keeping with the positions taken by the Association with regard to problems of modern war." Concurring, the executive board ruled that, in the future, questionable advertisements should be referred to the committee for decision, in accord with the policy that "The AAA will not accept advertisements or notices for positions involving research or other activities the products of which cannot be made available to the entire scholarly community through accepted academic channels of communication"—thereby registering its aversion to government, business, religious, and other organizations which require some degree of confidentiality. Thus, as government censorship dwindles, that of the anthropology association rises.[1]

The potential for censorship inherent in the strict enforcement of ethical standards was further manifested by the 1969 report of the ad hoc ethics committee, which recommended establishing a research registration system "to provide evidence of the *bonae fides* of all researchers in the field." The committee proposed that members engaging in research voluntarily submit curriculum vitae of those on their research team; provide data on the purpose, duration, sponsors, and location of the project and on scholarly contacts in the host country; and reveal whether "any restricted publication or

[1] Replying to complaints about his acceptance of the advertisement, Ward Goodenough, editor of the *American Anthropologist,* declared, "In the absence of instructions to the contrary . . . , it would be improper for the editor to exercise political censorship over paid advertisements relating to matters of professional concern." He received his political instructions soon enough (see *American Anthropologist,* October 1968, p. vi, and *Newsletter of the American Anthropological Association,* March 1969, p. 1).

reporting" or any other activity of a "commercial, political, paramilitary, etc." nature was contemplated. Additional information or "substantiation" might be requested by the committee which would then issue a certificate of registration or explain why a certificate was denied. "If anthropologists cannot regulate their own conduct and find ways to distinguish themselves from those who claim this title," the committee warned, "they will find themselves far more stringently regulated in, and in some cases excluded from, areas as large as new nations and as small as Indian reservations" (American Anthropological Association, 1969). Evidently, the committee wanted AAA to become a power whose agents were recognized by nations and reservations which deny recognition to agents of the United States government.

The political aspect of anthropological ethics and the severe divisions within the association were again manifested in the episode which began in May 1970 when ethics committee chairman Eric Wolf received from the Student Mobilization Committee to End the War in Vietnam papers on anthropologists' work in Thailand which a graduate student had xeroxed from a professor's files. Wolf wrote to four anthropologists named in the papers for an explanation, stating that "these documents contradict in spirit and in letter the resolutions of the American Anthropological Association concerning clandestine and secret research" and sent a similar statement to the AAA board. Whereupon the board unanimously rebuked Wolf and a fellow committee member, Joseph Jorgensen, for making public statements in the name of the association and for conducting unauthorized inquiries. Whereupon the two resigned from the committee and aired the matter at length in the *New York Review of Books* (Wolf and Jorgensen, 1970; Foster, 1971b). Whereupon a special committee chaired by Margaret Mead was appointed to investigate the whole business.

The Mead committee found that the ethics committee had "acted hastily, unfairly, and unwisely"; that "counterinsurgency" research was not "as sinister as it sounds" but merely a current funding "label" replacing such earlier labels as "mental health" and "community development." Nonetheless, anthropologists must now recognize that "publication of routine . . . data about identified village communities . . . might be used for the[ir] annihilation by bombing." Therefore field workers should consider delaying publication of such data and concealing the identity of villages; "what may be required is more secrecy, not less secrecy" (Mead, 1971).

When this report was discussed at the November 1971 annual meeting, a reporter wrote, "No one disagreed with that conclusion, but other sections of the report brought hisses and laughs . . . the association's younger members see . . . Dr. Mead as a kind of anthropological Uncle Tom." The report was rejected overwhelmingly in a "distinctly unintellectual uproar" (Isaacs, 1971).

The Mead report lambasted the registration of research projects and certification of field workers as "either a farce or a device . . . on the order of the various oaths . . . during the Joe McCarthy era. . . . It would serve no purpose except to provide opportunities for the persecution of individuals whose activities may be personally or politically repugnant to temporary majorities in the shifting membership of successive executive boards." Nonetheless, such registration and certification had already been adopted by a ballot of the membership in which 50 percent of those eligible voted. A resolution that anthropologists not engage in secret or classified research was adopted by a vote of 1077 to 941. "There is no question," Ehrich (1970) observed, "but that the Association has been drastically polarized, and that the rubric of 'Ethics' has become a battleground for political maneuvering." That a thin majority of voters, a minority of the membership, can impose their standards upon the entire membership is doubtful.

American Sociological Association

Fellows of the American Sociological Association have striven in recent years to transform themselves from a scholarly to a professional association. As students of social forms who recognize the part ethical standards have played in the establishment of professions, they have attempted to define some—as a start, almost *any*—standard which they could accept and which would not be so blatantly opinionated or self-serving as to raise more doubts than it would dispel about the service this putative profession provides. The struggle between academic and worldly, didactic and pragmatic members, between those who would attack society and those who would influence it, has been long and wearying.

Since 1960, the association's section on social psychology (American Sociological Association, 1960) has had a code and a procedure for investigating complaints and imposing sanctions, including "reprimand and warning, voiding the certificate awarded [to a Social Psychologist, Certified by the Section on Social Psychology], expulsion from the Section, and recommendation to the Council of the American Sociological Association for expulsion from the Association." The code, which every member must accept, declares that the social psychologist must "give primacy to the needs and welfare of the client so long as they do not violate the rights and integrity of other individuals or organizations and are consistent with high ethical principles." He pledges to maintain high ethical and professional standards, to represent his qualifications accurately, to promote "systematic and objective research procedures," to "minimize the possibility that findings will be misleading," to disseminate methodological knowledge but preserve confidential information.

Since 1945, the American Sociological Association has repeatedly appointed committees to investigate ethical problems, but it took twenty-five years to get a statement of standards. A committee on research ethics appointed in 1951 considered the relationships of nonprofit institutions to research sponsors, the problems of investigators "with both subtle and crude outside pressures," and the types of research which sociologists might properly conduct. However, it produced little more than a call for the appointment of a new committee to give special attention to "(a) the rights and needs of graduate students and (b) competition between academic and commercial research agencies" (American Sociological Association, 1953).

A successor committee inquired into the former (but not the latter) question by means of a brief questionnaire addressed to thirty-seven sociology departments. Chairman Bernard (1955) then drew up five "possible recommendations" on faculty relations with graduate students. Viewed from the hippie era, one recommendation is a textbook example of the bond between ethical principles and social mores: "Faculty has the responsibility for making suggestions to a candidate with respect to mannerisms, dress, personality quirks, etc., which they feel might militate against his professional success."

In 1955, a national furor was aroused by the covert research not of the government but of University of Chicago investigators who, with the consent of judges and counsel, had secretly recorded the deliberation of jurors in six civil cases in a Wichita, Kansas, federal court, leading to a Senate inquiry and the passage of legislation prohibiting the recording of federal jury deliberations for any purpose whatsoever (Vaughan, 1967). One sociologist who looked into the episode was disturbed at "the basic distrust of social scientists" which it revealed and suggested the "adoption of a formal code of ethics" and "a system of licensing," or both, to "provide assurance that social scientists are trustworthy" (Burchard, 1958).

Whatever was done in these directions was not done quickly. In 1961, the executive committee approved the plans of the ASA committee on ethics, chaired by Robert Angell, to develop a code. The ethics committee thereupon invited ASA members to submit cases posing ethical problems and received some sixty responses. A seventy-seven-page draft code dealing with teaching, research, consulting, professional practice, writing and publishing, and the profession and the public was circulated for comment and, after revision, the ASA council voted to "receive" the document "with thanks" but without action.

Becker (1964) found the code too equivocal: "To be of any use, a Code . . . must deal successfully with the moral problems generic to social science. But these are precisely the problems dealt with least adequately by the draft code. . . . It cannot, for example, say that undercover research roles are not justified: it must equivocate by adding 'unless they are clearly the only feasible means for reaching important scientific goals.' The code is equivocal or unenlighteningly vague in dealing with most of the problems distinct to social science . . . because there is not consensus about such problems." This statement is true, but a high order of equivocality and generality is characteristic of many codes. To my mind, the worst features of the code were its naive assertion of the primacy of pure or academic research over impure or applied research and its affirmation of a double moral standard condoning lying, deception, and the breach of confidence in academic research while condemning it in nonacademic research.

This conclusion cannot be demonstrated by direct quotation because, despite sociologists' opposition to restraints on publication, the committee's final report remains a confidential document that may not be publicly quoted. However, some apothegms can be cited from a paper by Angell (1967, pp. 725–740) based upon the draft:

> . . . there is a clear line of ethical distinction between pure and applied research. For the purpose of obtaining important new scientific knowledge, deception . . . may sometimes be ethically tolerated, provided also that those who have been duped are later given a full explanation. . . . There does not appear to be any such ethical justification in the case of applied research. . . . Applied research is not so important as pure research. . . . In the case of applied research it is clear that one cannot make the exception to absolute privacy that is sometimes made in pure research: that information may be shared in confidence with colleagues for strictly scientific purposes. . . . The very difficult question whether pure sociologists may ethically penetrate organizations that bar all study of them is not faced by the applied researcher. Since he has not the high calling of developing abstract scientific knowledge, he has no claim to the special privileges that are sometimes enjoyed by those so engaged.

In 1967, yet another committee was appointed to pursue the search for a code. The ASA executive committee felt that congressional hearings on the invasion of privacy and the new controls over research instituted by the Surgeon General and the Secretary of State lent the task a special urgency. The new committee, chaired by Schuler (1967), posed a series of questions about the conditions under which it was or was not proper to invade privacy, deceive or endanger subjects, misrepresent objectives, and falsify or suppress data; the extent of obligations to sponsors; when the ethic of science should yield to "a higher ethic"; the degree to which sociologists should obey the laws and mores of society; and whether a formal code with sanctions should be adopted.

After a year's work, the committee submitted a draft which so displeased the ASA council that it promptly established its own subcommittee to write its own report. The full Schuler committee draft has not been published, but the preamble was an abstract discourse on democracy and sociology that did not deal with the practical issues at hand and that was written in language less than clear and convincing.[2]

The council's draft, produced in only a few months—after the unrequited years of labor by many committees—was brief and clear. Affirming the autonomy and integrity of sociological inquiry, it also recognized that such inquiry "must itself operate within constraints" to protect the autonomy and integrity of others. "The sociologist must not use his role as a cover to obtain information for other than professional purposes" and "must report fully all sources of financial support . . . and any special relations to the sponsor that might affect the interpretation of the findings."

Altogether, thirteen principles were proposed that seemed reasonable, better balanced than the proposals of earlier committees in recognizing the rights of subjects as well as of sociologists, and practicable. Thus, whereas the Schuler draft had stated that a "sponsor should not be permitted to suppress . . . unfavorable results while presenting only the favorable aspects"—a negative injunction exceeding the power of the investigator—the council placed on the sociologist the positive and practicable obligation "to clarify publicly any distortion by a sponsor or client of the findings of a research project in which he has participated." Circulated to all ASA members in November 1968, the draft was submitted to voting members a year later and adopted by a vote of 2,369 to 236.

[2] For example, it stated that a central characteristic of democratic society has been the "opening of the social structure into institutional patterns of shared decision-making and into patterns of choice within the institutional framework [which] has been based on the assumption of the essential freedom of the human person. From this assumption of essential freedom and from the pressure for maximizing its institutional forms stems the other values which cluster around the person of modern man: dignity, privacy, and the positive assessment of reason." Sociologists, it announced, "believe in reciprocal freedoms among different social groups and they believe that these reciprocal freedoms, guarded by reciprocal responsibilities, will create more freedom for themselves and others" (*American Sociologist*, November 1968, 316–317).

In anticipation of that action, a standing committee on professional ethics had been appointed and asked to formulate "procedural guidelines to be used in cases of alleged violations of the proposed Code."

These were adopted by a referendum and became effective in September 1971. "Code of Ethics Given Teeth," stated the announcement in that month's *Socio-Log,* the ASA newsletter. However, association staff privately acknowledged that, having learned (unlike the anthropologists) the cost and care required to act with due process to guard members' rights that were still protected by the courts, the association would proceed with caution in exercising its new power. With such caution, indeed, that a year later the chairman of the ethics committee reported, "So far as I am aware, the only successfully transacted business of the Committee during the present year was the transfer of the Chairmanship. . . . We stand ready to serve when the occasion arises" (Erikson, 1972).

American Psychological Association

Since 1953, the American Psychological Association has had a comprehensive code of ethics and an extensive program for its enforcement and periodic revision. An important factor precipitating APA activity appears to have been the growing engagement of psychologists in clinical work and consultation; their contact with physicians and their wish for a comparable professional status, including APA certification and state licensure and ethical self-regulation; and the practical need of both professional men and their clients for that measure of comfort and protection afforded by a code.

The association began its formal work in ethics with the creation, in 1938, of a special ethics committee succeeded two years later by a standing committee which "handled complaints informally, adopting for itself certain rules or principles" (Helweg, 1967). In 1947, this committee recommended preparation of a formal code; the association agreed and proceeded after a laborious process to adopt a provisional code in 1952. First, a committee was appointed to determine how a code should be prepared. It recommended an empirical approach, and in 1948 a second committee, chaired by Nicholas Hobbs, was appointed to carry it out. Letters were sent to the seventy-five hundred APA members asking them "to describe a situation they knew of firsthand, in which a psychologist made a decision having ethical implications, and to indicate what the correspondents perceived as being the ethical issues involved" (American Psychological Association, 1953, p. vi). More than a thousand reports were received. Edited to remove identifying information, these were sorted into six groups that ultimately became the six sections of the final code dealing with public responsibility, client relationships, teaching, research, writing and publishing, and professional relationships. The proposed draft of each section was circulated to prominent psychologists with a special interest in the area, published in the *American Psychologist* for study and comment, and discussed at national and regional meetings and by psychology departments, students, and other groups. Some two hundred reports of such discussions were submitted to the APA, becoming the basis for further revisions until the final draft was accepted as official policy in 1952. The claim of the ethics committee that "Perhaps as much as any document can be, this statement of ethical standards was written by a profession" (1953, p. x) seems warranted.

The result was a 171-page volume outlining eighty-three ethical problems each illustrated by from 1 to 18 specific incidents and followed by a statement of one or more relevant principles. In toto, the volume contains about 476 incidents and 163 general principles of professional conduct (plus many subsidiary principles). Some may criticize the profusion of detail and wonder if the most conscientious psychologist could possibly remember or abide by every principle; even the nineteen-page summary remains a good deal longer than the ten commandments or the ten brief principles of medical ethics enunciated by the American Medical Association. One or another principle can always be faulted, but the statement is nonetheless more impressive—more mature, comprehensive, and judicious—than are most of the ethical statements produced to date by other social science associations; in view of the difficulty of the enterprise and the many ways it could have failed, it is a highly creditable achievement. Several factors may account for this success: the practical nature of clinical problems; the experience of physicians as a model for dealing with these problems; and the disposition of psychologists, seeking public acceptance and legal licensure, to stress their obligations to clients, society, and the law of the land—principles challenged by more purely academic associations, which emphasize instead their obligations to "truth" and human "welfare," domains so prodigious that each scholar can define them as he pleases. For example, the APA code states that "The psychologist's ultimate allegiance is to society," and "The welfare of the profession and that of the individual psychologist are clearly subordinate to the welfare of the public. . . . in service, the responsibility of most weight is the welfare of the client"; whereas the abortive 1964 code of the American Sociological Association stated: "Serve first the moral principles of your society, which include the universal decencies of mankind. Serve next the peculiar ethical standards that have been worked out by your sociological colleagues. Serve last the claims of any client or organization that has employed you"—which might lead some clients to suspect that they were getting short shrift (American Psychological Association 1953, p. 7, and Angell, 1967, p. 740).

   Though the entire APA code is worth careful study, much of it deals with client relationships, fees, and advertising. I note here only the provisions on research standards and then discuss arrangements for enforcement. The code holds the psychologist responsible "for planning his research in such a way as to minimize the possibility that his findings will be misleading." To produce distorted results deliberately by the biased selection of subjects, samples, questions, or methods "to yield predetermined outcomes . . . is unethical." Data which do not comport with the main conclusions must be reported or the reasons for not reporting them must be explained; findings should be withheld only if they are unsound or do not meet professional standards. However, in contradistinction to the position taken by the anthropology association, the right of a member to engage in employment involving limitations on research publication is explicitly recognized, as is the proprietary nature of data collected by an organization. "Materials prepared by staff members of an organization as a part of their organizational duties . . . are the property of that organization. These should be released . . . only with the authorization of that organization."

Exposing subjects to emotional stress or deception is permissible only "when the problem is significant and can be investigated in no other way" and when the subjects' voluntary consent has previously been obtained. The psychologist "must seriously consider the possibility of . . . harmful aftereffects and should be prepared to remove them as soon as permitted by the design of the experiment."

Enforcement of the code is the responsibility of a standing ethics committee assisted by a member of the APA professional staff. The APA bylaws specify that a member may be dropped or disciplined "for conduct which tends to injure the Association, or to affect adversely its reputation, or which is contrary to or destructive of its objects," and they instruct the ethics committee to investigate the conduct of any member which may be in violation of the code "whether or not specific allegations are submitted." They prescribe the procedures to be followed in filing charges against a member, holding a hearing, and dropping a member—the maximum penalty that can be imposed.

Additional detailed rules and procedures have been published by the committee (American Psychological Association, 1961, 1968). These indicate that the committee's functions are solely "investigatory and advisory," final responsibility for action resting with the board of directors—a division of responsibility which provides a fair process of adjudication and protects the association against legal action which might otherwise be brought by a member tried and found guilty by the same men who brought charges against him. The rules make clear that "Except in matters of ethics, [the committee] . . . shall not arbitrate controversies or censor publications. It shall not permit the use of its services for personal gain or vengeance nor allow information to be released about ethics cases with malice or primarily with intent to injure the reputation or means of livelihood of any individuals involved. The objective . . . shall in all cases be constructive and educative rather than punitive in character. . . . However, when the interests of the public or of the profession are in conflict with personal interests, the former must be of overriding concern." Committee inquiries "shall be courteous in tone and constructive in spirit." Where warranted, a subcommittee, usually of APA members from the local area, may be appointed to gather additional facts or the member may be asked to appear, or both. In either case, a full transcript will normally be taken. "No action unfavorable to a member . . . may be recommended . . . until the member has been offered an opportunity to appear." The member must also receive a copy of the recommendations and may appeal them to a special committee whom the member himself shall select from a panel designated by the APA president; prior to that special hearing, he must receive copies of all documents to be submitted in evidence and the names of all witnesses to appear against him. At the hearing, a representative of the ethics committee presents the evidence in support of the charges and the member may be represented by counsel. If the hearing committee concludes that the member should be disciplined, dropped, or permitted to resign, that recommendation is transmitted to the board of directors and the member may submit a further written statement before the board finally acts.

As can be seen, the procedures are semijudicial in character, laborious, protracted, and expensive. Whatever else it may be, such a process of determining beyond a reasonable doubt whether a man is guilty or innocent of a specified charge stands at an opposite pole from the process of asserting a political or moral principle; a fact which may help to explain why the social science associations trembling at the brink of enforcement have not yet plunged in.

In the average year, fewer than a hundred cases have come before the APA ethics committee, which has met perhaps three times a year to conduct its business; one or two dozen cases may be current at a time. Many complaints have involved questions of clinical practice, private consulting, professional advertising, and the endorsement of commercial products, and few are concerned with academic teaching or research. Ninety-four cases summarized in one publication (American Psychological Association, 1967) include charges of sensational, dogmatic, or unfounded public pronouncements; the misrepresentation of degrees and qualifications; sexual and other misconduct with a client; the indecorous solicitation of business; excessive or inaccurate professional claims; breaches of confidence; irresponsible failure to fulfill professional obligations; disclosing the contents or findings of psychological tests to unauthorized persons; plagiarism; and the failure to give coauthorship to a student assistant.

So far as can be judged from the brief accounts of each episode, committee opinions seem reasonable and judicious, varying in severity in accordance with the offense and the character and subsequent conduct of the offender. Where a member acknowledges his error and takes corrective action, the matter may be dropped. In more serious cases, the committee may ask the member to stop his misconduct; a letter of censure may be sent; he may be placed on probation or put under the surveillance of local psychologists for a designated period, and specified measures may be recommended such as a public retraction, the return of a fee, the modification of a listing in the telephone directory, or—for a member with emotional problems—undertaking a course of psychiatric treatment.

When an offense is serious and deliberate and a member is expelled from the association, which may happen once or twice a year, all APA members receive a confidential notice which gives the dropped member's name and lists the sections of the code which have been violated. According to the bylaws, a member who has been dropped may apply for readmission after five years "upon showing that he is ethically as well as technically qualified for membership"; his application is transmitted first to the ethics committee for its recommendation.

In 1968, a major venture was mounted to revise the code and extend it to new areas in which public interest had been aroused —particularly the protection of privacy, the rights of research subjects, and ethical issues in the sponsorship and use of research. Again, a large portion of the membership was contacted for information and opinion, and authorities such as journal editors, department chairmen, ethics scholars, and research administrators were consulted. Two drafts of proposed research standards have been published for comment and discussion (Cook, 1971, 1972). These stress the importance of obtaining ethical advice (for example, from an institutional ethics committee such as that mandated by the U. S. Public Health Service) and of obtaining the informed consent of subjects and protecting their privacy, welfare, and dignity. The drafts discuss, but offer no principles to govern, the sponsorship or utilization of research, merely noting that different opinions prevail on the influence of sponsors and the propriety of confidential research and assigning to the investigator the responsibility of deciding whether to conduct such research.

Initial reactions suggest that many psychologists felt the drafts placed too much emphasis on the rights of subjects and not enough on those of the profession. "The orientation was antiscientific and antiinvestigative," said Joseph Masling. "It needs a parallel section . . . on the right of the investigator to investigate . . . as long as the methods don't harm people" (Moriarty, 1972).

Summary

While the social science associations have been concerned about governmental threats to their freedom, the government has been concerned about the threats of research to the rights of citizens. Psychological testing and computer data centers are two examples of research instruments whose dangers have disturbed the Congress.

The Reuss respondents were reluctant to see the government directly involved in protecting the rights of subjects, fearing that the resultant regulation would be rigid, unrealistic, and obstructive. They preferred to see subjects protected by ethical standards voluntarily observed by investigators, their institutions, and their professional associations. This viewpoint has been supported by a panel of the Office of Science and Technology and by the Behavioral and Social Sciences Survey Committee, which asserted that the social science associations "bring effective force to bear" on the maintenance of ethical standards by social scientists.

Unfortunately, that statement is untrue. The American Psychological Association has been the only major social science association which has taken effective steps to see that members observe ethical standards. The American Economic Association has shown no interest in formulating any code to which its members would subscribe. The American Anthropological Association, the American Sociological Association, and the American Political Science Association have at least held discussions and prepared statements on selected ethical issues. But these statements have generally put more stress on the liberties of investigators than on the rights of subjects; and little or nothing has been done to enforce them.

4

Public Responsibility of Intellectuals

In his address on Government and the Critical Intelligence, President Lyndon Johnson (1966) took a strong stand on the public responsibilities of intellectuals. Because of their special education and talent, Johnson said, intellectuals have a special obligation to advise the government about what is right and wrong with its programs: "Their judgment may be wrong, and they must live with that knowledge as other men do who have been chosen by their fellow citizens to exercise the powers of government. Their judgment may be right and still not be accepted. . . . That is a risk that they all take along with everyone else. But they must provide it; it is an obligation of responsible intellect."

If the president is right, a great many social scientists are irresponsible, for they definitely do not agree with him. They put their obligation to their conscience, their profession, or their conception of human welfare above any that they may acknowledge to their government. Their stand is not simply a consequence of recent political disaffection but of a long-standing and entirely American attitude that does not accord automatic respect and priority to the needs of government over other human needs and institutions. Johnson (1958) himself expressed the same attitude in a statement that "I am a free man, an American, a United States Senator, and a Democrat, in that order."

In the Reuss inquiry, reservations about the scholar's responsibilities to government were voiced even by those who had been responsive to government requests. The predominant replies to a question about whether academic men have a "responsibility to examine issues of public policy, at the request of responsible public officials" were a much qualified "yes," an outright "no," or "no more than any other citizen." Thus, Alfred de Grazia stated that "the academic man has no more responsibility to spend his time examining issues of public policy than the next man, and . . . responsible public officials have no more authority to call upon them to devote themselves to these issues than any private citizens would have" (III, 73); and Frederick Thieme, who submitted a statement based on a discussion with eight faculty members of the University of Washington, of which he was vice-president, declared, "We recognize no such obligatory responsibility except as the individual scientist agrees to accept it in accordance with the dictates of his conscience or under a voluntary contractual relationship with a government agency" (III, 197).

Coming from an employee of the Oak Ridge National Laboratory who later worked with the Director of Research and Engineering in the Department of Defense, Davis Bobrow's reply carries special weight in conveying the skepticism with which many scholars regard requests from government officials: "The social scientist . . . has no obligation to advertise, justify, sell or front for specific policy positions or officials. He has no obligation to work outside of his competence. . . . He also has no obligation to assume that because a particular agency . . . tells him that a problem is . . . 'policy relevant,' the problem really merits priority in attacking national needs. . . . he has an obligation to treat responsible requests in a responsible fashion; public officials have an obligation to make responsible requests" (III, 32). Bobrow's skepticism is shared by other respondents who stressed that social scientists dare not take official requests at their face value but must make an independent assessment of their merit and the professional conditions under which the work is to be undertaken.

Who can disagree with such precautions? A man who undertakes research without regard to its value, feasibility, and probity must be foolish, hungry, or unprincipled. Disagreement arises "only" —which is to say, often enough—in the conclusions that radical and conservative, inexperienced and sophisticated, academic and nonacademic, government and private social scientists can reach about the value, feasibility, and probity of designated projects conducted under specified conditions for particular sponsors.

The main line of cleavage in responsiveness to government has run between academic and nonacademic social scientists. The simplest explanation may be that as the former are paid at least in part to teach, they need not, like the latter, constantly conduct research in order to eat. In principle, the best faculty at the best institutions are supposed to work only on problems that interest them and that are compatible with institutional mores. While the staff of high-caliber, affluent research institutes may enjoy comparable freedom, those at more competitive and less financially secure institutes cannot be so discriminating. Every institution cannot afford to adopt Lovejoy's principle of academic freedom: "those who buy a certain service may not (in the most important particular) prescribe the nature of the service to be rendered" (1930, p. 384).

The different conditions prevailing at academic and nonacademic institutions have generally been recognized by government administrators. Basic research grants awarded for unsolicited proposals have been concentrated at universities, whereas more tightly managed, applied research contracts, which may be awarded on competitive bids and contain publication restrictions, have been concentrated at research institutes. To be sure, the objectives and regulations of government research programs are not always to the liking of private scholars. Often they are out of phase, with the government either trying to stimulate research in a new area or lagging in its recognition of new intellectual and administrative problems. Government research and educational programs were particularly slow to acknowledge, comprehend, and respond to the massive tide of discord that has swept our campuses and cities.

Role of Private Scholars in Policy Formation

When differences in interest between scholars and officials have been accommodated and a bargain has been struck, "What help should, and should not, the federal government expect from private social scientists in the formation, implementation, and evaluation of national policies and programs?" (III, 6) The Reuss respondents agreed that social scientists could obtain and analyze information on a designated problem and perhaps indicate alternative courses of action and (more speculatively) their probable consequences. The kinds of knowledge that, in their opinion, could and should be obtained are discussed in the next chapter. Social scientists could also, respondents noted, evaluate the effects of existing programs; this type of evaluation is discussed in Chapter Six.

Respondents were divided on the issues of whether social scientists could and should go beyond neutral analysis to offer recommendations and whether, or to what degree, they are responsible for others' use of their work. Legally and administratively, it is improper for a private citizen to make policy decisions, which are the responsibility of appointed and elected officials. Yet the relation between facts and conclusions, and between conclusions and convictions, recommendations, and decisions, is so intimate that the social scientist can readily move from one to another. There is much debate about the legitimacy of his doing so, much ambiguity about the grounds for doing so, and yet much dissatisfaction when officials ignore recommendations that are offered.

A good example was provided in a lengthy statement by Ralph Beals (III, 18–27), who reported that some anthropologists had come to reject work for the government "because they felt that their main function was to justify or implement policies already determined and that any results or advice contrary to such determinations were ignored." Accordingly, Beals believed that anthropologists should respond to government requests only "where there is reasonable assurance that effective use will be made of the results."

What interpretation can be put on "effective use" other than action that accords with the policies anthropologists advocate? While thus setting as a precondition for research that officials heed anthropologists at least occasionally, Beals assigned to the officials unqualified responsibility for policy decisions, because these "are essentially political and often involve nonscientific judgments." Nonetheless, "where the scientific evidence strongly suggests the desirability of a given policy," he asked that the anthropologist be informed of "the bureaucratic or political considerations which have led to its rejection or the selection of a scientifically less desirable decision." Surely, the statements that policy decisions "are essentially political" and that "scientific evidence strongly suggests the desirability of a given policy" are contradictory. Or are only some policy decisions political while others can be made scientifically? That position must be rejected, for all policies that are politically possible are also scientifically possible; whereas whatever is scientifically necessary, like the flow of water downhill or the mortality of man, is not subject to political choice.

Beals's statement exemplifies the ambiguity of the social scientist's role in policy-making. Beals is not a flaming radical but a moderate and responsible senior statesman of his profession, who reached his conclusions after conducting a lengthy inquiry into the anthropologist's relations with government agencies. Indeed, his inconsistencies are partly attributable to his effort to maintain a reasonable middle ground (in which public policy is only partially founded on scientific evidence) readily outflanked by several more extreme, widely held positions, such as: (1) that public policy can and should be based more fully on social science findings; (2) that the social scientist can deal objectively only with facts—policy is a realm of value which he may, even should, enter as a citizen but not as a scientist; and (3) Myrdal's position, that the social scientist cannot deal objectively even with facts, because his observation, selection, and use of facts reflect values which may be recognized but not escaped.

Each of these positions is logically more consistent than

Beals's. Unfortunately, the deepest inconsistency of the social scientist's role in policy-making stems not from his logic but from practical circumstances. As a private scholar, he has no contractual right to be heeded, only to be paid. His resultant sense of frustration is entirely understandable, especially if "effective use" is made of his work for purposes he deplores. Some scientists hold the strange belief that they must prevent such use, although that belief is incompatible with the doctrine that scientific knowledge is in the public domain. Once it is made public, how can the scientist control the use that is made of it?

If (as I believe) there is no "scientific" way to formulate public policies, the social scientist is under no special handicap, except insofar as he lacks the ability, experience and knowledge which enables others (such as administrators, politicians, and lobbyists) to devise realistic policies. The experience and knowledge can be acquired by any able person who applies himself to the task. There are fewer intellectual mysteries and more pragmatic conclusions in public law and administration than in the arcane fields of social theory, and the social scientist who genuinely seeks such conclusions has a fair chance of finding them. These "pragmatic" outcomes of empirical research into social questions posed by government agencies are precisely those which left-wing critics have attacked as permitting only minor, not fundamental, changes in social policies and institutions. In part, this criticism reflects the fact that much applied research is avowedly and necessarily designed to improve the effectiveness of existing policies and programs. Administrators would be negligent if they did not sponsor such research, for every social policy and program cannot, need not, and should not constantly be transformed to test every untested idea. A people is not a hurdy-gurdy on which different social tunes can be played at will. In part, the criticism discounts the large volume of fundamental research which is constantly financed by government and which provides the factual basis for many new social policies and programs as well as for more radical proposals and critiques. The restraints that one agency may set on the bounds of research are breached by other agencies with different interests, so that the totality of government-sponsored research spans a broad spectrum of social and political opinion. And, in part, the criticism is sound, in the sense that no sane government can be expected deliberately to finance and publicize research into the means by which it might be overthrown or destroyed.

Does Social Science Solve Social Problems?

One way to assess the possible contribution of the social sciences to the resolution of present social problems is to identify their past contribution to the resolution of such problems. The Reuss respondents cited a considerable list of problems to whose solution they believed the social sciences had made a significant contribution. Controlling the "boom and bust" business cycle, avoiding excessive inflation or depression, and maintaining steady economic growth with a low rate of unemployment were the achievements mentioned most frequently by economists, though they would hardly be mentioned so frequently today. "All other contributions by the economics profession are minor by comparison," one remarked (III, 77), and the passage of time has lent that remark a certain piquancy. Other contributions include the systems of budgetary and program management introduced during the 1960s by the Department of Defense and other federal agencies which, by clarifying the resources required for and the benefits expected from alternative courses of action, "can lead to more prudent political and personal decisions" (III, 59).

The contributions of psychology—stemming from techniques of measuring individual differences in intelligence, attitudes, aptitude, and achievement—include improved methods of education through training, counseling, and placement; improved personnel selection and utilization; improved product design; and improved services and approaches in child development, physical and mental health, vocational rehabilitation, crime and delinquency, and treatment of the aged. Political science has contributed to the reorganization and improved management of federal, state, and local governments; to congressional reapportionment; to electoral reforms; and to "a heightened understanding of the policy process itself" (III, 11). Sociology and anthropology have helped to change public attitudes and behavior toward Negroes and ethnic groups; to improve race relations; and to improve educational, health, vocational, and other services rendered to many social groups.

In addition to such relatively direct help in alleviating social problems, respondents noted many indirect contributions made by influencing the outlook of other disciplines and professions (such as medicine, history, law, public administration, business, education, social work, and journalism) and both the informed and lay public. Because many Americans believed the prevailing data and ideas of the social sciences to be true, they came to influence our lives and government.

Were the ideas in fact true? Was their truth a critical or incidental element in the influence they enjoyed? Why did other truths exert less influence? And if the social sciences helped resolve so many social problems, why do so many remain? Do social scientists battle unaided a problem-mongering populace; do they create as many problems as they resolve; or do they not really help to "solve" any problem? Several respondents did, in fact, challenge the assumption that social problems can be solved like mathematical problems. "Most of the important and enduring social issues are not susceptible to explicit, once-and-for-all answers. . . . With rare exceptions, these are problems to be managed, to be resolved partially and repeatedly through the evolution of a social system" (III, 151).

Such reservations about the credit social scientists deserve for the solution of problems that are as persistent as sin are wise. If social scientists deserve credit for easing some of our problems, then they should also receive their share of blame for the persistence and aggravation of other problems. This uncomfortable but logical observation was made by the physicist Robert Krueger (III, 117) who, after citing our failures in race relations and "what appears to be a gradual moral decay of society," insisted that the "social sciences must bear some of the responsibility for failure to find solutions to the causes of crime and all of the responsibility for failure to find solutions to the political, economic, and psychological causes of war." To assign them total responsibility seems excessive, but to assign them none denies them any influence on the nation's affairs and modes of thought—in short, belies the testimony we have summarized.

Summary

Unlike President Johnson, our respondents felt that academic men had no special obligation to study public issues at the request of government officials and especially not to study them precisely as posed by the government, because that tended to produce narrow, self-serving research.

Social scientists' information and ideas have influenced national attitudes toward countless problems and the development of programs for dealing with them. But a social problem can rarely be solved like a puzzle; it must rather be managed, endured, outgrown, or, at best, reduced. Social scientists can claim success in dealing with social problems only at the risk of being also charged with failure—or are we to believe that they are influential only when they succeed?

5

What Research
Is Needed?

The word *balance* evokes an image of proportion and equity; of the blending of elements into a harmonious whole; of a healthy, natural, or organic equilibrium. In fact, the image can be so paradisiacal, so restrained and orderly, that it can appear less attractive to less restrained and less orderly Americans than it did to the classical Greeks. A balanced economy is not the goal of a one-industry town, a balanced government budget is not the goal of numerous economists, and balanced expenditures for every field of science are not the goal of scientists in every field. The attractiveness of such balance depends very much on which end of the budgetary seesaw one is sitting.[1]

Thus, the attitudes of high-energy physicists toward large government expenditures for accelerators are different from those of chemists and social scientists. The scientific committee which

---

[1] A modified version of this chapter appeared in *Minerva*, October 1972, as "Criteria of Choice in Social Science Research."

recommended that the National Science Foundation serve as a "balance wheel" to maintain the level of government expenditures for basic research despite cutbacks by other agencies had a high ("imbalanced") regard for basic research (National Academy of Sciences, 1965). Handler (1965) contends that balanced growth, planning, or allocations for science are less flexible and effective than *un*balanced growth—Charles Lindblom's "disjointed incrementalism" or what Handler terms "skillful opportunism," which capitalizes on unexpected opportunities. "Orderliness, balance, and detailed planning may be more satisfying to the planners than to the society they serve."

Imbalances in Government Expenditures

When, therefore, the Reuss inquiry asked for opinions about "the points of most evident present imbalance" in government expenditures for social research, for the kinds of research that seem to be either underfinanced or overfinanced,[2] it might have been inviting respondents to express their personal interests and values. This Don Price politely declined to do. "I could not answer the question as to what kinds of social research are relatively underfinanced except by expressing my prejudice that those fields in which I am personally interested are of course inadequately supported, and this view is not worth your consideration." Price noted that, despite many careful studies of the needs of individual scientific fields which the National Academy of Sciences has sponsored (including, subsequent to his reply, studies of the principal social science fields),[3] the Academy "has not considered it possible to

[2] The full question was: "Information on what the federal government is spending at universities and private organizations for research in the basic and applied social sciences, for research in various social science disciplines, and for research on various social problems is so inadequate and complicated that we cannot attempt to summarize it here. But we can, nonetheless, request your opinion on the points of most evident present imbalance. Viewed as a whole, what kinds of social research seem to be relatively neglected and underfinanced by the federal government? What kinds may be receiving relatively too much attention and money?" (III, 6)

[3] In addition to the comprehensive study *The Behavioral and Social Sciences: Outlook and Needs* (1969), the Academy has issued separate reports on anthropology, economics, geography, history, mathematics and computation, political science, psychiatry, psychology, and sociology.

express an authoritative scientific opinion as to the comparative
extent to which these fields deserve support. Such comparative judgments . . . include such a large measure of sheer political judgment that I doubt that anyone can pretend to answer them scientifically, and I would certainly not try" (III, 159).

Gerhard Colm, an authority on national economic planning,
sought a rational approach to the question of balanced expenditures
along the following lines. "In order to identify imbalances," he
commenced, ". . . one needs a notion of what a balanced distribution of funds would be." That idea, in turn, rested on one's
conception of why the government should support social research.
Colm saw two basic rationales: "One is that the Federal Government should support social science research work that directly aids
in the performance of recognized government objectives . . . [such
as] research work related to the anti-poverty program, to monetary
policy, tax policy, and so on. A second criterion would look at all the
social science research done within the nation. . . . Then presumably one could point to imbalances in the nation-wide social science
effort. . . . Only where . . . private financing is not likely to be
forthcoming one might say there is a Government responsibility for
filling such gaps" (III, 60). As it was "virtually impossible" to
reach "any reasonable conclusions" by the second mode of analysis,
Colm preferred the first approach. As examples of two problems for
which research funds appear to be inadequate in relation to the
possible significance of these issues for government policies, Colm
cited research on racial minorities and on foreign areas with "fast-
rising population, [and] low productivity." But "it is important not
only to consider the . . . urgency of the problem but also . . .
the likelihood that with additional research funds significant contributions for the guidance of future policies can be made" (III,
60–61).

All told, Colm's approach seems eminently reasonable; however, it is more applicable to applied and policy research than to
basic research, which seems to require a different rationale. Such
a rationale might be the support of the best ideas, men, or institutions, as determined by the best men one can get to make that
determination; but the criterion of foreseeable usefulness may be
unavoidably absent or attenuated.

All of this discussion remains on a very general level, and some may ask whether anything more specific can be said about imbalances in government research expenditures. Many answers to that question have been based on statistical evidence. Thus, after arraying agency expenditures for social research it is asserted that agencies which spend little (absolutely, or as a proportion of their total budget) should spend more and those which spend nothing should spend something. And if good research provides fresh information and fresh ideas, there is something to be said for this argument, especially in the case of stuffy agencies or those isolated from the normal forums of public debate. The State Department is a favorite example of the former kind and the Atomic Energy Commission of the latter. To be sure, research by itself may accomplish nothing, since a deadly agency is quite capable of commissioning deadly research; but the hope is that the research will be good and that the launching of good research program betokens the introduction of new personnel to administer and interpret it and a readiness by agency officials to give them a hearing.

A logical concomitant of this approach is that agencies with the highest research expenditures (such as the Office of Education and the National Institutes of Health) should lower them, or at least not raise them further. Though this argument is seldom made with the same zeal as that for expanding expenditures, it has a good deal to commend it insofar as we may assume that increments to already high budgets can be expected to yield a smaller return.

This approach takes *balance* to mean something very much like average or equal, an interpretation whose limitations are too evident to need detailing. Thus, in 1969, the average agency (which, of course, did not exist) allocated to social research 0.1 percent of its total obligations, 1.7 percent of its research and development obligations, and 4.9 percent of its obligations for scientific research. However, protagonists of research prefer to view the expansion of federal expenditures since 1945 as a portent of the future and, therefore, to take the larger agency expenditures of today as approximating the norm that most agencies should strive for tomorrow.

From similar statistics on expenditures for individual disciplines, subdisciplines, and purposes, one may deduce that too little

is spent on political science as compared to psychology and economics; on historical analyses as compared to quantitative ones; on
basic research as compared to applied research; and on the social
sciences as a whole in comparison with the natural sciences and
engineering. The trouble with these approaches is that they posit
what has to be independently established: that the comparison is
not only relevant but preferable to other relevant comparisons.
For example, if federal expenditures on social research are compared to those on historical and humanistic research, a comparison
for which a cogent case can be made, we would have to conclude
that it is not the former but the latter which should be raised.
While professors like to bemoan the low level of academic research
expenditures in relation to the high level of expenditures on defense
or space, it can be said with equal accuracy that it costs less to
sustain a welfare mother than a professor and that a mere hundred
million of the three hundred million dollars which the government
spends on social research would save many lives and shoe many
feet. We may fairly conclude that such statistical comparisons are
as much tools of political and moral persuasion as are transparently
emotional words.

When we turn from statistical to avowedly qualitative
assessments of the balances and imbalances of social research programs, many contradictory judgments are encountered. Thus, one
respondent asserted that too much research was devoted to "overly
broad subjects such as 'crime,' or 'poverty' " (III, 82)—and
another, to "narrow, circumscribed studies which produce results
of little generalizability" (III, 84). Respondents declared that too
much research was directed to goals which the government, rather
than the investigator, designated—and, contrariwise, that too much
was oriented to academic disciplines rather than to national issues.

Respondents contradicted each other and even themselves,
and if all of their testimony were to be given equal weight, it would
be difficult to know how federal research programs should be
changed. And, indeed, well-informed respondents could also be
found who were basically satisfied with the prevailing allocation
of federal funds. "On balance I believe present levels of support of
social research are adequately distributed over the various sub-
areas," said John Darley (III, 70). James Coleman agreed—"With

the exception of a few areas, I don't believe there is a great imbalance in expenditures at present" (III, 56)—as did Herbert Simon: "The present levels of research support are not greatly disproportionate to the numbers of social scientists, or to their capacity for imaginative(i.e., productive) research spending" (III, 186).

The questions about balance also elicited many replies of precisely the type that Don Price had shunned: that no kind of social research was overfinanced, all kinds could use more money, especially ———, whereupon a long or short list of topics was offered in areas of interest to the respondent or his institution. Unfortunately, the topics exhibited little discernible pattern and could readily have been extended to cover half or all or twice the social science universe.

The understandable reluctance of professional men to restrict the freedom of their colleagues, dictate their interests, or foreclose the possibility of fresh discoveries in any area of inquiry made it singularly difficult to obtain any positive testimony to the effect that research on *this* specific subject should be discontinued, because it was unlikely (no one could say "impossible") to prove rewarding. It is one thing to express such an opinion in a professional publication and quite another to present it as a guideline to be enforced in government programs. Again and again, in trying to set up hearings that might produce recommendations for increasing designated kinds of research and, conversely, not increasing or reducing other kinds (since we were skeptical of increases for *all* kinds), the Reuss inquiry staff sought and failed to obtain testimony that certain research should not be supported. Even scholars most critical of the quality of agency programs drew back from that sort of statement. Our resultant inability to make a cogent case for reordering social research programs in any definable and administrable manner was the main reason that hearings were never held.

If, in sum, the results of the inquiry about substantive imbalances in federal research programs seem inconclusive, the most likely explanation is that the question covered too vast a territory. It is simply not as practicable to evaluate the character of all research programs, taken as a massive ensemble, as to assess particular programs. When we inquired into research in six domestic areas,

respondents did offer detailed, substantive judgments of the needs
and deficiencies of several agency programs.

More and Better Data

I do not propose to discuss here the actual content of agency
research programs but rather alternatives which officials face in
designing them—the kinds of knowledge they can seek and can
realistically expect to obtain. Our point of departure is the question: "What kinds of new knowledge do we most need?"

Geoffrey Hazard, executive director of the American Bar
Foundation, dismissed the question by espousing the Sisyphean
doctrine of "more"—more money and research for more knowledge
which will never suffice and must constantly be replenished:

> . . . *most of the information that we have . . . in the*
> *area of criminal law and its administration . . . [is] obsolete*
> *or obsolescent. Moreover, rapid obsolescence will be a continu-*
> *ing characteristic of our knowledge and concepts for the rest of*
> *this century. Hence, the problem is not whether there ought*
> *to be a federal investment in building up a store of knowledge,*
> *as though that process could ever come to a halt or ever find*
> *definite results good for all time, but whether the federal*
> *government should make a materially greater investment in*
> *sustained processes of research, innovative experiment, criti-*
> *cism, reorganization of institutions, and then beginning the*
> *whole process all over again, generation after generation (II,*
> *30).*

The notion that social information goes stale and must constantly
be refreshed is more convincing than the static conception of social
knowledge derived from the model of natural science laws that
never change. We may also agree that an increase in the amount of
new information and the ferment that goes with new ideas are
needed, if not in all areas of American life (since there is more than
enough ferment in many), at least in the area of criminal law and
justice, where data are unsatisfactory, research has been at a low
level for many years, and practical problems have mounted so that
the ability of existing institutions to cope with them is in serious

doubt. Nonetheless, Hazard's reply ducked the question of research emphasis, which must be faced at every and any budgetary level.

Only a slight shift from more of everything—data, knowledge, ideas, and experiments—to more of some things was necessary to answer our question specifically. The most common answer was that more and better data were needed. Not just a chapter but a library could be filled with cogent specifications of the significant human problems about which existing data are unsatisfactory, dated, partial, unreliable, or in some other way inadequate for the reasonable needs of scholars and officials. Our authorities noted deficiencies in every area about which inquiry was made. Thus, one criminologist observed that "The basic statistical data which are the main guide to general policy regarding crime afford an altogether inadequate and misleading picture of the position" (II, 40); a second pressed for "uniform reporting systems for all agencies involved in criminal statistics" (II, 53); and a third called for "a reliable body of comparable information" in order to define rationally the objectives of both criminological research and of law enforcement (II, 32). In the area of education, respondents called for more information about "the absolute amount learned by students of various grades, ages, geographic regions, [and about] quality of schools" (II, 115); in poverty and welfare, for data on "who is served and what results are obtained" (II, 251), on disability, the adequacy of benefits, sources of income, and the racial and ethnic composition of the poor and of welfare recipients (II, 450, 452); in health, for data on the economic and social situation of affected populations (II, 378, 385); in urban land use, for data on "the types, amounts and costs of floor space and land area used for different purposes . . . the numbers of people and vehicles that go to and from the different parts of an urban area. . . . the number of people arriving at each land parcel and the number leaving it during each hour of the day, by different modes of travel, and . . . their origins and destinations" (II, 510–511). The ambitious proposal to establish a national data bank and national social indicators will be discussed in Chapter Eleven.

The need for more basic social data, which men such as Harold Lasswell and Kenneth Boulding deem to be as necessary to the creation of a true social science as were stellar observations to the development of astronomy, was set forth by Rensis Likert, director of the University of Michigan Institute for Social Research: "There is too little support for continuing, large-scale collection of basic social information of kinds that are needed both by social scientists for basic research, and by several government agencies, but not indeed enough by any one agency to warrant sponsorship. Examples: the existing programs are inadequate for getting comprehensive statistics relating to transportation, housing, crime, recreation, and race relations" (III, 125).

Data imply raw entries in a matrix whose coordinates are objectively determinable and pertinent to a full understanding of the phenomenon under study. However, the social sciences suffer from frequent disagreement about what coordinates are pertinent to full understanding; both the significance of coordinates and the data they measure are in constant flux; and few measurements can be made with full objectivity. Insofar as gross, pertinent, and reliable data cumulate faster than they are outmoded by events, they are naturally subject to continuing refinement. Is it any wonder, then, that reasonable demands for pertinent data are endless?

To many social scientists, more and better data are seen as the beginning of more and better understanding. To others, they lie closer to the end of understanding, since one cannot know what data to collect without first having made conceptual progress in ordering the confusion of events. However, the two positions are less sharply distinguishable than is often supposed. To the degree that social data and social concepts are fuzzy rather than clear, data do not exactly exemplify concepts, and concepts are not directly transcribed from data but rather imaginatively derived from them. One may say that social science theory distills a certain meaning from, and instills this meaning into, reality.

This process is an underlying weakness in the otherwise praiseworthy effort to improve social data or, as it is often put, to replace data gathered in the normal course of governmental operations by data specially gathered according to the specifications of social scientists. For ultimately the data will always pertain to people, not to social scientists, and will therefore always reflect the ambiguities and uncertainties of real people living in a real world, not social scientists' theories about that world.

Morgenstern has written a book about the inaccuracies of the data of economics, a field which nonetheless has enjoyed a vogue as the most practically successful of the social sciences, envied for its large volume of comparatively reliable and timely data. He combines an optimism about the progress of social science knowledge with a sharp degree of realism about its limitations:

> [*Economic*] *decisions made in business and in public service are based on data that are known with much less certainty than generally assumed by the public or the government. . . . even most widely accepted figures frequently have error components of unexpected magnitude, and consequently cast doubt on many currently accepted analyses in economics. . . . However, when the true conditions are realized, there will evolve a more powerful and realistic theory. We must carefully distinguish between what we think we know and what we really do and can know. . . . completeness is out of the question, since the number of economic data is limitless; and the task of scientific inquiry being an unending one, the problems of knowledge can never be resolved to our satisfaction [1963, pp. vii–viii].*

On the one hand, the quantity and quality of existing data seem never fully to satisfy our needs. On the other, the "limitless" number of data to which Morgenstern referred can utterly drown understanding. "The volume of purely economic data has most alarmingly outgrown the capacity of the human mind for absorbing and correlating it all," Clark (1927) lamented decades ago. Facts flood the mind in such profusion that only a residue of meaning remains for a time to mark their passage, like the silt deposited by a flood. That meaning is presumably what many respondents referred to as the knowledge or understanding which the social sciences need more of.

Vain and Modest Knowledge

As numerous illustrations of existing knowledge had been given in response to questions about social science contributions to

solving national problems, so other illustrations were readily offered
of the new knowledge that was needed to cope with current problems. But, though knowledge can be sought, it cannot be vouch-
safed. Therefore, the question ("What kinds of new knowledge do
we most need?") should perhaps be faulted more than the answers,
which included elusive kinds of knowledge that social scientists will
continue to seek and may conceivably find one day—or never.

For example, educators and psychologists emphasized the
importance of understanding human learning and motivation, not
just to advance knowledge but to provide a sound basis for improving the educational system. As Cronbach (1963) puts it, "Educational improvements that really make an impact on the ignorance
rate will not grow out of minor variations of teaching content and
process. Effective educational designs, worth careful development
and field trial, can emerge only from a deep understanding of
learning and motivation." Many respondents concurred: "We know
far too little as yet about teaching-learning processes" (II, 142).
"We need to know a great deal more about the nature of learning"
(II, 137). "Top priority must be given to the study of learning
process. We must understand how learning takes place so that we
can begin to identify the range of strategies and tactics that are
available . . . in a variety of learning situations" (II, 119).

In the field of mental health, Harvard psychiatrist Jack
Ewalt wanted more research "directed toward the discovering of
basic motivations of man" (II, 382). And to make progress in
solving urban problems, Frederick Aschman wanted more fundamental knowledge about the "quality of life," about "human needs,"
and about "people."

It is no disrespect to these respondents to say that, far from
meriting priority, such suggestions are too vague to promise meaningful scientific or practical results. Granted, a broad reply to a
broad question does not constitute a research design. Yet a common element can be discerned in these replies that is all too common in contemporary American social science: the notion that
enduring and significant knowledge about the nature and behavior of man (not just the specific behavior of specific men under
the particular circumstances of a particular investigation) can be
obtained by procedures outlined in methodological texts; and that

just about any question that can be asked about men can ultimately be researched and, hence, answered; or, to put it more conservatively, that a careful, objective, empirical approach can add something significant to our knowledge of any human question.

To call this a notion is less than just. It is a philosophy, an influential system of thought with innumerable proponents and practitioners, its own theoreticians, experimentalists, teachers, and politicians, its extreme and moderate leaders and followers in academic and practical affairs. It is also a superficial philosophy which, seeking a grand order of knowledge, produces too many petty facts and too readily misconstrues significant truths that sometimes lodge among them.

"We know far too little as yet about teaching-learning processes," says Julian Stanley. "As yet"? When will that statement not be true? What clear, hard, and significant knowledge do we now have about learning processes? If so little has been acquired in a century of effort, where is the assurance that another century will yield much more? Could human learning processes possibly be so varied, changeable, and interchangeable that they are not a fruitful subject for scientific investigation, let alone educational application? How long must how many social scientists investigate a problem before concluding that further investigation is also likely to be fruitless?

Lee Cronbach suggests that substantial reductions in "the ignorance rate" will come not from "minor" changes in "teaching content and process" but "only from a deep understanding of learning and motivation." Are doubling or halving school budgets, teachers, and students, then, minor changes? But they require no "deep understanding." What, indeed, does such an understanding consist of? If all educators and citizens must acquire it, the prescription for educational improvement is plainly futile. If they need not, then the greater understanding of a few social scientists can somehow work its weal on students despite the lesser understanding of taxpayers, legislators, teachers, parents, and, of course, the students themselves. Most likely, what is meant by deep understanding is simply the latest idea of a few social scientists, which becomes effective only when it is so widely shared and attenuated as to have been rendered superficial and been discarded by its originators for a newer idea. If so, major changes come not from deep ideas but from those which are widely held.

That the "basic motivations of man" is a large, ill-defined subject need hardly be debated. I do not mean to say that no one should ever conduct, or that the government should never support, research into large subjects, any more than that no one should ever try to write a history of mankind or could ever succeed in writing a good one. But it is one thing for an individual scholar to try a kind of research that requires for its success an exceptional order of talent and judgment; it is another to ask that large sums of money be allotted for such research by large numbers of people. Because a question is important does not necessarily mean that it can fruitfully be investigated by empirical procedures. What is the meaning of life? When will the next great religion emerge? Will America be torn apart by racial strife? How can we prevent war and death, loneliness, unhappiness? What is *the* nature of human needs, motivations, emotions, and ideas? What is *the* nature of man? It is painful but realistic to recognize the limitations of both man and his social science and to expect research programs to operate within them. There is much definable, obtainable, and significant knowledge that we lack; why devote greater resources to that which is poorly defined and in all probability unobtainable?

Abstract and Concrete Knowledge

These criticisms are directed at vacuous and vainglorious, not basic, research; the desirable balance of government expenditures between basic and applied research is a separate issue which has been debated too often to need restatement here. Although both academicians and men of affairs need knowledge that has practical usefulness in their work, the knowledge which is useful to the academician is, not surprisingly, of an academic or abstract character.

It is easy for the academic man to talk of the need for social change so long as that change takes place in society, not in his lectures. One cannot teach and yet constantly change what one is teaching so that what is said at the end of a lecture or book contradicts what was said at the beginning; instruction and the maintenance of a scholarly community demand continuity in the language and ideas of discourse. Scholarly theories and methods change, if at all, with generational speed; as Wilson (1958) remarks, "changing the curriculum entails all the physical and psychological difficulties of moving a cemetery." The most important means by which scholarly works are recorded, distributed, and absorbed by the academy—books and journal articles—serve to maintain the slow pace of scholarly change (while the books and articles that are produced more quickly seldom maintain traditional scholarly standards).

In this scholarly world, concrete data, examples, cases, and illustrations are not usually accorded great importance. The knowledge deemed most significant is the basic general idea or theory that does not change or changes slowly enough to be taught and to serve as a practical organizing principle to bind together, illuminate, and explain much of the data of the field (it never explains all the data or all aspects of any single datum). In short, that knowledge is most significant to academic men which has the greatest practical utility to them.

The same can be said of government officials; but theirs is a different kind of knowledge, the kind academicians use in their lives, not professions. Some general ideas and theories are there, insofar as they have acquired wide influence; but they are likely to occupy the background of attention because they do not serve adequately to organize, illuminate, and explain enough of the superabundant data and events of daily experience. In that daily life, concrete information is usually more helpful than abstract theory. Of course, ideas and insights are also helpful if employed by a flexible and adaptable intelligence. But it is never possible to understand all the people, events, and conditions one encounters daily; and where insight and understanding are lacking, a little information is a very good substitute. You may never really understand why your wife likes a certain hat, but the information that she does suffices to preserve your marriage. Thus illiterate peasants can live as wisely as educated men, and administrators can discharge their responsibilities well having less abstract knowledge than the academician needs.

Such differences in the needs of government and academic

men for concrete and abstract knowledge reflect differences in their tasks. But changes in the relative emphasis of government programs on practical or academic knowledge should reflect changes in national needs and circumstances. To all things there is a season. The economic and social crisis of the 1930s brought the social sciences to favor in Washington as aids to economic and social planning. During World War II, they aided military operations while basic research was necessarily neglected and impoverished; but thereafter it was rightly nourished with sharply increased government expenditures. And in the present season of social discord and discontent in which the nation wallows, the government would be negligent if it did not, once more, put such increased practical demands on the social sciences as they can meet.

Integrative Knowledge

In both basic and applied social research, the richness of experience and the poverty of explanatory theories and integrative systems have created an anarchy, a superfluity of unconnected findings. "A major deficit of the research funded by federal programs is that it tends to be disparate and unintegrated, noncumulative," observed a sociologist (II, 396). This situation has been at least as characteristic of independent as of federally sponsored research. ". . . the chief deficiency of contemporary empirical social research is the absence of general theory and the virtually random scatter of concrete attention," wrote Shils (1949) more than two decades ago. Cottrell (1952, pp. 21–36) sees "pressing needs . . . for a more consistent, coherent, and additive program of research" in the social sciences; while Odegard (1966, pp. 65–66) speaks of "the monumental accumulation of data and the meager crop of significant concepts" in contemporary political science. "Gaps, overlaps, every man for himself—at least superficially, social science appears to be a chaos of laissez faire," writes Lindblom of public policy analyses (Braybrooke and Lindblom, 1963, pp. 105–106).

Many of the suggestions respondents offered about the kinds of new knowledge that were most needed were directed at this situation. By intellectual or administrative means or both, they sought to organize the research and information generated by a major program. Thus, after criticizing the poor coordination of federal research programs in crime and law enforcement, one respondent suggested that what may be needed are "a national plan or strategy within which the mutual responsibilities and working relationships of these agencies will be more carefully defined and [establishment of] a system of administrative control, information exchange, and program review" (II, 37). Another proposed that the Office of Education develop and disseminate a ten-year plan for educational research in the 1970s similar to one it had issued in the 1950s (II, 149). And a third respondent suggested that "a total strategy for research on urban problems and . . . a continuously updated agenda with research priorities" be prepared by a new government institute under policy guidance from a national urban research council modeled on the National Science Board (II, 504).

There were calls for comprehensive "models" and "systems" analyses. So, an educational psychologist advocated "the development . . . of a more complex model of the learning situation" which would make possible more sophisticated educational experiments, which "might disclose that a particular educational treatment has different effects on learners with different backgrounds, interests, or abilities. This finding would mean that there is no single best method and that learning would be maximized by suiting the educational procedure to the individual. Ultimately such experiments might require study of interactions of a wide variety of attributes of teachers, teaching methods, content areas, and pupils" (II, 140). Or, it would seem, after several fittings to make sure that it is well tailored, one might develop a dynamic model of the entire educational system that might explain the individual and group consequences of all critical combinations of educational inputs. Or might not.

A systems approach was often advanced as more promising than single-factor approaches which had been tried and found wanting. Thus, Leslie Wilkins rejected "simple cause-effect" analyses for social systemic causes which might explain the incidence of crime and offer hope for its economical reduction. "We may never abolish crime, but we can reduce its dysfunctional features if we can ascertain more of the factors which make up the mutual causal system" (II, 39). Stuart Chapin warned against "single-purpose [urban] research objectives," urging "a systems approach to urban problems, where the behavioral systems actually define to an important degree the requirements for the facility systems" (II, 504). William Wheaton observed that "No university has been given the resources to make an exhaustive study of the effect of highways on urban development generally. Consequently, no such knowledge exists in organized form, although this is obviously far more important than the several hundreds of millions of research money spent on how to build highways" (II, 526).

That nations, cities, and individuals are not simple elements may be allowed; indeed, it may be insisted that they are not even (as many systemicists assume) unitary systems so much as complicated and volatile, compatible and incompatible sets of half-open systems. Assuredly, where a system is sufficiently closed and stable and data on the behavior of its parts are sufficiently accurate, timely, numerous, and regular, systems analyses have yielded much useful knowledge about it. (Often these data pertain to the physical or mechanical aspects of a system having both mechanical and human dimensions, such as the location, distribution, and movement of vehicles, goods, ammunition, and people. It is debatable whether such antiseptic analyses should be regarded as part of social science, of engineering, mathematics, statistics, econometrics, or simply of "operations research"—that is, a field of its own.) However, the availability of those data, the stability of the system, and therefore the potential fruitfulness of systems analyses of a particular problem cannot be assumed; they must be demonstrated in each case. The need for such a demonstration is all the greater as the expense of data collection and analysis mounts, for it is hard to say what systems analyses devour more of: data, programers, computers, or money.

Therein lies the principal reservation that must be expressed not about systems analysis per se but about the excessive expectations many analysts hold out for it. Thus, Wheaton complains that, because no university has been given the resources for an exhaustive study of the "effect" (sic) of highways on urban development, invaluable knowledge does not exist. What can this statement possibly mean? That a very large sum devoted to a very large study of the many effects of highways (the effects of other methods of transportation will presumably require still greater sums) will yield such powerful and useful insights about the past development (physical growth? industrialization? changing volume and density of housing and population? economic, social, and cultural specialization?) of American cities as to usher in a beneficent new era of urban and highway planning? If knowledge were so effective, it would indeed be invaluable; but if invaluable knowledge could so readily be purchased, it would lose its value.

Large-Scale Research

The sheer magnitude of truly systematic study evidently commends it and other large and comprehensive study to many persons as a solution to the problem of proliferating disjointed fragments of knowledge. "Experience suggests that it would be wiser to mount larger scale attacks on major problems, rather than scattering small-scale investigations conducted by relatively inexperienced researchers," former U. S. Commissioner of Education Francis Keppel stated: not in itself an extreme or unreasonable position (II, 127). Welfare problems, Robert Morris complained, are as serious as health problems "but have not been the object of so intensive, nor concentrated, nor massive a study [sic] as that represented by the [National] Institutes of Health" (II, 458). Again, the peculiar and mistaken singular form of the noun. Does this usage imply that a singular order of significant knowledge about any domain of nature or society can be produced by a singular concentration of research expenditures? (Massive, NIH expenditures may be, but concentrated they are not.)

Imperceptibly, the advance from small-scale to large-scale projects and expenditures, from limited to prodigious quantities of data, brings a shift from modest to immodest claims for the resultant knowledge, as if truth, like an automobile, is worth approximately what it costs. Large expenditures had produced the atomic bomb, lunar exploration, and major medical advances: Would not comparable expenditures produce comparable knowledge—and the advances that, many fancy, flow from such knowledge—in education, welfare, and other social areas? And so are launched the pretentious claims that beset social science in the public arena.

Plainly, a group of collaborators and assistants can generate, assemble, and examine a large volume and variety of information. By specializing, they may raise the quality of a complex study, yielding results more comprehensive, accurate, and balanced (or, mayhap, neutral and conventional) than any that an individual could obtain alone in the same time. But collaboration does not alter the process by which each individual gains knowledge and understanding or the nature—durable or ephemeral, clear or ambiguous, certain or dubious—of the knowledge itself. It is an egregious assumption of the scientistic social sciences that forced quantification and rigorous manipulation can somehow transmute ambiguous opinion and mutable conduct into unambiguous and immutable truth.

Large masses of data can be analyzed systematically only when reduced to a quantitative form that disregards the qualitative aspects of the human experience. But what can be done with that raw experience—a million taped interviews, a thousand life histories, or two presidential archives—except to classify and file it? Its qualitative meaning can be abstracted only by the same process of reading, selective note-taking, and intellectual synthesis that characterizes traditional scholarship; and every scholar can perceive a slightly different meaning in the same documents. Once the mass of qualitative information exceeds the volume that one scholar can absorb, augmenting it further merely aggravates the problems of intellectual digestion.

The most practical and economic way to handle the large masses of data gathered in contemporary social research is to work out a scheme for classifying and counting them in advance of collection, with the consequence that new data mainly illuminate old ideas (though they may also inspire new ones). To hold off classification until the data are collected is possible only in part (verbatim replies can be recorded for subsequent coding, but they remain replies to predetermined questions) and magnifies the labor and expense of analysis. A large survey is as time-bound as a small one and is more vulnerable to the errors that arise when instructions and data, passing through many hands, can lose something of their original meaning or accuracy at any stage. Large surveys therefore require a strict discipline and inflexibility that limits their capacity to absorb new ideas or subtle information; the information gathered must be gross enough to be comprehended by the lowliest interviewer and respondent and processed consistently, in accordance with instructions, by the lowliest clerk and punchcard operator. Insofar as survey data do, in fact, measure what they purport to measure, a larger sample or complete census increases statistical reliability and permits a more complete—and, by the same token, more complex—picture of the phenomena being studied. As the scale of research and the volume of data increase, permitting the introduction of additional explanatory factors and the examination of smaller and smaller subgroups, we come ultimately not to the clarity of definitive truth but back into the inimitable complexity of life.

The scale and sophistication of quantitative research do not, of themselves afford assurance of definitive results, as is demonstrated by the controversy over the interpretation of the findings of the Coleman study *Equality of Educational Opportunity* and, for that matter, virtually every important study invoked to justify a controversial policy. No study is impeccable, without flaw, compromise, or weakness in design, execution, or interpretation; no large and intricate body of social data lends itself unequivocally to only one interpretation and only one consequent social policy. The more a policy is contested, the more assiduously will opponents search out the flaws in the data and the reasoning on which it is ostensibly founded. Conversely, the more widely a study is accepted, the more likely does its acceptance rest upon the palatability, rather than the flawlessness, of its conclusions.

Despite the inevitable limitations of its ideas and data, the large-scale study normally carries an authority that is politically attractive to its sponsors. Smaller studies can be readily reproduced (with one or another decisive modification) by intellectual and political rivals whose arguments are then as strongly based on fact as are the original investigator's. But by its scale a very large study becomes historically unique, so that its data can only be challenged by internal weaknesses which cannot be concealed or are voluntarily disclosed. Even should a rival study of comparable magnitude subsequently be mounted, it can neither erase nor exactly reproduce the original, which to that extent is invulnerable. Who can say with comparable authority that there really were three or twenty or no social classes in Newburyport, Massachusetts, from 1930 to 1934, instead of the six which Warner and Lunt (1941) found and thereby imposed on subsequent analyses of American communities? Who can duplicate the data gathered in Project Talent, the Coleman study, or the forthcoming national educational assessment? Because our knowledge of man and society always has a historical dimension and because the very large study is at least a minor historical event of its own, its findings are definitive not in the same sense as important findings in the physical sciences (which, being reproducible, are correctable or confirmable) but in the sense that selected facts have been permanently incorporated in the public record of the time.

The very large study which does not rely upon data produced in the normal flow of affairs but requests special answers to specially designed questions—and this is the ambition of the social sciences as they become increasingly specialized and professional— poses an additional problem that is growing as the volume of research mounts. This is the problem of saturation, or imposing on the time of the public and especially of key persons. Overburdened industry and university officials are rightly wary of additional requests for information. Protests about the volume and frequent duplication of government information requests (many of them stimulated by social scientists in universities and industry) led to the 1942 Federal Reports Act under which the Bureau of the Budget has since reviewed government data requests and tried to make them less burdensome. For many years, the American Council on Education has circulated long lists of the questionnaires being sent to universities and colleges, in an effort to discourage duplication; on occasion, educational officials have been known flatly to refuse what they considered excessive, uninformed, or otherwise unreasonable requests for information. "I think the poor have been overly exploited by research experts and officials," observed Winifred Bell (II, 444), an opinion voiced increasingly by Negro spokesmen and by both conservative and liberal critics of the relatively large sums spent on social research and the relatively large income of social researchers as compared to that of the poor whom they study.

The problem of saturation and of questioning the social scientist's legitimacy is a domestic version of the difficulties that have arisen in some overseas areas from too heavy a concentration of too naive American social scientists and a resultant questioning of their motives, their political and intellectual sophistication, their knowledge, and their judgment. The lesson is better learned before the problem becomes acute: the volume of social research and hence of social data on certain critical public questions is not infinitely expandable. Though social scientists' thirst for new data may be infinite, as a practical matter their possibilities of acquiring it— especially key data from key people—will be limited. Increasingly, they will have to decide which data are indispensable and which they can forego.

Social Experimentation

Another body of respondents placed their hopes for fruitful knowledge less on research per se than on experimentation and demonstration—that is, on substantial, deliberate experimentation not in the laboratory but in the real world. They seemed to say that abstract knowledge could never suffice to guide complicated social programs, but perhaps a combination of the knowledge and experience gained by practical experimentation would.

For example, Norval Morris wanted more experimentation on different modes of probation and citizen protection in the "national laboratory" of the United States (II, 33). Winifred Bell wanted extensive and varied experimentation and demonstration with new means of welfare assistance (II, 444). Francis Ianni would correct "the fragmented and incremental [educational] research we have today" with a "future-oriented, systems-conceived research effort" on the scale of the space program, a vision of radically new, expensive, experimental schools or educational "systems" which gained in ambitiousness what it lacked in clarity (II, 125).

As their resources and influence have increased, social scientists have talked increasingly of such large-scale national experimentation, and examples can be cited in which such experiments have been undertaken. In Project Vicos, Cornell anthropologists for many years experimented with various means of raising the living standards of a group of Peruvian Indians; the Office of Economic Opportunity has been experimenting with negative income tax payments in New Jersey; Nourse (1969) has characterized the eleven-billion-dollar tax cut of 1964 as "a more daring and more professionally designed experiment with a total economy than we had ever experienced before." Concluding a book on the contribution of social scientists to recent public policies and searching for some approach which may be more successful than existing methods of program evaluation, systems analysis, and cost-benefit analysis, Rivlin calls for "systematic experimentation" to find out "what works. . . . These experiments should be carefully designed, on a large enough scale and with sufficient controls to permit valid conclusions about the relative effectiveness of various methods. . . . In other words, the conditions of scientific experiments should be realized as nearly as possible. . . . Information necessary to improve the effectiveness of social services is impossible to obtain in any other way" (1971, pp. 87, 91, 108). The last sentence (can *everything* else that social scientists do be *that* irrelevant to social services?) may indicate the current discomfort of some analysts. Confident of their craft in the early 1960s, when prosperity and reform accompanied their counsels, they have been perturbed by the subsequent economic and social malaise which they have been unable adequately to relieve or to comprehend. As they took too much professional pride in what were national achievements, they are now professionally too distressed by national failures. Whatever may be the exact intellectual status of their disciplines, it certainly has not changed greatly in the interim.

Every significant new social program or institution; every new stock issue, factory, product, city, neighborhood, or school; every new election and administration might be considered as a kind of economic or social experiment. At times, entire nations (particularly those, such as Sweden or Russia, whose economic and political systems differ substantially from ours) and peoples have—indeed, mankind itself has—been regarded as an "experiment"; but this usage puts a decidedly looser construction on the word than does its scientific usage of controlled and reproducable observation. In a strict sense, the word should be confined to cases in which a "control" population is compared with an experimental one or in which a specific factor is changed and anticipated consequences subsequently are measured.

Setting aside the fearful complexities which render tenuous the equation of even such strictly defined experiments with physical science experiments, it is probably more accurate to refer to them as social rather than social science experiments, insofar as: (1) They involve many people and much money, so that final moral and practical responsibility must be assigned to individuals with the requisite authority to sanction the project; hence the final control is social, not social scientific. (2) The primary purpose is social, not social scientific. The simplest test of this definition is that a social experiment such as the construction of a new town or model city can succeed even though it adds little to social science knowledge, because we do not really know why it worked or because the critical conditions of its success were unique and cannot be duplicated elsewhere.

However, insofar as the opposite is true and final authority is exercised by social scientists whose primary purpose is not social action but the acquisition of knowledge, then, for good or bad, we have a case of full-fledged, real-world social science experimentation. Since the authority necessary for a major real-world experiment lodges with officials of government and the many organizations whose cooperation is vital to success, the most that social scientists can normally hope for is a collaborative or subordinate role in which they work within restraints imposed by these officials and by social convention.

Serious criticisms can be lodged against real-world social science experimentation, and the better an experiment is, technically (the stricter the controls), the more serious must some criticisms be. Such an experiment is probably the single most expensive way to gain knowledge, and on that ground alone it should be the last, not the first, resort of investigators. Morally, experiments can represent social scientists at their worst, for regardless of their personal sensitivity—and all are by no means inhuman monsters; some are hard-headed, narrow-minded "realists," but many are well-meaning pragmatists and idealists; and some newer recruits are economists who know more about methodology than about society—experimenters are inevitably put in the position of playing with other people's lives. The willing consent of the subjects (how correctly that word indicates their status!) may alleviate but not alter that position. If the consent is genuine, representing a free choice made after a balanced presentation by persons with no special interest in the work, it can impair the representativeness of the experimental group. A self-selected group may not be representative of the entire population; and the subjects' very consciousness of the experiment can yield results inapplicable to an ordinary population receiving no special attention from investigators, journalists, politicians, and administrators.

But the primary criticism of social science experimentation must be leveled at its assumptions: that one can identify, isolate, and control discrete, enduring, and manipulable factors in society as in nature; and that society is such a comprehensible, closed, and consistent mechanism that the operation of one factor is necessarily the same at one time and place as at another. Quite to the contrary, it must be asserted that, in society, a "factor" is as narrow or broad as the imagination, and the imagination of each citizen differs, though each is homogenized in the experimenter's mill. Quite contrary to the logic of the painstaking experimentalist, it must be asserted that we will gain no more authentic knowledge from real-world experiments than from other empirical methods. "Under precisely controlled conditions," the Harvard Law of Animal Behavior states, "an animal does as he damn pleases." We can expect no less of men.

Longitudinal Research

One recurrent suggestion was that more longitudinal studies are needed which follow a cohort over many years. For example, in studying the causes of poverty, Harold Watts would put more emphasis on "processes extending through time—the dynamic relationships that shape family formation, growth, and dissolution; evolution of careers, choices involving earning and spending income. These are extremely pertinent to the problem of poverty reduction, and as yet only poorly understood. The main obstacle here is the lack of data on families, earners, youth, and so on, over a period of time" (II, 267–268). Daniel Price, Harold Sheppard, and Elizabeth Wickenden also stressed the need for long-term longitudinal studies, and Charles Lebeaux for very long-term ones "running over several generations" (II, 454). Even the redoubtable Moynihan (1969b), who succumbs to the conventions of the guild less readily than most, has asserted that "the federal government must begin to sponsor longitudinal research . . . to follow individual and communal development over long periods of time."

My reservations about such research are based partly on its expense: for it is *very* expensive, and very expensive studies should supply specially valuable results. Good longitudinal research is also technically very difficult, because it is hard to keep a qualified staff together and intellectually alive for the long period needed to complete the study (Lebeaux's staff would have to be immortal). The alternative (often dictated by events) of changing the staff in midcourse endangers the comparability of the data gathered at different intervals. The longer a study lasts, the more likely it is that some of the ideas and problems with which it started will have been modified or discarded by subsequent developments, rendering earlier data to that degree irrelevant to the issues of the day. It is also difficult to keep track of a large and mobile population that must be tested and interviewed periodically over the years. Though allowance for shrinkage can be made by drawing a big enough initial sample, the lost members may well differ in important respects from those who remain, thereby reducing the representativeness of the surviving population. The added dimension of time enormously compounds the complexity of analysis, bringing the size of the population in some critical cells below the level of statistical reliability so that the final analysis does not merely open up new knowledge but brings us inevitably to many dead ends of ignorance.

When all the hazards have been surmounted and after five, ten, or twenty years the magnum opus is published and the stacks of punch cards are made available to the fraternity for additional analysis: what then? Assuming that the study was a success, we will know more about what happened to a group of people five or ten years before, under the circumstances which then prevailed. We will have such insight as sociological or psychological and statistical analyses can provide about processes and events of the past. But social scientific analysis of historical events and processes does not alter their historical character or provide any assurance that the lessons of one decade will be applicable to the next. The successful longitudinal study can add significantly to our knowledge of the past —as can any other successful historical study. But the relevance of that knowledge to the current scene must be established by current evidence. It is true that most empirical social knowledge is dated and must frequently be updated: that is an inescapable difficulty with which we must live and labor. But the difficulty is aggravated and not eased by longitudinal study; and the more protracted the study, the greater the likelihood that it will add only to our knowledge of lives that have been lived.

Unexceptionable Knowledge

This recital of the kinds of knowledge that are most needed may be completed with a kind that is, I believe, unexceptionable, being modest, clear to understand, practicable to obtain, and patently relevant to the improvement of public programs and services. It is, very simply, knowledge about the availability and nature of the services that are provided to different groups and communities and of the social and geographic distribution of the problems which these services are supposed to deal with. Thus, Eli Ginzberg asked for more information about "the ways in which different sub-groups in the population—by income class, location, ethnic background, etc.—seek medical attention and follow through on the services which they obtain" (II, 385). Similarly, Michael Davis wanted more information about the incidence of disease among different economic and social groups, so that preventive and corrective measures could be designed more intelligently (II, 379).

Sylvia Lauter of the National Urban League made a case for collecting detailed racial data in all fields of social welfare (II, 451–453). Obviously, data of this sort are not merely of practical help in allocating funds and personnel and improving welfare services; they are also politically helpful to any group—inner-city residents, children, mothers, Negroes, or the unemployed—which can thereby be shown to need additional services or to lack its fair share of services available to others. But viewed solely from an intellectual standpoint, the request for data on a particular factor such as race represents an assumption that this factor is relevant to a particular social problem or service. When that assumption is no longer correct, racial data will no longer be illuminating and our racial problems will have ended.

Summary

What kinds of new knowledge are most needed to improve the effectiveness of domestic social programs? All kinds had their advocates, and if all responses were taken with equal seriousness, it would be quite impossible to set any priorities in government research expenditures. There were calls for more program evaluation; for more large-scale, long-term, and longitudinal research; for systems analyses; and for more large-scale social experimentation. Most frequent of all was the call for more and better data on all conceivable and some inconceivable problems.

At the same time, many respondents recognized the profusion and fragmentation of existing data and sought both intellectual and administrative ways to order them. Among the suggested ways were theoretical advances; reviews and summaries; the development of typologies, classification systems, models, systems analyses, and comprehensive research plans; and the formation of many research institutes.

A number of respondents detailed specific kinds of information which could plainly be obtained and appeared needed to understand better the incidence and nature of a social problem and to improve the effectiveness of relevant services. But the overall impression given was one of striking out in all directions at once; of the absence of clear and convincing priorities; and of a widespread inability to distinguish between the order of knowledge which can and that which cannot be obtained by empirical research.

6

Program Evaluation

If there is one kind of research that social scientists familiar with governmental affairs agree is much needed at the present juncture, it is that which evaluates the effects and effectiveness of governmental programs. Some social scientists contend that program evaluation is too narrow and servile a use of first-class talent, which should rather be devoted to fundamental research, the examination of large national issues, or the formation of national policies. But that opinion about the best use of the best talent does not really dispute the judgment that more and better evaluation of governmental activities is needed and that social scientists are able to conduct it.

Only a few years ago, the phrase *program evaluation* rarely occurred in the social science literature, though *program analysis* has had a longer history as a recognized, if often humble, phase of government administration. Since the 1960s, however, as new domestic programs multiplied fissiparously—"between the presidential elections of 1960 and 1968 . . . the number of domestic programs of the federal government increased from 45 to 435" (Moynihan, 1969b)—the need to evaluate their merits also grew;

118

and it has not diminished under the Nixon Administration, which inherited this vast and not entirely welcome progeny together with a war and inflation. That need was formally recognized in President Johnson's statement extending to the rest of the government the PPB (planning-programing-budgeting) system that Secretary McNamara and economist Charles Hitch had earlier instituted in the Department of Defense. "Once in operation," the statement said, the new system would enable the government to "(1) Identify our national goals with precision and on a continuing basis (2) Choose among those goals the ones that are most urgent (3) Search for alternative means of reaching those goals most effectively at the least cost (4) Inform ourselves not merely on next year's costs, but on the second, and third, and subsequent year's costs of our programs (5) Measure the performance of our programs to insure a dollar's worth of service for each dollar spent" (1965, p. 917). Insofar as budgeting is a forecast of future expenditures, PPB is a kind of near-term futurology; but inasmuch as budgeting is a selective projection of past experience, it inevitably involves some assessment—be it methodical or impressionistic—of that experience. And commencing in 1965, government budgeting put formal emphasis on the kind of methodical program assessment for which empirically minded social scientists are qualified.

In his address at the Brookings Institution thirteen months after the inauguration of the PPB system, President Johnson (1966) stressed that the nation "urgently needs" independent evaluation of public programs and policies. Such evaluation, he acknowledged, "is less glamorous than the power to create new ideas; it is less visible and less publicized than the power to administer new programs." But it was no less important; and he went on to praise it as an activity worthy of the best minds.

Assuredly, more and better evaluation of government programs, old as well as new, is needed, and social scientists are qualified to undertake it. But it should be undertaken with a realistic appreciation of the difficulties entailed and with correspondingly modest claims and expectations for the usefulness of the results. Excessive claims are as reprehensible in social research as in other areas of merchandizing.

The difficulty of conducting sound program evaluation is

so great that evaluation is often distinguished from research; and the difficulty of meeting normal research standards is partly responsible for the reluctance of social scientists to undertake evaluation. "Research," one writer suggests, is marked by "flexible deadlines" and "sophisticated treatment of data that have been carefully obtained," whereas program evaluation commonly faces a fixed deadline and tends to use available data and such additional data as can be "expeditiously collected" (Wrightstone, 1969). There are "very few evaluation researches which have the elegance of design and clarity of execution which would achieve widespread admiration among social researchers," Rossi observes (1966, p. 127).

The poor quality of the resultant evaluations has been widely remarked. "Although there are notable exceptions, most of what passes for evaluative research in most fields of public service, such as health, social work, and education, is very poor indeed," Suchman concludes in his book on *Evaluative Research*. "By and large, evaluation studies of action or service programs are notably deficient in both research design and execution. Examples of evaluative research which satisfy even the most elementary tenets of the scientific method are few and far between" (1967a, pp. 20, 74). Levine, who headed the research and evaluation efforts of the Office of Economic Opportunity, remarks that "the state of evaluation of educational programs is such that we cannot even be sure that when favorable program results are obtained, they are the result of good program design . . . [and not] merely a Hawthorne effect" (1966, p. 345). Wildavsky (1969) has caustically condemned the quality of most PPB policy analyses conducted by government staff. "The data inputs . . . are huge and its policy output is tiny."

These judgments by protagonists of program evaluation are cited not as the final gospel truth (though contrary judgments are not encountered as often) but simply to temper the more intemperate assertions about the contributions social science can make to the evaluation of government programs and policies. The poor quality of much evaluation is not attributable solely to factors which can be changed—the quality of investigators, methods, data, and conclusions—but to ineradicable difficulties. Only a few need be mentioned.

One has already been noted: the difficulty of getting a good research design and good data. This problem is not an accident but a consequence of the normal situation in which most program evaluation takes place. When, as is customary in research, one starts with a question, one can consider various methods by which it might be answered and eventually elect those that appear most promising. But program evaluation starts with a program—with an ongoing activity already shaped by forces and events which cannot be reshaped to suit the investigator's convenience. The question comes second; the research design, third. Necessarily, the quality of the design suffers. The situation can be improved but not transformed when social scientists are involved from the outset in planning a program so as to facilitate its later evaluation, for they seldom can (or should) dominate the planning process. Subsequent developments are, in any event, likely to disturb the initial design, for governmental programs function with real people in the real world, not obedient students in a classroom.

The model cities program affords an example. Social scientists on the staff of the Department of Housing and Urban Development worked out a scheme for the evaluation of the seventy-five proposed model cities, which they helped to select. Unfortunately, senior officials thereupon substituted a number of other cities, and the White House reputedly then made fourteen further substitutions. These changes may have strengthened the program politically, but they definitely upset the staff's evaluation scheme.

To my mind, the best evaluation design is flexible and adventitious, adjusting its methods and even its questions to changing realities and capitalizing on unpredictable data-gathering opportunities. However, social scientists are taught to avoid this approach, and a proposal which did not set forth its procedures in advance would probably be rejected for one which, doing so, was more proper if less realistic.

Yet proper and rigorous methodology is rare, expensive, and pedantic, demanding a rigid adherence to the initial design regardless of the political and human realities and consequences. The evaluator cannot act as a friendly observer, passing along information and advice that may help a program to succeed. He must be a stern taskmaster, insisting on obedience to the design even if this threatens the success of the program, for the success of a program can depend on the very factor that makes rigorous research fail: a readiness to change.

Marris and Rein (1967) describe this conflict in the effort to evaluate the "grey area" demonstration projects to combat delinquency: "As soon as the [program] staff . . . discovered a better way of serving trainees they adapted their procedures . . . accordingly. It was impossible to be inventive, flexible and expedient on the one hand and at the same time do careful, scientific, controlled research on the other. . . . the claims of research and action were hard to reconcile. As this became apparent, a subdued but fundamental controversy arose . . . [between] the research directors . . . who insisted on the methodological rigour implicit in the commitment to experimental demonstration, and those who were prepared to improvise a more speculative evaluation with whatever resources lay to hand" (pp. 198, 200). They conclude that "research and action . . . each inhibits the other from following its bent. . . . the projects could not realize their claim to be experiments without abandoning their determination to benefit the communities in which they worked" (p. 206).

A basic difficulty that frequently plagues those who seek to evaluate the effectiveness of federal social programs is that, in the community, these programs are not discrete and isolable. When federal funds for education, job training, or health are merged with funds from state, local, and private sources, how can the effects of one dollar be separated from those of another?

Evaluation faces the same problem of time that confronts all policy research: the more time is allowed, the sounder—and less useful—will the findings be. "The better the study, the longer it takes, and consequently the less usefulness it may have. Conversely, the sloppier the procedure, the more likely it is to provide information on questions of interest even though this data will be of doubtful validity" (Mann, 1969). One writer remarks caustically that "the Head Start program, which moved public education into an entirely new area, which involved the training of vast numbers of personnel for new teaching and aide roles and which required materials that were in process of development as the program got under way—this program was nevertheless 'evaluated' in its first summer!" (Fox, 1967). Preposterous, perhaps; but also necessary. The need to conduct *some* kind of early evaluation to be assured that a program is going well, to improve its administration, and to obtain evidence to justify continued appropriations (first to departmental superiors and then to the Congress) is responsible for the poor quality and self-serving character of much evaluation. So long as these needs continue, there will be a demand for, and supply of, "quick and dirty" evaluation.

Evaluation also faces a set of interlinked moral and practical problems that impair its objectivity, insight, or candor. Agency staff and clientele who know most about a program are least able to view it objectively; whereas the outside investigator's objectivity is purchased at a considerable cost in naivete. However, the longer a study lasts and the more knowledge he acquires, the greater is his moral indebtedness to informants, which inhibits the candor of his reporting. And as his naivete declines and his knowledge grows, the investigator becomes committed to a particular analysis and conclusion: in the course of becoming an expert, he becomes a partisan. Thus he eventually falls from his state of intellectual innocence to a position of personal and social responsibility akin to that of agency staff.

A final problem should be mentioned which is widespread and intractable: identifying a program's goals. Obviously, the effectiveness of a program can be determined only if its goals are known, but these often resemble Winston Churchill's description of Soviet policy: "a riddle wrapped in a mystery inside an enigma." There are ostensible or formal goals, put out for public consumption, and real goals which cannot be advertised. Commonly, social programs are marked by the multiple and even conflicting interests that generated them. ". . . only in logic are contradictions unable to exist: in feelings they quite happily continue along-side each other," Freud once remarked, and the remark is just as apt if *feelings* is replaced by *politics*. Congress must serve diverse interests and constituencies and can do so more easily by amalgam and compromise measures, which offer something to many different groups and are lent a semblance of unity by goals broad enough to embrace the spectrum of interests involved. Would legislation be possible without such words as *community, welfare, freedom, education, health, equality,* and *opportunity?*

Coleman (1968) observes that the first difficulty confronted in his effort to evaluate the equality of educational opportunity was "to determine precisely what the request means. . . . various members of government and of society have different conceptions of what such equality consists." Five separate conceptions had to be considered in designing the study: "first, inequality defined by degree of racial segregation; second, inequality of resource inputs from the school system; third, inequality in 'intangible' resources such as teacher morale; fourth, inequality of inputs as weighted according to their effectiveness for achievement; and fifth, inequality of output as prima facie evidence of inequality of opportunity."

Daniel Moynihan (1966a) relates how "at least four distinct—and, generally speaking, incompatible—understandings" became intertwined in the phrase *community action* and the legislation governing that OEO program: (1) the "Bureau of the Budget Concept," which viewed community action as a device to promote program coordination and administrative efficiency; (2) the "Alinsky Concept," which saw it as a means to help the poor to gain "power, and a sense of power" by community organization and by "inducing conflict"; (3) the "Peace Corps Concept" of providing services to, and promoting self-help among, "the underdeveloped peoples of the United States"; and (4) the pragmatic and politically minded "Task Force Concept," which sought to gain political support for the President and reduce unemployment by creating new "urban, ethnic political machines."

Schultze (1968), who as Budget Bureau Director was responsible for implementing the PPB system, points out how diametrically opposed are the evaluator's need for a clear statement of program goals and the contrary need for vagueness in getting a program adopted in the first place:

> *The first rule of the successful political process is, "Don't force a specification of goals or ends." . . . [The] necessary agreement on particular policies can often be secured*

*among individuals or groups who hold quite divergent ends.
. . . The Elementary and Secondary Education Act of 1965
. . . was enacted precisely because it was constructed to
attract the support of three groups, each with quite different
ends in view. Some saw it as the beginning of a large program
of federal aid to public education. The parochial school interests saw it as the first step in providing . . . financial assistance for parochial school children. The third group saw it as
an antipoverty measure. . . . If there had been any attempt
to secure advance agreement on a set of long-run objectives,
important elements of support for the bill would have been
lost, and its defeat assured.*

*Another example is the wheat price-support program
enacted in 1964. . . . This program secured the support of
two quite distinct groups. One group sought a subsidy program acceptable to farmers. . . . The other group saw in the
direct payment scheme the possibility, at some future time, of
placing a limit on the subsidies paid to high-income farmers.
. . . The two groups had diametrically opposite objectives.
Yet both were able to agree on the same program—precisely
because ultimate goals and objectives were not forced into the
debate [1968, pp. 47–49].*

But how can programs with diffuse and equivocal purposes be
evaluated sharply and unequivocally?

To set a narrow goal is to risk attaining it—and terminating
the program. To set a rigid goal is to hazard the future of a program by perpetuating the circumstances prevailing when it is
adopted, whereas the ability to adapt to new circumstances is the
ability to survive politically; and, once launched, the real goal of
many programs is the same as that of many persons: to survive.

Enough has been said to indicate some of the obstacles to
good program evaluation. My conclusion is that good evaluation is
difficult and that large claims for the potential of social scientific
evaluation are unwarranted. The function of program evaluation
in not to convert society into a laboratory and citizens into experimental subjects but to improve a community and to help its people.
That kind of evaluation cannot be conducted by a set of artificial

rules that can be imposed on laboratory mice and classroom students. Successful evaluation requires as much adaptability, ingenuity, and respect from the investigator as he requires sympathetic cooperation from the community and agency staff. The final product will not constitute the pure distilled truth but the useful judgment of an informed, careful, and relatively impartial observer. There will usually be many people informed about the program and motivated to criticize whatever conclusion is reached.

7

Location of Research

A comprehensive empirical analysis of federal research allocations cannot be attempted here, for this examination would require a book in its own right; and it would not be an easy book to write, because many of the critical data—on the volume and location of expenditures; the number and types of recipient institutions; the number, field, and qualifications of investigators—are incomplete or nonexistent. Lacking better data, we must make do with poorer; if half a loaf is better than none, so, presumably, are a quarter and a sixteenth. My fractional analysis is based mainly on selected expenditure statistics and on the judgments of Reuss respondents about the kinds of research that should be conducted by different kinds of institutions.

Allocations by Sector

Unfortunately, the National Science Foundation, principal source of statistics on government scientific research expenditures, does not normally obtain information on the allocation of social research expenditures among different kinds of institutions or even on the proportion of funds which are used extramurally. Therefore such information must be derived by ad hoc inquiries and estimates.

The Reuss inquiry took one statistical step forward by requesting each federal agency to determine the amount of its 1967 extramural social research obligations. Overall, agencies obligated $240 million for research performed by nonfederal organizations, or 76 percent of the $315 million then estimated to have been obligated on social research. Subsequently, the Behavioral and Social Sciences Survey Committee independently estimated the extramural portion for 1967 at $220 million or 74 percent of all social research obligations (which had shrunk, in the interim, to $297 million). It further estimated that of the $220 million, 65 percent ($143 million) went to universities and the remaining 35 percent ($77 million) to nonprofit institutes, profit-making firms, state and local government agencies, and individuals (1969, p. 14), thus providing statistical evidence that, in extramural research, the major practical choice facing government agencies is that between universities and all other places. (However, the BASS Committee may have overstated the volume of social research funds that universities receive.) In the collection of social and economic statistics, the government exercises less choice, 96 percent of its $100 million reported obligations for this purpose having been used intramurally in 1967 (National Science Foundation, 1967, p. 243).[1]

BASS estimated all national expenditures not only for social science research but for a previously undiscovered phenomenon titled "development in the behavioral and social sciences." For reasons to be stated, I believe that this concept and the statistics purporting to measure it should be deposited in the vast attic of quaint ideas beside the Loch Ness monster, extrasensory perception, flying saucers, and other curiosities which have eluded all efforts at empirical observation. Nonetheless, as this concept has been lent authority by an important and, in most respects, commendable

[1] However, the distinction between "research" and "statistics" or "data collection" is not sharp. Apparently using a more relaxed definition of statistical activities than that of the National Science Foundation, the House Subcommittee on Censuses and Statistics reported that, in 1969, "$69 million, or more than 20 percent of the . . . total expenditures for federal statistical activities," was spent extramurally (*Federal Statistics*, 1971, p. 58).

report, it deserves at least the attention required to dismiss it (Table 3).

The National Science Foundation, from which both the BASS and the Reuss inquiries derived many of their statistics, defines *development* as "systematic use of the knowledge and understanding gained from research, directed toward the production of useful materials, devices, systems, or methods, including design and development of prototypes and processes." By definition, successful research augments knowledge and successful development does not. Research is scientific while development is an engineering activity. Though industry used 70 percent and academic institutions only 13 percent of the $27 billion national expenditures on R&D in 1970, the academy employed 58 percent and industry only 26 percent of the nation's 125,000 Ph.D. scientists, because industry worked predominantly on the D and universities on the R of R&D.[2] Although some persons with a science Ph.D. may be involved in development, that does not transmute it into a scientific activity any more than marketing, administration, warfare, education, or journalism become scientific upon employing some science Ph.D.s. The BASS Committee's mistake is to single out some development activities in which some social scientists are engaged together with computer programers, social workers, teachers, business executives, and members of many other occupations and professions, and allocate their entire costs to the social sciences.

The National Science Foundation does not make that mistake, for it classifies only *research* expenditures by discipline and *development* expenditures not by discipline but by agency, institution, and industry. Similarly, the Office of Management and Budget reports development expenditures by agency and objective, such as aircraft, missiles, ships, reactors, air pollution control, and improving health care or education. This is the only sensible approach because a technical product—a radio, book, or bomb—cannot be developed (that is, brought to the stage where it can be produced routinely) solely with the ideas and work force of a single intellectual discipline, be it physics, psychology, typography, or metallurgy.

[2] Of course, not all Ph.D. scientists were engaged in research. These statistics are drawn from National Science Foundation (1970, p. 29, and 1971, p. 13).

Table 3

RESEARCH AND "DEVELOPMENT"[a] OUTLAYS IN THE SOCIAL
SCIENCES, 1962 AND 1967

Source of Funds	Million Dollars		Percent	
	1962	1967	1962	1967
Federal government	$188	$388	49	48
Research	120	291	31	36
"Development"	68	97	18	12
Industry	130	289	34	36
Universities and colleges	24	48	6	6
Foundations	23	24	6	3
Nonprofit institutions	14	39	4	5
State governments	5	15	1	2
Total	$384	$803	100	100

[a] I have put "development" in quotes to indicate its dubiousness.
Source: Behavioral and Social Sciences Survey Committee, 1969,
p. 15.

BASS was evidently led into error by the fact that several
federal agencies whose research expenditures are confined to the
social sciences also report expenditures for development; ergo, it
reasoned, the latter expenditures should also be assigned to the
social sciences. "Because all of the Office of Education's reported
research obligations are for the behavioral and social sciences, we
can assume that the total amount for development can likewise be
assigned to these fields" (1969, pp. 293–295). But that assumption
is mistaken, since agencies whose research is confined to the natural
sciences—such as the Post Office, the Bureau of Mines, and the
Atomic Energy Commission—do not and cannot assign their development costs to these fields.

However, mistakes can be instructive. If we examine the
statistics of agencies confining their research expenditures to the
social sciences, some intriguing information emerges (Table 4).
In 1969, two-thirds of the extramural research expenditures of these
agencies went to academic institutions, the same proportion which
the BASS Committee estimated for all government agencies. However, more than half the *development* expenditures of the Office of

Education and the Office of Economic Opportunity went to independent nonprofit organizations.

What activities does development embrace here? Illustrations that BASS would classify as "social science development" include "a specific plan for urban renewal [prepared by architects, engineers, surveyors, and draftsmen?], a decision on the site of a new power plant [by engineers and administrators?], the preparation of audiovisual aids for instruction [by cameramen, script writers, artists, and teachers?], or a program for a computer [written by an applied mathematician?]" (p. 25). Social science, no; but the last two examples would evidently constitute educational "development" if financed by the Office of Education. A physicist who writes a book on an NSF grant is doing "research" in physics, but the same book prepared for a regional educational laboratory apparently is educational development.

"Development" expenditures of the Office of Education included the entire costs of the twenty nonprofit laboratories and some costs of the ten research centers which it sponsored, and the costs of "all projects or programs which have as their aim the production of materials, techniques, processes, hardware, or organizational structures for instruction and education" (Office of Education, 1969, p. 127). Those of the Office of Economic Opportunity were, evidently, mainly for demonstration projects in manpower, legal, health, and community services and in education. In addition, the putative "research" budgets of these agencies may fund research training, facility construction, information dissemination, planning and programing projects, and occasionally even direct operations.

To sum up, in recent years about three-quarters of federal obligations for social research but less than 5 percent of those for social data collection have been allocated to nonfederal organizations. Of the extramural research funds, roughly two-thirds have gone to universities and the residue to nonprofit institutes, profit-making firms, and state and local government agencies. In several important domestic programs, a majority of "development" funds have gone to nonprofit institutions, many formed specifically to advance agency purposes. All told, a large portion of the "research" budgets of domestic social programs are, in fact, used for other purposes.

Table 4
Selected Agency Obligations for Extramural Research and Development by Different Sectors, 1969

Agency	Sector					Million dollars
	Academic	Nonprofit	For profit	Other[a]	Total	
Social research						
Office of Education	75%	14%	—	10%	100%	$57.7
Office of Economic Opportunity	51	11	36	3	100	21.5
Economic Development Administration	30	6	7	57	100	7.1
Office of Manpower Research	83	15	3	—	100	3.6
Other agencies[b]	62	16	8	14	100	1.8
Subtotal	66	13	9	12	100	$91.7
Development						
Office of Education	42	51	2	5	100	$72.7
Office of Economic Opportunity	20	52	19	9	100	26.4
Economic Development Administration	26	5	29	41	100	9.8

Office of Manpower Research	83	15	3	—	100	.9
Other agencies[b]	—	—	—	—	100	—
Subtotal	36	47	9	9	100	$109.9

Research and development

Office of Education	57	35	1	7	100	$130.4
Office of Economic Opportunity	34	34	27	6	100	47.9
Economic Development Administration	27	6	20	47	100	16.9
Office of Manpower Research	83	15	3	—	100	4.5
Other agencies[b]	62	16	8	14	100	1.8
Total	49	31	9	10	100	$201.5

[a] Mainly state and local government.

[b] The Agriculture Department Economic Research Service and Farmer Cooperative Service, the Social Security Administration, the Interior Department Bureau of Outdoor Recreation, the Bureau of Labor Statistics, the State Department, Peace Corps, Federal Home Loan Bank Board, and Small Business Administration.

Source: Estimated obligations of agencies whose research obligations were confined to the social sciences and psychology, fiscal year 1969 (National Science Foundation, 1968b).

Let us now examine the opinions expressed by Reuss respondents—themselves affiliated with universities, nonprofit and profit-making organizations, and state and local government agencies—about the kinds of social research federal agencies should conduct themselves or sponsor at various organizations.[3]

There was widespread agreement that, whatever generalizations might be made about the desirability of conducting one or another kind of research in one or another kind of institution, no such generalization should become a dogmatic policy, since the most important criteria for the conduct of research remained the quality and usefulness of the product, which were governed by pragmatic considerations. Therefore, it was often said, research should be placed wherever the men best qualified to conduct it happen to be. When several equally qualified men are available, the work should be placed where it can be done most cheaply; and conflicts of interest should be avoided. Some overlap and even duplication of work by different organizations was desirable as a check on quality and bias and to obtain the special perspectives afforded by different kinds of institutions: "institutional pluralism is as important as individual pluralism" (III, 153).

Prescriptions about the kinds of research that should be assigned to different institutions were partly descriptive of prevailing institutional competence and partly ideological statements about the functions that they should exercise in principle.

Intramural Research

A few respondents would have dispensed entirely with intramural research because they felt it virtually impossible to conduct genuinely objective research within the political constraints of

---

[3] As expressed in answers to two sets of questions. In the general inquiry, respondents were asked: "What kinds of social research should federal agencies conduct themselves? What kinds should they sponsor at universities? At independent nonprofit organizations? At profit-making organizations?" (III, 7). Similar questions were asked in each of the six substantive areas: "What kinds of educational research [welfare research, research on urban problems, and so on] should the federal government conduct itself? What kinds should it sponsor at universities? At state and local agencies? At independent nonprofit institutions? At profit-making organizations?" (II, 27, 109, 250, 377, 442, 499).

government. Alvin Gouldner elaborated the point: "I do not think that federal agencies should *themselves* conduct *any* kind of social research. My reason is that the value of any kind of social research is greatly influenced by the amount of autonomy of the researcher. I think that it is very easy for intra-agency social research to become a political and policy football. While this danger can never entirely be eliminated . . . it is greatest if and when conducted within a specific operating agency. I therefore tend to believe that *all* social research should be given to outside contractors" (III, 102–103). Respondents believed government staff are singularly ill-placed to conduct politically hazardous research or to evaluate their own programs, both of which require a protected and independent institutional location.

Most respondents readily assigned to government agencies the function—often, it is true, not dignified as research—of collecting statistics, particularly of a recurrent nature, relevant to their administrative responsibilities. Other research which might best be left to government staff included that involving classified information, sensitive questions of national security or politics, and data not available or conveniently processed outside the government; longitudinal studies requiring continuity of personnel; research needed to check on work conducted by outside organizations; questions requiring quick answers and research needed to maintain a staff qualified to answer them; even some basic research which can help to retain good staff au courant with new knowledge in the field. A general degree of research competence was needed not only to meet internal agency needs but to administer, evaluate, and make perceptive use of extramural research.

Taken together, the foregoing might seem broad enough to encompass almost any research an agency might wish to do, but plainly, except for the collection of statistics, respondents envisaged a modest role for the government compared to that of nongovernmental organizations.

State and Local Government

If a modest role was seen for federal agencies, that of state and local agencies was more modest still. They had few staff competent to conduct research and were so heavily involved in operational responsibilities as to lack the money, time, or detachment for research. However, their cooperation was indispensable for much research by other organizations and especially for evaluating new departures in education, health, welfare, law enforcement, and other state and local programs. Again, it was argued that until local agencies recruited qualified social scientists—which hiring, in turn, might require that they themselves conduct a certain amount of research—they would be unable to make effective use of the research conducted by other organizations.

A strong case for building up the research capability of state and local agencies was made by psychiatrist Harold Visotsky, then Director of the Illinois Department of Mental Health. The major deficiencies of existing research on mental illness, poverty, and other social problems, he contended, were their "piecemeal nature" and the failure to translate their findings into action; both deficiencies could be corrected by establishing in federal, state, and local agencies research institutes to mount major, focused studies of problems now investigated by scattered contracts and recruit staff able to implement the findings, staff now employed by private organizations with government money (II, 404).

Universities

The university was held best suited to basic, theoretical, and long-term research by one or a few investigators, which permits intellectual, methodological, and administrative freedom and flexibility. Many respondents cautioned against using academic men for short-term answers to pressing problems; would as many hold the same view today, in a time of heightened social crisis?

Opinion differed on whether universities were suited for interdisciplinary and applied research. Though holding that faculty should do less applied research, James Coleman suggested that such institutional adjuncts as the University of Chicago National Opinion Research Center and the university R&D centers financed by the Office of Education could fulfill the same purposes as independent institutes like RAND (III, 57). Several respondents stressed that, whenever possible, the government should have its research conducted at universities, where it is usually cheaper and helps to promote their training function.

Among the kinds of research singled out as inappropriate for universities were projects entailing secrecy, providing quick answers, or "likely to develop permanent dependence on . . . action arms of the federal government" (III, 34). John Kofron, research director of the market research firm the Chilton Company, charged that surveys were often awarded to "name" universities which lacked the resources to do a good job. "This often leads to the use of students as researchers in ways in which they are not well trained . . . and . . . often produce low grade research" (III, 112).

Research Institutes

The nonprofit research institute, it was stated, was well placed to supplement internal government research and to undertake confidential or applied research inappropriate for educational institutions. The large institute was "particularly valuable for conducting multidisciplinary research on a quick response basis," for handling large, complex projects, and for "subcontracting with many outside organizations" (III, 29). Davis Bobrow added that it was well suited to "design, manage, conduct, integrate and evaluate research and pilot efforts involving large problem-oriented programs," because at an institute, "unlike the university or the federal agency, systems research and planning does not conflict with another primary mission" (III, 35).

Walsh (1969) concludes an article on the Stanford Research Institute, which was in the throes of severing its ties with Stanford University, by remarking that "SRI in transition could find it less difficult to weather the cutting of its bond to Stanford than to answer some of the basic questions about its own identity." A weakness of certain institutes—as of certain universities—is the obverse side of their ready adaptability and availability for virtually any research purpose: a lack of cohesion and central purpose. Gerhard Colm, who was attached to an institute which had such a purpose, the National Planning Association, observed that "Independent nonprofit organizations usually have (or should have) a focal 'mission' of their own. They should undertake contract research only if such work falls clearly within the line of their mission, so that at the same time they are doing something which the Government finds useful they are also adding to their general services to the community (which alone justifies their tax-exempt status)" (III, 61).

For-Profit Organizations

For-profit research organizations were, some respondents insisted, qualified to conduct the same kinds of research as non-profit institutes. Herbert Simon saw "no essential distinction between the . . . two categories of organizations" (III, 188) and Kofron deemed many "so-called" nonprofits "in fact profit making in every sense of the word with the exception of . . . tax status" and "often very competitive with the profit making organizations who are not tax sheltered" (III, 112). Robert Krueger, president of the for-profit Planning Research Corporation, said with some acerbity, "I am well acquainted with the functions of non-profit institutions. Generally, their overheads are higher than those of profit-oriented organizations and their costs are therefore higher. It is not unusual for a non-profit to win a contract for a research project and then sub-contract the project to a profit-oriented firm" (III, 119). One possible implication of Kofron's and Krueger's remarks was openly advanced by Alfred de Grazia—that the government "should attempt to favor research done by profit-making organizations as opposed to independent non-profit organizations" because the former "may well have better efficiency records and furthermore pay large sums of taxes on their profits" (III, 74).

Profit-making organizations found more advocates off campus than on. The academic respondent usually considered them qualified only for routine work and the quality even of such work, Ralph Beals felt, would be assured only if carefully inspected by independent scientists. Kofron conceded that "All commercial organizations are . . . not providing quality research" but "a substantial number . . . do." The government should use them especially "for very large scale survey research programs . . . because of their ready made staffs, rather than attempting to use the average university or non-profit group [which] . . . invariably will not have the ongoing staff of trained people working as a group in these fields every day" (III, 112).

Obviously, the availability of qualified profit organizations will vary with the type of research service required and the problem at hand. Margaret Gordon considered few to be qualified for studies in the welfare field, and Gerhard Mueller saw "no use" for them in criminal justice research, but that situation may change as additional appropriations attract firms to the area. The burgeoning market in educational materials and equipment has generated considerable commercial interest and competence in the research and development underlying that new technology. Writing as chairman of the board of the General Learning Corporation, former Commissioner of Education Francis Keppel naturally sympathized with such efforts by profit-making organizations which were "particularly qualified to conduct research on the relation of the new educational technology to the improvement of schools and colleges" (II, 128). However, Keppel's predecessor as commissioner, Sterling McMurrin, graduate dean at the University of Utah, was decidedly more reserved about the proper function of private enterprise in government-financed educational research: "The government should . . . move with the greatest caution in granting public funds to profit-making organizations, doing so only when it is absolutely clear that such action will bring the largest possible gain to education. Profit-making organizations expecting to gain from educational research should normally be expected to fund their own activities" (II, 131).

Morton Schussheim felt that some federal agencies have been "too doctrinaire" in not contracting with profit-making firms which have qualified staff and a good record of completing projects on schedule (II, 524). In contrast, William Wheaton felt that, though "of immense value in technological research," profit-making organizations had little to offer in policy-oriented urban research. Wheaton drew an interesting distinction between professional services, which they could offer, and research services, which they could not. "The tendency of professional offices or firms and profit-making firms to treat their discoveries as secrets, rather than to widely disseminate them, limits the usefulness of these organizations outside the field of professional services" (II, 528).

Contracting with industry can pose two dangers less likely to arise in contracting with nonprofit institutions: one is the possible conflict between the government objective of advancing knowledge by widely disseminating the results of research and the profit-making organization's interest in obtaining proprietary knowledge to secure a commercial advantage over competitors. Should a government contract give one firm a special advantage in marketing a new text, audio-visual aid, or calculator, it might be charged that "the public's money is being invested for private profit" (II, 146). Then, too, a profit-making organization which either has a commercial interest in a particular product or conducts research for a firm with such an interest faces a conflict between the dispassionate pursuit of knowledge and the danger of uncovering truths harmful to that commercial interest; it is likely to concentrate its attention on profitable truths.

Historical Changes

In the early years of this century, as now, the collection of social and economic statistics by the Departments of Commerce, Labor, and Interior was conducted intramurally, as was the work of economists in war planning and of psychologists in troop testing and training during World War I. However, significant exceptions to this pattern of intramural work occurred. The Department of Agriculture block grants to land-grant universities helped support considerable work in agricultural economics and rural sociology. In the 1920s, the newly formed National Bureau of Economic Research and the Institute for Government Research (subsequently, the Brookings Institution) undertook government-sponsored research in economics and public administration. During the 1930s, social scientists benefited from federal work-relief grants. Prominent private scholars served as advisers to government statistical and research programs and, at higher levels, to the economic and social planning of the New Deal. Nonetheless, the dominant mode by which the (by present standards) low volume of social and economic research was conducted was within the government. The aversion to regular programs of extramural research was illustrated by the fate of a 1934 proposal by Massachusetts Institute of Technology president Karl Compton that the government award scientific research grants to be administered by the National Academy of Sciences. That proposal was rejected and was opposed by many Academy members, who objected to the principle of government research sponsorship (Lyons, 1969, pp. 68–70).

The large R&D programs which the Office of Scientific Research and Development and the Manhattan Project contracted for during World War II set a new administrative pattern. After the war, many of these projects and laboratories were transferred to new and expanded agencies, particularly to the Atomic Energy Commission, the National Institutes of Health, and the Office of Naval Research. Subsequently formed agencies such as the Air Force, the Office of the Secretary of Defense, the National Science Foundation, new Institutes of Health, the National Aeronautics and Space Administration, and the Office of Economic Opportunity adopted the same pattern. Thus, newer agencies have tended to allocate more of their R&D funds to extramural organizations than have older agencies. Of the ten departments and agencies which used more than a third of their 1966 R&D budget intramurally, only one, the Arms Control and Disarmament Agency, was established after 1941; and of the ten using less than a third intramurally, again only one, the Post Office Department, was established before 1941 (Orlans, in press, Table 5).

Too much should not be made of the date of formation of many agencies, especially those established by reorganization, since their ancestry can usually be traced back much further. The significant point is that the modern style of government is to "contract out" much research and development, not to mention management and other services, formerly performed by government staff. As strenuous efforts were made to convert the Office of Education from a statistical agency to an influential one, a major program of extramural research heralded the conversion. Efforts to invigorate the Justice Department and the new Department of Housing and Urban Development were accompanied by new extramural research programs; to many observers, State Department unwillingness to sponsor extramural research is another sign of its antiquarian ways. The habit of contracting for talent and services has become so entrenched that voices must now be raised, as in the 1962 report of a committee chaired by Budget Director David Bell, to defend the legitimacy of intramural research and the importance of maintaining within the government staff qualified to govern in the public interest and of mastering the knowledge necessary to do so.[4]

That the government should be competent to govern and that first-class staff can help to maintain that competence are reasonable, even banal, propositions. However, it does not follow that first-class staff can be induced to serve only agencies which conduct a substantial volume of intramural research. The two matters—good staff and good intramural research—are separable, so much so that the contrary argument—that a program of extramural research is desirable to keep really good staff in touch with the best national authorities—is equally plausible.

Extramural Vs. Intramural Research

It would be foolish to prescribe the proportion of either intramural or extramural research that any agency should conduct, which must be determined by its special history, needs, circumstances, and opportunities. But a strong argument can be made against a completely self-contained intramural program and for at least a minimal amount of extramural research and (its cheap substitute) consultation.

Inasmuch as democratic government exists not to perpetuate itself but to benefit the public, so should its research. The knowledge research yields should enlighten the citizenry as well as improve the government; if final power resides in the public, not the bureaucracy, the public must receive enough knowledge to enable it to change any policy of which it disapproves. And the public is more likely to receive that kind of knowledge from extramural research

---

[4] Though approving heavy extramural contracting, the Bell report stated, "No matter how heavily the Government relies on private contracting, it should never lose a strong internal competence in research and development. By maintaining such competence it can be sure of being able to make the difficult but extraordinarily important program decisions which rest on scientific and technical judgments" (1962, pp. vii, 21–22).

conducted by independent investigators than from intramural research fully controlled by government officials.

In turn, government officials are more likely to obtain from independent scholars than from their staff knowledge and candid opinion free from any commitment to established agency policy. "It is no accident that the best diplomatic service in the world is the one in which the divorce between the assembling of knowledge and the control of policy is most perfect," Walter Lippmann wrote in 1922 of the British foreign service. ". . . the power of the expert depends upon separating himself from those who make the decisions, upon not caring, in his expert self, what decision is made" (1946, p. 288). Lippmann envisaged the development of an American civil service with independent status, quality, and repute comparable to those of the British service. Each department should have a high-level intelligence staff whose independence would be assured by employment conditions like those of tenured faculty. Others have had a similar vision of the American higher civil service. But the conditions which Lippmann postulated for truly independent research staff have yet to be realized within the government, while they exist to varying degrees in private organizations. To obtain these conditions, the government must sponsor research with such organizations.

Academic Vs. Nonacademic Research

Most respondents' judgments about the strengths and weaknesses of the different kinds of research institutions seem reasonable, if inevitably colored by conflicting experience and interests. What is missing is a sense of change in the national research structure. Though the overwhelming majority of social science Ph.D.s have been employed by universities, it is likely that, as the teaching needs of higher educational institutions are saturated, the number in the nonacademic sector will rise. A substantial corps of full-time social research personnel—in 1968, 36 percent of all Ph.D. social scientists whose "primary work activity" was research and development[5]—

[5] According to the National Register of Scientific and Technical Personnel, which probably gets a fuller count of academic than of nonacademic Ph.D.s, 5716 Ph.D.s in five social science fields reported their "primary work

already resides outside the academy and competes successfully with it, especially for applied research.

Many faculty are convinced that the professional men who are at universities are better than those who are not: for did not the faculty themselves select them and did they not select the best? With the best talent on campus, what can remain for the rest of the nation but the second-best and downright bad? "The university . . . tends to send into society those who are not quite the best, keeping the very best for itself," writes Weinberg (1964), director of the Oak Ridge National Laboratory and a leading critic of the power of university scientists in Washington, thus conceding an important point to his opponents. Is the Ph.D. not a higher degree of ability as well as endurance? Relatively more social scientists with Ph.D.s and fewer with master's and bachelor's degrees are employed on campus than off. Do publications, awards, and comparable indices of professional distinction not provide objective measures of intellectual ability? Then academic men are undoubtedly more able than nonacademic.

The trouble with such evidence is that it is circular. Of course, academic men are better able to do what academic men do. But the same can be said of nonacademic men. It is a common enough experience of governmental and applied research organizations that staff newly recruited from the academy must go through a period of retraining before they can meet the requirements of nonacademic employment.

Unquestionably, too much poor quality social research is conducted both off and on campus. But if the character of academic and nonacademic research differs, then a different quality test must be devised for each; and if the quality of academic and nonacademic investigators is to be compared fairly, a "culture-free" test must be devised which gives each group a fair chance to meet an independent standard of ability. Such a general test of ability would be difficult to prepare and the results would be of little help to

---

activity" as R&D in 1968. Of that number, 2041, or 36 percent (40 percent of the psychologists, 39 percent of the economists, 27 percent of the anthropologists, 23 percent of the political scientists, and 21 percent of the sociologists), worked for government or private organizations or were self-employed (National Science Foundation, 1969, pp. 75–76).

government administrators in deciding where to conduct specific inquiries. The usual answer to that problem is to give the work to the best man available at a reasonable cost, regardless of where he is located. But the cumulative effect of such individual decisions does not necessarily produce allocations which are in the national interest. Each agency must know its large research objectives and adopt allocation policies calculated to advance them; and national policies may also be needed to amalgamate divergent agency objectives into a semblance of common purpose.

Factors in Sector Allocations

Among the considerations which should be taken into account in formulating agency policies are the following: does the government have a responsibility to subsidize academic institutions as an important national resource; and, if so, should the desirability of aiding them affect agency allocations? Since 1945, the answer to the latter question has generally been "yes, other things being equal." If the tumult on campus and decline in the esteem of the academy have called forth any new government policies toward academic research, they have not yet been enunciated.

Carnegie Corporation president Pifer (1966, 1967) argues that a new type of nonprofit "quasi nongovernmental organization" has grown up in recent years to perform research and other services for the government. However, to perform these services adequately, these organizations require a degree of financial stability which they have not been able to acquire under ad hoc project financing. Accordingly, Pifer calls for some system of government fees or block grants to ensure their viability and independence. The proposal has been received with resounding silence in Washington. Fees paid by the Department of Defense have given some stability and independence to its nonprofit contract centers such as RAND and the Aerospace Corporation—and have been the subject of repeated inquiries and criticism. A report by the Comptroller General (1969) has challenged the use of these fees to shift the work of a center into new fields or "to enable it to compete in the private sector for non-Government business" (p. 7).

Patently, it is unfair for the government to set up an organization and subsidize it to compete with privately established organizations. Or is it? The rules governing such competition require considerable clarification. Some years ago, the federal "contract research centers"—government-financed, privately managed R&D institutes and laboratories—were required to work exclusively for their sponsoring agency. However, as budgetary ceilings have been imposed on nuclear and defense centers, that rule has been liberalized. In 1969, Secretary of Defense Melvin Laird went so far as to invite the secretaries of all government departments to make use of the "unique capabilities" of the defense centers (Orlans, 1972, p. 111).

There are numerous government research programs for which only universities are eligible but, I believe, none from which they are excluded. Several Budget Bureau circulars have attempted to set forth an equitable basis by which government agencies can determine the relative costs of contracting with for-profit companies and conducting work intramurally, making reasonable allowance for the taxes paid by the former and the difficulty of establishing comparable overhead and depreciation charges; but apparently no such guidelines have been issued regarding the comparative cost of work conducted by nonprofit and profit-making organizations.

A critical factor in agency allocations is control over the release of research findings. Good universities usually disdain any controls, whereas profit-making firms and most nonprofit institutes accept them. This point should be borne in mind by those who would like institutes to play a more important role in the national research enterprise: for the public generally receives less published information per dollar from institute research than from university research.

A good institute appears to offer so many advantages to a government agency, so many opportunities to research promoters, and so much hope for maximizing the benefits of research that not a day goes by without one being proposed and not a week without one being established. A well-funded institute can attack a problem intensively with diverse, full-time staff; acquire cumulative expertise in a special area; provide the supporting services and conditions to fulfill contractual obligations, ensure timely reports, and control their distribution; and budget for the follow-up activity necessary to implement research findings. One of the primal choices facing a research agency is whether to sponsor a new institute, to allocate funds to an existing institute, or to sponsor only discrete projects. When a research budget is low and agency needs change frequently, individual projects are the most practical alternative; but when budgets are larger and objectives more stable, an institute becomes more attractive. However, an institute represents a heavy commitment of agency resources, reducing budgetary and programing flexibility; and serious conflicts can develop between agency personnel and institute staff who can deal directly with senior agency officials. A serious charge against the "captive" institute is that it degrades the status of agency staff and assigns an important policy function to private persons responsible only to the officials who commission them.

The public has not derived as much benefit as it should from government-sponsored research at private organizations. The confidential nature of this research, the limited distribution of reports, and the devotion of the organizations to their sponsors all reduce the direct value of their work to the public. In contrast to academic work, which is freely published and subject to constant professional criticism, that of most institutes is not routinely evaluated; neither the public, the professional community, nor the government official has an adequate way to judge its quality. These are weighty arguments against assigning too large a role to institutes in research programs outside the national security area.

Summary

About a fourth of government social research funds have been allocated intramurally and the rest to nonfederal organizations, among which universities have received the largest proportion; independent nonprofit institutions have played a larger role than have universities in development and demonstration work.

Most respondents assigned to the federal government a modest role in research, except for collecting statistics, and a still more modest role to state and local governments. They deemed universities best suited for basic and long-term research in which the investigator enjoys great freedom, while independent nonprofit and

profit-making institutes were considered best for applied and interdisciplinary work. Some professors held that profit-making organizations did low-quality work at high cost, an opinion that officials
of these organizations did not share.

The proportion of agency funds that should go to different
kinds of institutions cannot be determined by formula. But awarding funds solely on a pragmatic, ad hoc basis is not an adequate
policy. The national interest calls for clarification of policies governing the support of research at nonprofit institutions and the terms
under which competition between nonprofit and profit-making
organizations should be permitted. An important factor which
should set limits on the use of nonacademic organizations for
domestic research programs is the relative inaccessibility of their
findings to the public.

8

Freedom to Publish

Restraints on the release of government-financed research findings are central to determining the character, location, and usefulness of this research. The prevailing doctrine among academic social scientists, a view which has generally been accepted by university administrators, is that they should conduct only research which they are free to publish. But every choice has consequences, and one result of the freedom-to-publish requirement is that research must be confined to subjects which can fruitfully be investigated with information that is readily accessible or in the public domain. Another result is that informants are likely to withhold information that could hurt them if published, and because this information is necessary to a balanced understanding of government policies, published research on such policies runs the danger of being at least partly incomplete and unbalanced, or overtaken by events. As officials will still want to control the release of certain kinds of research, a third consequence is that this research will be conducted by government staff themselves or by private organizations prepared to accept such controls.

The Reuss inquiry took several approaches to the problem

of publication restraints. Respondents were asked to recount their experience with any restrictions on their freedom to publish; university business officers were asked to report their experience in dealing with government agencies on this matter; and then questions about their publication policies were put directly to government agencies. The results of each are summarized in succeeding sections.

Experience of Respondents[1]

There was a marked difference between the experience of social scientists attached to universities, few of whom had encountered publication restrictions, and the experience of those at independent research organizations, many of whom reported such restrictions. Testimony about the freedom of publication was particularly forceful with respect to university research on medical and educational problems. Thus, Eli Ginzberg "was very impressed with the freedom to publish fully that was the underlying policy of the National Institute of Mental Health (NIMH) during the years that I served on the [NIMH national advisory] Council (1959–63)" (II, 386); and Jack Ewalt, chairman of the Harvard department of psychiatry, stated that "There are no restraints whatsoever on publication. To my knowledge, and we have had extensive research experience with federal agencies, there is no attempt to change the reports or in any way influence the findings" (II, 384). The agencies he specified "with which I have dealt personally" included the National Institutes of Health (NIH), the Department of Defense, and the Vocational Rehabilitation Administration.

Though government agencies sponsoring biomedical research have a clear record of publication freedom in their grants to universities, two points which are less widely known should be

---

[1] Specific questions asked were: "Have you encountered any restraints on freedom of publication in any government grants or contracts for social research? If so, what have they been; what projects and agencies were involved; and what position did you take with regard to these restrictions? How was the problem disposed of?" (III, 7) and "Do you know of any significant restraints on the freedom to publish fully the findings of government-sponsored research? If so, please give the agency involved, the nature of the restraint, its effect on the content of the final report, and your opinion of whether the restraint was reasonable and in the public interest" (II, 27).

noted. First, NIH and NSF, in common with other agencies, may impose publication restrictions in research *contracts,* as distinct from grants. Second, at many medical schools, research reports are cleared with department chairmen.[2] This practice, particularly common with regard to the research of younger men in clinical departments, is designed to maintain professional standards of quality and propriety; the power to censor inherent in such clearance has attracted surprisingly little notice.

As respondents indicated, the Office of Education (OE) has generally imposed no restrictions on research publication. But here too, closer inspection disclosed a number of inhibitions on publication. At least some OE nonprofit centers have developed publication controls similar to those of other research institutes. Thus, the Center for Urban Education in New York requires the director's approval for any publication or other use of the findings of center work;[3] and it may undertake confidential work. Also, OE

---

[2] For example, in describing the measures taken to evaluate the results of research conducted at the Baylor College of Medicine at Houston, Baylor University president Abner V. McCall reported that "When the investigator is ready to present his results at a scientific assembly or to publish them in a scientific journal, a manuscript is prepared. The departmental chairman reviews the manuscript, making suggestions for change if necessary, and authorizing the presentation or publication (which authorization is required before the results may be made public)" (Interstate, 1964, p. 77). Cornell University vice-president Franklin A. Long indicates that "The results of the research of the individual investigator [at Cornell Medical College] are reviewed by the chairman of his department. All research publications must also be approved by the division or department chairman" (Interstate, 1964, p. 80). At the Johns Hopkins Department of Medicine, the review of manuscripts was taken quite seriously. In February 1968 one member stated that he had just finished reviewing a paper whose senior author was a full professor; he thought it quite poor and would recommend against publication.

[3] ". . . the Assistant to the Director for Communications . . . provides for necessary corporate processing which includes the obligation of the Director of the Center to determine publishability. . . . The Director is also responsible for determining when and in what manner the author may publish or otherwise use the findings of Center sponsored research and development in whole or in part. . . . The Center has been accepting the release date set by the client, but will whenever possible ensure that a reasonable date for the release of a Center report to the public is agreed to at the time the contract is drafted. . . . However, the possible adverse effect on the research underway of publicizing its report prior to completion of the work is obvious. . . . The Board does not in general favor confidentiality, but if

contracts and grants for a certain period contained a clause requiring approval of the contracting officer prior to publication. However, according to OE, that requirement had been designed only to obtain compliance with government printing and binding regulations (IV, 549).

Sar Levitan attacked the Office of Economic Opportunity (OEO) for restrictive policies that I will examine later, and academic respondents singled out the Agency for International Development for sharp criticism. Stephen Bailey reported that the experience of Syracuse University with the AID publications policy had been "extremely unhappy" (III, 12). And William Wheaton declared that AID "has a reputation . . . for being so heavily laden with red tape and Federal censorship as to be impossible to deal with" (II, 528–529).

The dominant tone of satisfaction with the freedom to publish was accompanied by observations that this was not an absolute freedom to be exercised in the face of every other consideration; voluntary restraint had at times to be exhibited. The preservation of anonymity can pose a quandary in applied research where academic generalities give way to concrete particulars—to the specific responsibilities, successes, and failures of specific individuals and organizations. Some compromise is necessary with the principle of disclosing the truth, the whole truth and nothing but the truth.

Robert Charpie of Union Carbide was confident that "In every case of publication restraint in urban research where I know all of the details . . . extenuating circumstances explain the government's position and were more important in the national interest than the issue of freedom of publication" (II, 507). In *every* case? Of course, "extenuating circumstances" arise and assuredly "the national interest" should come first, but are government officials always best qualified to define that? Harold Watts, director of the University of Wisconsin Institute for Research on Poverty, was less confident that such restraints were always for the good. "In general the sponsor-scientist relationship and expectations about further support probably leads to some regrettable 'voluntary' censorship

there are compelling reasons of public welfare and program values, the Board would be willing to accept this condition in certain circumstances" (Stewart, 1968).

whether or not there is an explicit power over publication. I see no way . . . to prevent some cases of unfortunate suppression of research results" (II, 272).

Sar Levitan of the Upjohn Institute spoke more strongly about the danger of "thought controls" in government-sponsored research. "Universities with faculties engaged in critical evaluation of government programs may find that federal spigots eventually run dry." Accordingly, many faculty preferred to conduct basic research that would not endanger their funding; and as full public candor could not be expected from those who did engage in government program evaluation, Levitan argued for increased support of evaluation by private foundations and the universities themselves (II, 254–261).

Don Price suspected that the Harvard policy of not accepting secret research partly explained why so few attempts to restrict publication had come to his attention as dean of the John Fitzgerald Kennedy School of Government. Some "borderline problems" had arisen; he did not object to giving "a sponsoring agency reports shortly before releasing them to the public, and in many cases certain types of data need to be kept confidential for the protection of the privacy of individual respondents" (III, 160). Rensis Likert stated that his University of Michigan Institute for Social Research has "undertaken only one study that was classified. . . . We presently decline financial support from any source . . . that is not accompanied by assured freedom to publish. Some agencies have taken steps to influence the content of our reports or to delay publication, but these cases have been instances of legitimate concern for their responsibilities and all have been resolved without compromising our obligations to make scientific results public" (III, 127).

Nonacademic research organizations are so accustomed to government publication controls that they commonly accept them as reasonable and warranted. "In some 15 years," said John Kofron, vice-president of the Chilton Company, "I have not been aware of any real restrictions on freedom of publication in any government grants or contracts for social research. The restraint which requires that data be provided to the sponsor first before any publication certainly seems to be in order and most understandable" (III, 113).

Stuart Rice, former head of the Budget Bureau Office of Statistical Standards, stated: "two decades of experience with statistical and research activities as a Federal employee lead me to regard unwarranted [publication] restraints . . . as rare. The withholding of publication at government expense . . . may, of course, be warranted if the work performed departs from specifications, or if the results fail to serve the purposes intended. . . . Even so . . . such departures from specification have usually been accepted by the initiating agency" (III, 172).

Rice's assertion that "unwarranted" restraints are "rare" can be taken as an acknowledgment that warranted restraints are not rare. This viewpoint was expressed by respondents from Abt Associates, RAND, the Research Analysis Corporation, and other institutes accustomed to doing confidential work for government and private clients and to accepting a greater degree of corporate responsibility for staff research than does a university for the research of its faculty. Hoping to maintain continuing contractual relations with a government agency, they are anxious to please, and their considerate regard for the judgment of agency officials can strike academic men as an unseemly sacrifice of professional independence. "I have not encountered any restraints on the freedom of publication that disturbed my professional ethics," observed Thomas Rowan of the System Development Corporation. "Obviously, a sponsoring agency has the right and, indeed, obligation to see that published results are of high professional quality and are not idle conjectures that may be misleading" (III, 183).

Not all institute respondents viewed publication controls with such equanimity. That clearance was at least a nuisance was hinted by Norman Christeller of the Institute for Defense Analyses (IDA): "We encourage our staff to publish in professional journals . . . but we retain the right to approve such publication. This latter safeguard is essential if we are to satisfy the publications provisions that are included in most of our contracts with the Federal Government. . . . While there may occasionally be some impatience with the delays incidental to obtaining government permission for publication, we have not encountered serious problems in obtaining such permission" (IV, 599). IDA psychologist Jesse Orlansky reflected a greater annoyance at the clearance procedures: "I find it burdensome to submit drafts of unclassified material for government review before submitting them to a professional journal or before giving a public speech in order to check them for security purposes. This is a condition of employment with certain organizations doing highly classified work for the government. I do not suggest that any change in these arrangements is possible or desirable. . . . I know of no single case where an individual's private views were interfered with. Nevertheless, the current arrangements are burdensome and probably tend to reduce the number of unclassified reports which get into the professional journals" (III, 145).

At RAND, Herbert Simon observed, publication restraints "were usually administered intelligently" (III, 189). Smith concurs that the Air Force has "generally allowed RAND staff members to speak their minds freely even on subjects of official concern to the Air Force." However, in his opinion, RAND clearance increased in strictness in the early 1960s, in response to "a more hostile external [political] environment. . . . publications have been subjected to more rigorous pre-publication criticism and review before being released to the client or the public" (1966, p. 144). Controls were tightened again in 1971 following the release of the "Pentagon Papers" by RAND alumnus Daniel Ellsberg. An economist who spent some time at RAND in the 1950s wrote: "I had to have clearance on anything I wanted to publish. . . . [My manuscripts] were cleared only because I deleted certain kinds of material . . . to avoid offending the Air Force—questions of tact and good relations."[4] RAND clearance rules have been extended to its work for the New York City government. "It was a condition imposed by the city . . . that nothing be released to the public without explicit approval," Peter Szanton, director of the New York City-RAND Institute, has stated (Tolchin, 1970).

The charge that an agency had suppressed, modified, or delayed a publication for political reasons was made by several respondents under cover of anonymity for themselves or the agency. For example, Davis Bobrow stated: "A paper written some time ago was withheld for several months until after an election. Given

---

[4] Letter to the author, December 11, 1966.

the unfair criticism that part of the government had been receiving because of its important mission, I agreed with this action. The paper was subsequently released. We all know that many research reports are withheld or 'de-sensitized' for reasons of agency security as contrasted with national security. This situation is unhealthy, but it is an unhealthy response to unhealthy expectations and constraints put forward by political critics" (III, 35). Theodore Vallance, former head of the Army Special Operations Research Office (SORO), related an episode that may just possibly have involved the Army contract with American University for the administration of SORO when the Camelot episode broke: "A university-based, government funded social science project . . . became the subject of some international controversy, being described in the press as espionage, undercover, war-like and with other opprobrious though untrue terms. The sponsor invoked the terms of its contract which vested in the sponsor the final approval of publication . . . and requested the university to refrain from issuing any statements about the research. . . . The university authorities agreed" (IV, 610).

An economist at a well-known nonprofit institute stated: "I am not aware of any government agency which has not placed or tried to place some restrictions on the distribution of sponsored research. By and large, however, the Department of Defense has had a commendable record. . . . Even in those areas . . . in which the department may be potentially embarrassed, they have generally permitted distribution and discussion of this research within the professional community. Our own experience with such agencies as OEO and the Federal Aviation Agency (FAA) has been somewhat less favorable. . . . A private research organization, however, has no ultimate course of appeal, as our contracts give the sponsoring agency full property rights and the use and distribution of our research" (III, 79).

Experience of University Business Officers

At the request of Reuss subcommittee staff, Howard P. Wile, executive director of the Committee on Governmental Relations of the National Association of College and University Business Officers, circulated an inquiry about publication restrictions to business officers at the seventy-eight institutions which were then members of the committee plus eight which were not.[5] Of the forty-seven who replied, only twelve cited examples of restrictive contracts, whereas the other thirty-five reported none. Considering the large number of contracts received by most universities, the overall incidence of restrictions was very low. Such cases were reported more frequently at institutions with a large volume of research than at low-volume institutions; this fact is probably attributable to the increased likelihood of encountering a few cases there and, perhaps, to their administrators' alertness to restrictions (due to their greater experience) and to a certain pugnaciousness in opposing them. The few publication controls that the inquiry documented affected a minor portion of academic research and academic institutions. The net impression was of a generally successful vigilance by administrators and faculty to maintain publication freedom.

The Reuss inquiry did not obtain a complete inventory of all restrictive clauses in force at universities. However, the care with which respondents itemized every contractual clause that might restrict publication suggests that, collectively, their replies gave a good picture of the kinds of controls that existed in unclassified research projects and the agencies most likely to impose them. The Agency for International Development was cited most frequently, and complaints were also leveled at two other foreign affairs agencies, the Arms Control and Disarmament Agency and the Peace Corps, lending credence to the comment of David Heebink, Stanford research administrator, that "The closer the work of the agency impinges on foreign policy, the more restrictive its publication policy is likely to be" (IV, 509).

Alban Weber, counsel of Northwestern University, gave the

---

[5] Member institutions (listed in IV, 488–489) included most of the universities and institutes of technology which are best known and highly regarded and most of those with the largest volume of federal research and development funds. For example, they contained eighty-five of the eighty-six departments of anthropology, economics, political science, psychology, and sociology whose faculty were rated as "distinguished" or "strong" in the Cartter study (1966) and all of the thirty institutions receiving the largest amount of federal obligations for research and development in 1966. The eight nonmember institutions, added at my request, largely to sample a few liberal arts colleges, were Amherst, Birmingham-Southern, Grinnell, University of Hartford, Howard University, Oberlin, Reed, and Swarthmore.

following account of an episode which indicates the practical limits on enforcing publication restrictions if investigators decide to disregard agency objections:

> *We have recently had an extended controversy with the Agency for International Development, in connection with a [contract] . . . for a survey of the economy of Liberia. . . . which stated that the report to be made was to be the property of . . . [the agency]. Several of the researchers . . . prepared a book incorporating much of the data in the report which had never been declared confidential by either government. . . . Because the name of the book was "Growth Without Development" and because it was highly critical of the Liberian Government . . . AID made strong representations that the book not be published, and, in fact, claimed that its publication would violate the property rights of AID. . . . The authors and the Northwestern University Press proceeded to publish the book several weeks ago over AID's objections. We have been informed that AID intends to take no further action (IV, 498–499).*

The basis of the AID contention that the report should not be published, Weber said, lay in a common "boiler-plate" clause giving the government rights to the data and the report. Such a clause can be used to promote a policy of open domain, since if the government "owns" a report, it has the right to publish it and to permit anyone else to do so. However, in the Northwestern case, it was used by AID officials to show "that the Government had the right to suppress it" (IV, 623).

A similar clause was included in a Peace Corps contract at Princeton, which accepted it, with some modifications, on a non-precedent-setting basis. Stanford has had the same experience with Peace Corps officials, who insisted on the right to approve publication (IV, 509).

Publication restrictions by a third foreign affairs agency, the Arms Control and Disarmament Agency (ACDA), were incorporated in university contracts that were unusual in several respects. They required the contractor to "request in writing and obtain . . . the consent of the Agency prior to the public release of any information relating to the contract." Though consent "shall not be withheld unreasonably or in such a manner as to restrict the Contractor's independent position," it was necessary even after the end of the contract "for a reasonable time" not to exceed three years after final payment (which generally occurs after acceptance, not submission, of the final report). ACDA also could forbid a contractor to state that his work was sponsored by ACDA or the U. S. government. That is, the agency could legally require a university investigator to break the ethical principle that he disclose his research sponsor, a principle which has been endorsed by several social science associations (IV, 505, 580) as well as by the Foreign Area Research Coordination Group, to which ACDA supposedly subscribed.

The business officers registered four complaints against Department of Defense (DOD) research contracts, one involving the Army and the other three the Air Force Office of Scientific Research. However, in view of its $8.5-million volume of social and psychological research at university campuses in 1967, few publication problems seem to have arisen in Defense Department contracts —probably fewer, proportionate to the number of contracts, than in the university research programs of civilian agencies and, especially, foreign affairs agencies. Donald S. Murray offered a likely explanation: "It is my feeling that language in contracts of the non-defense agencies tends to be more restrictive than in those of the Department of Defense. This may be because the non-defense agencies do not have the same rigid standards for identifying privileged information nor the well established procedures for handling it that one finds with the DOD" (IV, 499–500). As Murray indicated, DOD does have a carefully worked out gradient of policies that may give it greater flexibility than civilian agencies have in handling various categories of privileged information. In addition, as the department has long-established relations with nonacademic organizations accustomed to confidential research, it probably has less need than other agencies have to place politically sensitive research at academic institutions. Publication restrictions reported for domestic agencies included contracts of the Civil Rights Commission prohibiting publication without prior approval and similar restrictions in several contracts of the Department of Health, Education, and Welfare (HEW), the Labor Department, the Veterans Administration, and other agencies.

Government View

On receipt of the business officers' responses, an inquiry was directed to the agencies cited in cases of significant restrictions. In addition, agencies sponsoring one million dollars or more of extramural social research in fiscal year 1967 were asked: "1. What are the Department's policies regarding the release of the results of unclassified social research performed under contract . . . ? 2. What rights, if any, does the Department retain to limit, delay, or prevent the release of the findings of such unclassified research? 3. Under what circumstances are these rights most commonly exercised? 4. How frequently are these rights exercised?" (IV, 516).

"Never" or "rarely" was so invariable an answer to the last question that nothing more can be said about it other than that this query was plainly not the best way to gather incriminating statistics. With a few exceptions, the inquiry may fairly be characterized as an exercise in mutual misunderstanding or obfuscation or both. Repeatedly, it proved necessary to send a second letter before publication controls were acknowledged; and time did not permit the additional investigation needed to determine the extent of such controls and the degree to which they were warranted.

One reason for this difficulty in communication was the native disposition of officials to admit nothing (particularly to the Congress) which might be construed as an error. Another was that, though agency staff might "limit" or "delay" publication, they were blind to the fact because they were convinced that their actions had such legitimate objectives as improving a report or combining it with other data. Yet another was that agencies regard a certain genre of contract work not as independent research which may enjoy the right of publication but rather as an extension of internal operations or of management study. And perhaps the most important reason was that publication problems rarely arise with compliant and cooperative contractors who are often not interested in publishing, let alone in making a public issue over it. The preparation of a publication requires, in addition to data of public signifi-

cance, time, money, and qualified professional and editorial staff—
or, altogether, a certain academic outlook, an interest in knowledge
for its own sake. This atmosphere or outlook is simply not typical of
many organizations which are happy to conduct proprietary work
for industry and the government, with no questions asked about the
disposition of the product.

One test of the absence of agency controls is that the investigator may publish without prior review by the sponsoring agency.
Review need not imply control; and it need not be a bad thing,
since staff comments can help to improve the final report. But if a
review is not required, nothing is available for agency officials to
control, and the investigator is in the position of any citizen, free to
say what he pleases to whoever may listen.

On this test, the government programs which exemplify a
model of freedom are the research grants of the Public Health Service (PHS) and the National Science Foundation under which investigators publish without agency review. However, as will be
noted, PHS and NSF research *contracts* contain publication controls. Programs with similar publication policies included Agriculture Department awards to agriculture experiment stations; Welfare
Administration research grants; doctoral dissertation grants and
other grants of the Labor Department Office of Manpower Policy,
Evaluation, and Research (OMPER); National Aeronautics and
Space Administration grants and contracts—except for certain
contracts regarded as adjuncts to its internal operations; the Smithsonian Institution programs; Advanced Research Projects Agency
basic research contracts at universities; and Office of Naval Research (ONR) unclassified contracts. ONR added the additional
injunction that an investigator had an *obligation* to publish. "A
basic tenet of ONR is that our investigation is not completed until
the investigator has reported his results to his interested professional
colleagues in all necessary detail." Though this report did not constitute a "review," ONR also required that "All significant information developed under a sponsored program must be disclosed first to
the sponsor and to the sponsor's sister agencies" by means of semi-
annual progress reports "and such other technical reports as may be
required by the Scientific Officer" (IV, 540).

Only very limited restrictions distinguished several other programs from the foregoing. Thus, extramural research supported by the Vocational Rehabilitation Administration could be published without prior review, subject only to the protection of individual confidentiality. A similar rule applied to Welfare Administration contracts, which were employed infrequently, in lieu of grants, when information had to be obtained from personal interviews or case records. On request, reports emerging from OMPER research contracts or institutional grants could be withheld from publication for ninety days. Labor Secretary Willard Wirtz said that the delay enabled the department "to schedule the timing of release of important research findings, and allows full exploitation of the program and policy implications . . ." (IV, 555).

The difficulty of getting full and frank information about publication controls can be illustrated by the example of the two exemplary agencies, the Public Health Service (PHS) and the National Science Foundation. In his official response to the Reuss inquiry, Berwin Cole stated emphatically that PHS "does not retain any rights to limit or delay or prevent the release" of unclassified research performed under contract or grant (IV, 545–546). Yet the following National Institutes of Health (NIH) memorandum plainly qualifies that unqualified declaration:

> *Subject: Restriction of Contractors' Publication Rights*[6]
> *. . . Each institute and division director is responsible for deciding when a contract sponsored by his organization should include a provision limiting the contractor's publication rights by requiring prior approval of any publication. . . .*
>
> *In general, a contract provision limiting the contractor's publication rights should be used when there is a possibility of—*
> *(a) Damage to public health;*
> *(b) Violation of proprietary rights, confidence, patient privacy;*
> *(c) Hindrance of scientific progress;*
> *(d) Embarrassment to NIH.*

[6] National Institutes of Health, Policy and Procedure Memoranda, Office of the Director, Office of Administrative Management, November 29, 1967.

*. . . If a contractor refuses to accept the restriction,
the institute or division director may reconsider his judgment
in the light of the contract project's importance and the need
for that contractor to perform it. . . .*

Cole's response was dated January 1967 and this memorandum, November 1967, but it is difficult to imagine that the memorandum initiated rather than codified policy. In fact, it is difficult
to imagine a major agency operating without *some* publication control over *some* of its extramural contracts. Until receiving general
authority in the latter 1950s to contract for research,[7] NIH used
selected and more closely administered grants to achieve program-
atic purposes (as did NSF in some grants as well as contracts).

Of the four criteria designated in the above memorandum,
the first two are patently justified and the third conceivably justifi-
able, though it carries a taint of political censorship.[8] (If a report
will hinder scientific progress, why not leave that judgment to the
editors and reviewers of scientific publications? And what special
qualifications do government officials have that private scientists
lack to foresee the future of science?) The fourth criterion is so
embarrassingly frank that it is kindest to pass it by without further
comment.

The last paragraph of the memorandum is also unusually
frank in recognizing the bargaining that normally ensues in negotiat-
ing a contract. A contractor who is hard to get can exact more
favorable terms than one who is more readily available; for evidence, one need only compare the Harvard response to our inquiry
with that of certain other universities.

The Reuss subcommittee letter to the National Science
Foundation said, "We are particularly interested in your policies in
research performed under contract." This elicited the reply that
"Contracts and grants for research awarded by the Foundation's
Office of Economic and Manpower Studies operate under the same
general policy" as do other NSF grants. "Wide release is encour-

---

[7] For some years before 1965, when it received general authority to
enter into research contracts, the contract authority of the Public Health
Service was provided in annual appropriation acts.

[8] That seemed to be the case when a government report on birth
control research was suppressed in 1962 (Hunter, 1962).

aged, subject only to restrictions on the disclosure of information which is privileged or identifies individual respondents" (IV, 591–592).

Very likely, that reply was an honest error, but it was an error nonetheless. In a second communication, the agency noted that NSF contracts normally provided that all data collected become the property of the government and that disposition of the data shall be made "in a manner mutually agreeable to the Contractor and the Foundation." Now it was explained that "it is the intent of the Foundation to make data fully available to the public as soon as possible. . . . In some instances, however, there have been delays . . . because the contractor's initial submission was incomplete or because we required additional information needed for full understanding and correct interpretation of the results" (IV, 595).

That response got closer to the heart of the matter. For what can happen in the course of a contract at NSF, as at other agencies, is not that a villainous official suppresses a report to keep the truth from the public. Rather, the contractor has not done precisely what was requested: the stubs in Table X are not the same as in another report; or the analysis is very interesting but ignores the position taken by the director in recent testimony; or the quotations from Congressman P seem inappropriate in a statistical report; or the implications of Table Z should be brought out more clearly in the text; or Part II is excellent but what has it got to do with the contract and where are the breakdowns by designated fields that were supposed to be obtained? All of this in the name of quality—and, after all, who is in a position to judge that but the investigator and foundation staff monitoring his work? Both want to wind up the work, but unfortunately the staff cannot accept the report until the requisite changes are made. One delay succeeds another; deadlines are extended and broken. The investigator grows weary, then exasperated: does NSF intend to publish the report or not? If not, he would like to publish it elsewhere; already it has lost much of its timeliness. Only then does the full significance of the "mutually agreeable" provision become apparent because, with the deepest regret, NSF staff feel it necessary to defer agreement until such and such is done. Without allocating blame to either side, this account accurately describes what has happened in relation to some NSF contracts.[9] *Suppression* is not the right word for it; *attrition* is better. When something goes wrong, the normal process of administering the normal government contract provides ample opportunity for the attrition of patience, tolerance, and the best of intentions.

The quality issue also emerged as a significant factor in the publication controls of the Departments of Agriculture, Commerce, and Interior; but quality, though no doubt a genuine consideration, can be a euphemism for statistical or political compatibility. The importance of statistical compatibility was clear in the contracts of Agriculture's Economic Research Service (ERS) with nonpublic organizations, in which information could be released "only at the discretion of the Contracting Officer . . . under such conditions as he . . . may prescribe and with such credit or recognition or collaboration as he may determine" (IV, 518). The reason, ERS administrator M. L. Upchurch stated, was "to assure adequacy of treatment and conformance with publication standards of the Department. . . . If the manuscript . . . does not meet these [standards] . . . then our rights to change the manuscript are exercised. . . . The contract reports . . . are sometimes not intended for publication as received, and must be elaborated on or collated with other materials before final publication is made." If ERS did not use a report, the contractor could issue it at his expense only with approval (IV, 518, 520). These contracts, in effect, seemed like subcontracts for work to be written up by agency staff and published by the government. Contractor reports were published, an ERS staff member explained, "on *our* responsibility." A representative report bore the signature of an ERS economist, though the preface noted that "Data collection and preliminary data summaries were the responsibility of staff members of Agri Research, Inc., of Manhattan, Kans., under contract #——." The credit given here is greater than that received by many contractors. For instance, a major nonprofit institute received no credit for a volume it prepared

[9] One example can safely be cited, because the two principals, good and honest men caught in a vise of their own devising, are now dead: a study conducted under NSF contract by Alexander Korol of the Massachusetts Institute of Technology which dragged out for more than five years, though it was originally to take two, and was finally published at *Soviet Research and Development* (Cambridge: M.I.T. Press, 1965).

that was published by the Office of Economic Opportunity as if it had been a staff product; the report of a for-profit firm was published by the Economic Development Administration with no mention of the author's name.

At the Office of Transportation Research, then in the Commerce Department, contractor reports were treated as confidential until written approval for release was given, and a stringent penalty clause provided that unauthorized disclosure "shall constitute a breach of this contract upon which the government may . . . terminate . . . this contract, [and] recover damages to the extent of any loss of value suffered hereunder" (IV, 525–526). Confidentiality was necessary, department spokesman Chester Holden said, to protect government interest in "undue escalation of costs, employee morale, etc."—and perhaps, as Holden did not say, to reserve to the department greater freedom in policy decisions or justifications than would be possible were all reports immediately released. The period of confidentiality, Holden observed, "would be of a temporary nature only . . . to give OTR the opportunity to make suggestions for editing and revising" (IV, 525).

An Interior Department spokesman stated, "it is our policy to publish all research findings promptly . . . consistent with good quality reporting" and that "Rights to limit publication are exercised only[!] to be sure that publication is consistent with departmental policies or interests." These rights were maintained by prohibiting publication without approval "for one year following the submission of the final report." Reports were reviewed for both "technical and policy considerations" (IV, 551–553).

An example of "policy considerations" leading to the "temporary" withholding of reports was afforded by studies of the supersonic transport for which the Federal Aviation Agency contracted. The story was related by *Wall Street Journal* reporter Fred Zimmerman (1967): "economic studies done by several outside research concerns and just delivered to the FAA are so critical of the project's optimistic financial assumptions—including those about market demand, likely fare levels and the balance-of-payments effect—that the FAA has decided to keep them secret. When the FAA commissioned the studies early last year at a cost of more than $650,000, it is understood to have said it would make them public when completed. But as it began receiving the reports and discovered almost all conclusions were unfavorable to the SST, it quickly stamped them 'for official use only.' "

The preservation of confidence while policy deliberations were afoot was an explanation advanced by the Commission on Civil Rights for publication controls in certain contracts with universities and other nonprofit institutions which were part of a commission investigation of racial isolation in city schools requested by President Johnson. "These contracts were very different from . . . research grants. . . . Their specific purpose is to obtain information for use in the Commission's reports," Commission director William Taylor declared. "One purpose of this restriction is to prevent the results of a report being prepared for the President or Congress from being prematurely released by a contractor. . . . Apparently many universities fail to distinguish between Government subsidized research and a contractual arrangement requiring the preparation of a particular report or the collection of specified data. . . . This restriction is to preserve the discretion of the President with respect to the use of any information requested by him. . . . It seems only appropriate that the same rationale which protects interagency communications within the executive . . . should apply to work done by contractors on this project" (IV, 587–589).

Taylor's arguments summarized the outlook of many officials about the proprietary right of the government to contract research findings. Each argument alone has more merit than all taken together, for though in any particular instance there may be good reason to keep a release date, to protect a confidence, or to preserve a policy option, what meaning can possibly be attached to the "purchase" of a report and the "discretion" of *not* using it but the right to forget, to bury, or to suppress it? The commission would have had an easier time contracting with commercial or nonprofit research organizations which sell their intellectual services more forthrightly than do leading universities.

Office of Economic Opportunity

The Reuss subcommittee's interest in the publication policy of the Office of Economic Opportunity, sponsor of one of the largest programs of extramural social research, was aroused by an editorial, "Publish and Perish," in the *Washington Post* of September

20, 1966. This stated that OEO research contracts "give the OEO
the power to forbid publication of the scholar's findings. The OEO
observes that it has never exercised this power . . . but its very
existence is a force to coerce a sympathetic view of the agency's
embarrassments."

Inquiry verified that OEO controlled publication in many
of its contracts. For example, publication without prior written
consent was forbidden in contracts with the International Business
Machines Corporation for computer simulation studies of the national economy, with the Hudson Institute for an analysis of the
position of poverty in American society, and with Kirschner Associates for the evaluation of Small Business Development Centers.
All told, such controls had been placed on eighty-four projects
costing $12.4 million in 1965 and 1966.

Joseph Kershaw, first OEO research director, contrasted the
publication restraints of other government agencies with the freedom
permitted by OEO (II, 252–254). But Levitan, a close student of
OEO, conveyed quite the opposite impression. "An increasingly
dangerous practice is . . . [OEO's] contracting with private consulting firms and academic institutions for survey and evaluation of
public programs. The products of the outside experts become the
property of the contracting agency and are not frequently published.
. . . Thus far, the product of the OEO [intramural] research staff
remains largely in the files of the 'Poverty House' " (II, 256–257).

When Levitan's criticism was brought to Kershaw's attention, he responded that, nonetheless, "OEO has been pretty good"
about making evaluation reports available. However, "researchers
ought to have the courtesy to allow an agency to digest its recommendations and results before they are made public, and I am sure
that OEO has asked researchers to observe this courtesy" (IV,
651). He did not deal with the greater power to prohibit publication that OEO had reserved in its contracts. Perhaps, as has been
the case at other agencies, this right was a provision, retained by
agency lawyers in certain contracts, that research staff disliked but
could not readily make a public fuss about.

One can make a case for reducing publication restrictions or
for retaining reasonable controls in the contracts of any agency. But
OEO had been subjected to so many other political attacks that it

seemed unwise for it to invite the additional charge of suppressing information. In October 1966, OEO research director Robert Levine had said that a more liberal policy would shortly be adopted in OEO contracts. But much of January passed into history without any further sign of action from OEO, which was doubtless fighting many battles on other fronts. Whereupon, Congressman Reuss wrote OEO director Sargent Shriver: "My subcommittee was told that the OEO policy of restricting the release of contract research findings would be changed in 'the middle of November,' but it is the third week of January and nothing has yet been done. Until these restrictions are lifted, the public will think that OEO permits its contractors to release only those facts it wants the public to know. Congress will believe that OEO is playing politics with its research funds, rather than conducting a dispassionate search for the truth, letting the facts fall as they may" (IV, 653–654).

This letter, together with documentation of the nature and extent of OEO publication control, was released to the press and received modest attention. In February, Shriver replied that he had "recently approved a new clause to be contained in all contracts for evaluation or for a research or demonstration project" permitting publication after sixty days' notice. OEO had never prevented the release of findings. "At worst, it seems likely that the effect was to delay making public certain information rather than not making it public at all" (IV, 656–657). Probably that statement was true for OEO, as for most other government agencies; but as sufficient delay can reduce or vitiate the value of reports, it has undoubtedly contributed to the nonpublication of many.

So persistent are the forces of governmental caution and control and so luxuriant is the growth of contractual clauses in semi-tropical Washington that it is not the least surprising to note in the boiler plate of a prospectus for an evaluation contract issued by OEO in 1968 that "The Contractor shall not publish or reproduce [any] . . . Data in whole or in part . . . without the written consent of the Government."

Pentagonal Policies

The Department of Defense (DOD) is so vast, more like a nation than an organization, that formal policies and pronouncements issuing from the Office of the Secretary can hardly be accepted as evidence of actual practice in the administration of thousands of individual projects. Nonetheless, these policies merit attention because they have been worked out with manifest care. DOD staff may be no wiser than the staff of other agencies or quicker to confess error, but they are more likely to have a policy directive filed and producable for any occasion.

The department has established five categories of restriction for the distribution of documents, limiting circulation to progressively smaller circles (IV, 527–533):

1. *No prior approval required for public distribution.*

2. *Prior approval required for transmittal to a foreign government or foreign national or government*—to protect information furnished by a foreign government, to keep proprietary information from foreign firms, or to protect technical "know-how."

3. *Prior approval required for transmittal outside the U. S. government*—when ethical considerations arise in tests of commercial products, and to protect private property rights.

4. *Prior approval required for transmittal outside the Defense Department*—for documents involved in negotiations between government agencies, in evaluations of the contractors or programs of other agencies, in the protection of trade secrets, and in related causes.

5. *Prior approval required for transmittal outside the controlling DOD office*—to protect documents containing administrative data, staff studies evaluating other DOD components, inventions by DOD personnel, and related causes.

Each of these categories bears a designated "distribution statement" which must appear prominently on all copies of documents generated by DOD staff or contractors. The 1965 directive establishing these categories stated that their objective was to permit the "widest possible distribution" of documents consistent with the necessary protection of privileged information.

A 1957 directive issued by Secretary of Defense Charles Wilson mentioned "without limitation" ten kinds of official information protection "in the public interest," including the protection of personnel and medical records, confidential informants, proprietary data, information that might "adversely affect morale," and privileged executive communications (IV, 533–536). One can recognize in that list categories of information singled out by other agencies as grounds for publication control. Each category appears reasonable of itself, though permitting ample latitude for restrictions serving political purposes. Recognizing that danger if they could not obviate it, the two Defense Secretaries under whom the foregoing directives were issued both issued resounding declarations against their use for such crass purposes. Secretary Wilson declared that his directive did not authorize the withholding of information which "might tend to reveal administrative error or inefficiency, or might be embarrassing" (IV, 536). And Secretary Robert McNamara declared, "We are under a special obligation to disclose mistakes and ineffective administration and operations. . . . In no event should overclassification be used to avoid public discussion of controversial matters" (IV, 542).

The general testimony of social scientists in our inquiry was that the Defense Department gave contractors commendable freedom to express their views on contentious issues. And as the waves of protest about military and classified research on campus have mounted in recent years, the department has reduced the volume of classified research on campus. The department has sought to maintain its ties with sympathetic and productive faculty, meeting university demands for unfettered publication while retaining controls in off-campus research.

Senator J. W. Fulbright has provided evidence that the latter controls can, in the judgment of political critics, be used for political purposes. In 1968, Fulbright charged Defense with needlessly classifying a Douglas Aircraft study of "Strategic Alignments and Military Objectives." He criticized the Defense Secretary for refusing to give the Committee on Foreign Relations an Institute for Defense Analyses report on 1964 incidents in the Gulf of Tonkin and attacked DOD publication policies: "public funds are spent for research purposes, but . . . the results . . . are not made available to the public unless such results seem to serve the purpose of those administering the programs. . . . I think it is outrageous that . . . the results of the studies are denied if they do not suit their purposes. This is not research at all. This is spending enormous amounts of money to gather information to support administrative theory, and if the study does not support their preconceived notions of what our foreign policy should be, the study is buried" (1968). A year later, Fulbright returned to the theme. "No congressional committee," he declared, "should be denied copies of any research reports, paid for with taxpayers' money, except on grounds of executive privilege." In response to a written request by any congressional committee, he contended, the Secretary of Defense should be required to submit a copy of any "report, study, or investigation . . . made in whole or in part with Department of Defense funds" (1969).

A basic contradiction in the DOD control system is that although no prior review of unclassified basic research reports was supposedly required, *some* prior review of all DOD-generated reports was supposed to be made to ensure that they contained no classified information. "It is clearly the responsibility of the Department," Defense spokesman Colonel Richard Taylor observed, ". . . to protect classified information, regardless of whether it is generated under a classified or an unclassified contract." In practice, DOD programs enjoyed "a considerable amount of discretion" in deciding whether or not to require prior review. The Office of Naval Research dispensed with it in unclassified contracts, but reviewed reports in applied research projects. The Air Force required clearance even in some unclassified contracts at universities (IV, 538–9).

Foreign Affairs Agencies

That the university business officers had grounds for their complaints against foreign affairs agencies was attested by agency representatives. The overall policy of the Agency for International Development was to require prior approval for the publication of any material prepared under its contracts. Since its policy at universities, which generally required "review" but not "approval," was regarded as "an exception to this rule," let me consider the paramount policy first.

AID had had, Curtis Barker stated, "no apparent problem" in its contracts with nonacademic institutions, under which "results may be made known to the public only at the discretion of the Contracting Officer . . . and with such credit . . . as he may determine"; all data and writings "shall be the sole property of the government" (IV, 573). The publication controls in these contracts were said to be, in words popularized by Students for a Democratic Society, "not . . . negotiable." AID deputy general counsel Stanley Siegel explained the reasons for these controls:

> *We want our research contractors to report their findings and conclusions to us in full candor and without self-censorship. . . . The right of approval before the first publication is a means to assure the Government of this objective and, at the same time, to guard against overseas reactions that would be self-defeating. . . .*
>
> *There is a presumption in favor of release. We would be concerned, however, about the dissemination of opinions or data obtained in confidence which would jeopardize foreign assistance objectives . . . or the possibility of doing further research in that or other countries. . . . A report sponsored by AID which would . . . endanger the development objectives shared by it and the United States might be withheld (IV, 575–576).*

Publication clearance might also be required, by mutual consent, in a university contract. However, the prototypical university contract merely stated that "Neither party shall publish . . . without giving thirty . . . days notice . . . , together with a copy of the proposed article" (IV, 572). During that period, "the Agency may . . . comment on the scientific soundness of the manuscript, which the contractor is free to accept or reject." AID is "obliged to identify breaches of security. . . . [and may also] raise concerns of national interest" (IV, 571). Gardner has observed that AID concern about security is decidedly overdeveloped. "The problem that publication poses for A.I.D. is not one of security but of discretion. . . . The faculty member who exercises admirable discretion when surrounded by his colleagues at home may be far from discreet . . . when he is halfway around the world. And the consequences of such lapses overseas may be far more severe than at home" (1964, p. 29).

In conversation, officials confirmed the main points in the episode about AID objections to the publication of *Growth Without Development* by Northwestern University Press. They intimated that a difference of opinion prevailed within the agency between the lawyers, who sought to retain tight controls in contracts, and other staff who felt that such clauses were, in any event, ineffectual should an investigator reject agency judgment.

Granted, when the two are in serious conflict, the national interest should come before the interest of scholars. But is the nation so frail that its interests can be jeopardized by every word a scholar may write, so that they must all be screened by officials? Something is wrong either with that assessment of our strength or with the measures AID has taken to protect it—for, as the Northwestern case demonstrated, these measures cannot forestall the release of information AID deems harmful. Therefore the policy of attempting to control some academic publications is unnecessary or unrealistic, because the agency cannot, in fact, control them, and if the national interest would indeed be jeopardized by certain findings, it should not contract for them. But the nation has survived the failures of AID publication policy, and universities will doubtless survive its successes.

State Department Review

Some of the frankest and most thoughtful observations on publication controls received during the Reuss inquiry were submitted by Raymond Platig, director of the State Department Office of External Research; his response may demonstrate either that it is possible to be frank and a government official or that Platig had only recently entered government service.

In the wake of the Camelot fiasco, President Johnson instructed the Secretary of State in an August 1965 letter "that no Government sponsorship of foreign area research should be undertaken which . . . would adversely affect foreign relations. Therefore I am asking you to establish effective procedures . . . to assure the propriety of Government-sponsored social science research in the area of foreign policy" (1965, p. 832).

In implementing this instruction, the department (Department of State, 1966) defined the scope of its review authority as "research programs and studies in the social and behavioral sciences dealing with international relations, or with foreign areas and peoples, whether conducted in the United States or abroad, which

are supported by agencies of the United States." Agencies were required to clear any project that "might have potentially adverse
effects on U. S. foreign relations"; and clearance was specifically
required for projects sponsored by military and foreign affairs
agencies which involved foreign travel or contacts with foreign
nationals. Research financed by the National Science Foundation,
the National Institutes of Health, the Fulbright-Hays programs, and
the Office of Education was exempted from review, with a few
exceptions that had long been in force.[10] The review of research
sponsored by such domestic agencies as the Departments of Agriculture, Labor, and Health, Education, and Welfare was expedited,
"since the sensitivity of such work in most cases is relatively low."
The department was advised about all proposed research and retained the option to review any. Each agency was held responsible
for ensuring that the contents of unclassified reports "will not adversely affect U. S. foreign relations." If there were any question
about the "propriety" of releasing an unclassified report, the agency
should consult the department about its disposition "and possible
classification" (Department of State, 1968).

These criteria and review procedures had been in force for
little more than a year when we inquired about their effects on unclassified research. In describing its review process, the department
had declared that "very few proposals offer difficulties that interfere
with speedy clearance," and "the review implies no right or effort
to influence the content or conclusions of the work to be performed." I challenged the latter claim: "While this may be true in
a certain formal sense, can it be true in a more realistic sense? Does
not the very fact of the review imply an influence over the content
of the research that can be sponsored by designated agencies, or the
conclusions that can be released to the public? One must suspect an

---

[10] ". . . grants to, or contracts with, *foreign* institutions made by the
National Science Foundation, the Office of Saline Water, and the National
Institutes of Health, as well as most agencies supporting scientific projects
abroad using U. S.-owned excess foreign currencies, were cleared with the
Department under statutory requirements or administrative arrangements.
. . . Occasionally, also, the administrators of exempted agencies and programs may seek Department advice on political or other circumstances
abroad that may affect grants to or contracts with American individuals or
institutions" (Department of State, 1968).

influence on the nature of individual projects; but even if this were not the case, such a review would still influence the nature of sponsored research in a broader sense, by clearing only certain kinds of projects. Indeed, if the review exerts no influence on the nature of government-sponsored research, why conduct it?" (IV, 568).

Platig replied "Yes," the review did effect the nature of research in the sense that "certain kinds of research should not be performed under certain kinds of government sponsorship" because that has "often been found to damage United States relations with foreign countries, and . . . [to diminish scholars'] access to the minds and even the data of foreign countries." The character of the sponsoring agency was critical to the acceptability of some projects: "some agencies [such as NSF and NIH] can do things with impunity that other [military, intelligence, and foreign affairs] agencies could do only at the risk of trouble." Platig rejected my suggestion that the claim not to influence the content of research was only formally true. "We contend that the statement is true with more than formal validity, and that the answer is 'No,' review does not so influence the projects undertaken—because once the contractor signs up to perform a project under the agreed specifications, the review process . . . does not affect what he says and what judgments he reaches." He conceded that "the specifications themselves have an influence." For example, a proposed DOD project might be modified to sanction only research within the U. S. or to delete part of the projected work. "Manifestly, then, the review can affect the scope and the method of the proposals. . . . but this fact does not mean that review influences the content of the project once the mind of the scholar is at work on his research."

To the question whether departmental review influenced "the conclusions that can be released to the public," Platig replied " 'Yes.' It would be a serious limitation on the agencies' use of contract research if all conclusions had to be made public. Agencies must be allowed at times to profit by research into hypotheses and contingencies the very consideration of which would cause sensations and misunderstandings if known and expecially if associated with certain official sponsors." Normally, the investigator should know and agree to this condition at the outset—"unless," Platig allowed, "world situations change."

Departmental review had seldom led to the classification of an originally unclassified proposal. Review staff were professionally committed to research and one of their basic objectives was, "when possible, to suggest ways of adapting a proposal so that it need not be classified" (IV, 568–570). Of more than four hundred review actions taken by the department as of January 1967, only five (all involving military or foreign affairs agencies) had been approved conditional on later clearance of the report, with the understanding that it might then be classified.

In December 1967, the interagency Foreign Area Research Coordination Group (1968) issued guidelines for the conduct of contract research, which sought to placate the academic community about the reasonableness of review procedures. They affirmed that the government should protect academic integrity, promote the advancement of knowledge, and "as a general rule . . . encourage open publication." Beyond that, things got stickier. There was no way around it, the general rule had sometimes to be broken. "Material which cannot be declassified must sometimes be used in research required for important purposes. . . . The government often needs research-based analysis . . . which, if made public, could produce serious misunderstandings and misapprehensions abroad about U. S. intentions." If classification were necessary, the "university is its own judge of whether or not it wishes to contract for research in this category." The government should ensure that the researcher knew in advance of, and accepted, any classification that might be imposed and of any anticipated uses of the findings. The guidelines for nonuniversity contractors did not differ radically from the academic guidelines, except that the right of the government to classify and control publication was here so obvious that it was not even mentioned.

The statistics of actions taken in the State Department review bear out the department assertion that the projects of foreign affairs and military agencies have been controlled more closely than those of domestic agencies. The conditions set for approval have included (most frequently) consultation with U. S. overseas missions and (sometimes) with foreign governments; (in a few cases) security classification or the submission of the manuscript for State Department review; (frequently) the acknowledgment of government sponsorship to foreign colleagues and perhaps to foreign officials; (occasionally) the submission of field-work plans for consideration by the department; and (in a few cases) the cancellation of field-work abroad. Partly because the academic research supported by NSF, NIH, and Fulbright awards was not subject to review, well over half of the projects reviewed were conducted by nonacademic organizations.

The department (Department of State, 1968) declared that its review is concerned "only with sensitivity which may properly concern the Government" and that it is not designed to endorse the quality or importance of the research per se; its standards are political, not scientific. Yet this assurance was precisely what discomforted Wolfle (1966) in a *Science* editorial: "The State Department . . . is properly concerned to avoid any political risk or embarrassment to the United States. The more zealously risk is avoided, the more likely it is that proposals that others consider valuable will be banned. . . . The risk should be weighed against the potential gains. Yet the State Department, which does not claim to be strong scientifically, has announced that it will not consider scientific or other aspects of a proposal, only its probable impact on foreign relations."

Returning to the subject three years later, Wolfle (1968) reported that he had heard a few criticisms of delays but "no strong protests over the way in which the Department of State has carried out its project-screening responsibilities." The general opinion was that "the easiest way to get a project approved is to promise to classify the results. . . . Multiple reviews . . . [and congressional criticism of] foreign area research . . . are reported to have reduced the amount of research and to have shifted some agency programs into safer directions. . . . Playing it safe has never been the best formula for achieving . . . productive research results."

Discussion

It is easy to endorse freedom of publication as a First Amendment right essential to a free and sovereign citizenry and to condemn the suppression of information by the bureaucracy to conceal wrongdoing, incompetence, and the pandering to special interests. When such information about public programs is suppressed, not just academic truths but important public interests and important principles of democratic government are jeopardized.

However, there are also legitimate reasons for drawing a veil of privacy over many governmental affairs. Indeed, there are good reasons to darken the almost transparent veil that gives officials too little opportunity to consider future policy free of public pressures (which include the pressures of powerful private interests). On the whole, our government is too open, not too reticent; it has no Official Secrets Act like that which binds British civil servants to disclose no official information they have learned in government employment, without prior authorization. Formulating policy under TV klieg lights does not advance good government, as trying a man in the press does not advance justice. The doctrine of executive privilege is essential to preserve even a semblance of rationality in government.

Restrictions on the freedom to publish research reports ultimately rest on that doctrine. These restrictions can be meaningful or formalistic, some agencies reserving rights of review that they do not actually use. If all university research and none that is conducted elsewhere were free of such restrictions, then about three-fifths of federal funds for social research—all that conducted within the government and by independent nonprofit and profit-making organizations—would be under some publication control. Can anything be done to reduce this large volume of research that is screened before release?

An initial step would be to oblige agencies to identify the volume of research whose publication is controlled. Congress might then choose to limit that volume. It would have the information enabling it to do so, and that fact alone might induce officials to husband this power. A second step would be to require the public listing of all research projects in progress, the degree to which any publication restriction applies, and the date and conditions under which it will be lifted. It might be useful also to give an investigator the right to appeal an agency ban to a board lodged in a body such as the Office of Science and Technology, the Office of Management and Budget, or the National Academy of Sciences.

Since the failure of many reports to see the light of day is due to many factors other than suppression, an agency—perhaps the Clearinghouse for Federal Scientific and Technical Information—should be made responsible for inventorying and stocking all available contractor reports and providing copies at cost.

Uniform rules cannot deal adequately with the varying objectives and circumstances of research undertakings; even without formal controls, an agency can prevent or delay publication—for example, by subcontracting for parts of a work which are meaningless unless assembled with the other parts or by conducting the work with its own staff or with consultants who have the status of government employees. The conflict between the public's wish to know and the agency's wish to withhold certain information will persist regardless of administrative rules and arrangements. Repeated public scrutiny of these arrangements and how they function should help to keep sponsored research as open as possible.

Summary

The remarkably consistent, independent testimony of respondents, university business officers, and government officials about publication controls in government-financed research yields the following picture:

University investigators can publish freely under the terms of all research grants and most contracts; however, some contracts require agency approval prior to publication. Little remains of the substantial volume of classified work conducted on campus following World War II, and most universities now require freedom to publish as a condition of accepting government funds. Government agencies have developed a twofold policy under which no control, or a minimal notification, obtains at universities, whereas research with more severe controls is conducted elsewhere.

Few independent research institutes insist on reserving their freedom to publish. Accustomed to proprietary work for industry, institutes will normally accept comparable work for government agencies. The assumption of corporate responsibility for a project; the contributions of many staff to the work; the need to maintain the continuing confidence of sponsors; the applied, individualized nature of research problems; and prevailing working conditions limit the right, interest, or ability of staff to publish freely without prior approval of the sponsor and institute management.

In sum, private research institutions are of two types: the academic, in which publication control rarely applies, and the nonacademic, in which it is the rule. Each practice is posited on a different kind of information and institution. University investigators subsist on information of an academic—that is, general or public—order at an institution which has little administrative interest or ability in restricting their freedom; while nonacademic investigators rely on information of a more nonacademic—concrete, specific, and often confidential—order at institutions organized to maintain such confidence and to discharge other corporate contractual responsibilities.

The large number of extramural projects subject to agency publication controls should be publicly identified and regularly accounted for. Continuing public scrutiny should serve to reduce such controls to the minimum level genuinely required to maintain the confidentiality of executive deliberations.

9

Quality of Sponsored Research

The independent evaluation of government domestic programs has been receiving increased attention in recent years. However, the evaluation of the quality of independent social research itself remains neglected. A similar failure to evaluate the quality of government-sponsored research in the natural sciences can also be noted, and a similar cause is suspected: research does not prosper by arming its enemies.

Quality is not a matter on which everyone will agree, and it would be a mistake to expect, to seek, or to obtain unanimous opinion. An evaluation which concludes that all aspects of a program are equally excellent is as valueless—uninformative and unbelievable—as a unanimous plebiscite or poll. The few public evaluations of government research programs often have that taste of saccharine advertising rather than astringent knowledge.

A good example is the report of the Wooldridge committee (1965) which judged the research sponsored by the National In-

stitutes of Health to be "typically of high quality. . . . Despite the
tenfold increase in NIH support of research. . . . there is good
evidence that the average quality is steadily improving." However,
that "good evidence" was not presented. The committee did indicate that of 240 grants which were investigated, its consultants "expressed serious reservations about 9 projects and adjudged an additional 7 to be unworthy of support" (p. 3). The distribution of the
remaining 224 cases among the many other grades of quality—high,
good, ordinary—and their geographic, disciplinary, and institutional
location were not divulged.

In an effort to learn about the frequency and nature of research program evaluation, the Reuss subcommittee requested each
department and agency financing extramural social research programs to submit "Any available (official or unofficial) analyses of
the degree to which they are achieving their objectives, and of their
overall adequacy and quality" (II, 600). The responses may be
called comical or sad, but not informative.

Of the twenty-one governmental units which obligated one
million dollars or more on extramural social research in 1967, ten
either disregarded the question or submitted material that was not
germane to it. Five others acknowledged the question but for one
reason or another did not really answer it. One, the Agriculture Department Economic Research Service, stated that "There are no
broad general statements available dealing with the objectives and
justification for extramural research. . . . [We] know of no analyses
of the degree to which such objectives are being achieved" (II,
600). Two, the Advanced Research Projects Agency and the National Aeronautics and Space Administration, explained that their
programs had not been under way long enough to be evaluated,
although the latter also added that its social research program "has
improved the understanding" of the national role of the NASA
R&D activities (II, 617). And two—the Army and the National
Science Foundation—replied that no special evaluation could be
provided because evaluation, like breathing, went on constantly.

Of the six remaining agencies, two stated that their normal
procedures ensured the high quality of sponsored research. William
Gaud put much confidence in the Research Advisory Committee of
the Agency for International Development and the "thorough and

painstaking" system of reviewing and selecting research proposals to ensure that projects "accord with the Agency's overall objectives, make sense in terms of scientific merit and feasibility and have a potential payoff for AID's assistance efforts" (II, 616). Similarly, the Office of Education stated that "The selection-rate (about one proposal in five is funded) has been sufficiently rigorous to insure that only high-quality proposals would actually be supported." Additional tests of research quality were the approbation and participation of leading members of the professions and bibliographic citations:

> *One index of the quality and effectiveness of extramural research is the general recognition and approval of the programs by pertinent professional groups, as evidenced by submission of research proposals by capable researchers and by the willingness of leaders in the professions to serve as field readers, consultants, and advisory committee members. . . . Further evidence of quality is found in the favorable reception accorded OE-supported research presentations at meetings of professional societies. Still another proof of quality is the heavy representation of OE-supported research in the bibliographic citations in the* Review of Education Research *[II, 603–604].*[1]

The Labor Department Office of Manpower Policy, Evaluation, and Research declared that its findings had contributed "significantly to the solution of serious manpower problems"; the number of investigators and institutions receiving grants was also cited to show that they were achieving their objectives of involving more investigators and institutions in manpower research (II, 615–616).

Three agencies—the Air Force and two NIH institutes—submitted material which came a little closer to the substance of genuine research evaluation. The Air Force provided the report of a 1966 meeting of an advisory committee of the Behavioral Sciences Division of the Office of Scientific Research. There was nothing

---

[1] The report on *Educational Research and Development in the United States* reviews a number of more serious evaluations of educational research undertaken after this reply was prepared (Office of Education, 1969, Chapter X); see also Organisation for Economic Co-operation and Development (1971).

particularly remarkable about this report; agency files must contain hundreds like it. Why more are not published is something of a mystery. Perhaps they are deemed too insubstantial to warrant, or to withstand, public scrutiny—but important decisions are nonetheless based on them. Perhaps publication might breach the confidence of private deliberations, but approval of the participants could often be obtained. This precedent is worth repeating.

For example, psychologist Harry Helson stated that the research sponsored by the division "has shown steady improvement year by year. Average-quality projects have been eliminated and replaced by work of decidedly superior investigators." Anthropologist Ward Goodenough considered investigators to be "of top quality." Committee members (seven of the eight came from universities) opposed confining OSR basic research to subjects obviously and immediately relevant to Air Force interests. One said that "relevance . . . should not be a criterion for . . . support, at the sacrifice or neglect of quality"; another, that "The only concern should be with quality, not wholly with relevance. If the quality of research is maintained it will eventually prove useful"— and cited work which, after forty years, had assumed "tremendous importance to perception during space flight." (Scientists might patiently wait that many years for research to prove useful, but their foolish fellow citizens might prefer to sponsor it somewhat closer to the time that space flight could be envisaged). The committee also made three recommendations for maintaining quality, each of which probably ran counter to higher government policy: research should be funded for about three years; more research should be sponsored overseas where a dollar could still buy more good research than it could in the United States; and quality alone, not geographic location, should be considered in awards (II, 601–602).

The National Institute of Child Health and Human Development submitted a set of abstracts which demonstrated one simple way, mysteriously avoided by other agencies, of evaluating quality. The agency commissioned the preparation of abstracts and quality ratings of reports it had sponsored. The examples submitted were rated either A or B, and "excellent," "important," or "very worthwhile" littered the appended comments; but in one case critical comments were included—"the relative lack of specificity about the results. . . . It was disappointing that the author did not attempt . . . ; it might have been appropriate to have used a control group." Published reviews commonly assess the quality of books, but comparable assessments of professional papers remain hidden in the files of journal editors. Might it not occasionally be useful for them to see the light of day, with such emendations as may be charitable to protect the lives of reviewers and their victims? This method provides an economical way to assess the quality of research in a given field.

Finally, the National Institute of Mental Health submitted the evaluation of its activities that had been conducted by a panel of the Wooldridge committee, whose overall report on the National Institutes of Health has already been mentioned. NIMH singled out for special note the panel statement that "The industry and competence of the supported research scientists are extraordinarily high, and set the standard of excellence throughout the world for work in their fields. In only a small proportion of cases has the research failed to meet satisfactory standards and the maintenance of high quality in the face of the great expansion of the total program is particularly worthy of note." The panel cautioned against the frequent emphasis of the Congress and the department on useful research in neglected areas, which, it felt, could divert scientists from more promising scientific work and "increase the probability of errors in scientific judgment"; and it recommended the formation of a special study section to review and, if necessary, reject "urgent or large-scale projects not initiated by scientists" (which would properly admonish both the Congress and the Executive!). The panel appeared to favor small research projects and to be more skeptical about expensive clinical research centers and large, centrally directed collaborative projects which required "extra care" and special review mechanisms to assure their success. Noting the difficulty which the beginning or unorthodox investigator experienced in getting NIMH support, it suggested that small grants and general institutional grants be expanded (Wooldridge, 1965, pp. 130–140).

The panelists' report presented a viewpoint so characteristic of academic scientists that a special study was hardly needed to produce it; members did, in fact, acknowledge that their observations derived not only from an examination of the projects sampled by consultants but "from our general experience." The panel's high praise of the quality of NIMH extramural research was not shared by all the Reuss respondents. Pioneer health economist Michael Davis, psychiatrists Jack Ewalt and John Knowles, psychologist Brewster Smith, and sociologist Robin Williams agreed with the panel, but economists Victor Fuchs and Eli Ginzberg and psychiatrist Harold Visotsky were more caustic about the social and economic research sponsored by NIMH and the Public Health Service (PHS). Fuchs wrote that "Research on the economics of health has generally not been of as high quality as other economic research, but the situation is improving" (II, 384); while Ginzberg declared: "By and large the quality of research on the social, psychological and economic aspects of health and medicine being conducted in the United States . . . leaves much to be desired. It is very hard to identify ten first-rate items over the last ten years. . . . much more planning should be devoted to establishing three or four major centers . . . in critically important areas. To do so one would have to avoid frittering away a lot of money on small unimportant project grants" (II, 385). Visotsky felt that "the most significant feature missing . . . is a sense of planning in which the selection of programs to meet carefully evaluated alternative needs is provided with a rational basis. . . . One of the major characteristics of Public Health Service research is perhaps its diffuseness and its lack of defined program focus" (II, 400–401). Plainly, whereas the academic men on the Wooldridge panel were delighted with the entire system of NIMH grants to individual investigators, Fuchs and Visotsky, who were not attached to a university, and Ginzberg, who was at a graduate school of business, believed that this kind of research was "frittering away" large resources which should be used in a more concerted manner—precisely in the manner that the panel considered unwise and unproductive.

An interesting evaluation of NIH-sponsored research was offered by a sociologist who had been an NIMH study section member:

> *Some of the very highest quality social research has been produced under . . . [PHS] auspices. . . . There is,*

*however, unevenness in the rigor demanded of applications
from different disciplines, with low rigor and high approval,
for example, for projects in anthropology and high rigor and
low approval for projects in social work or education. Highest
rigor is reserved for psychology and psychiatry with moderate
rates of approval. Sociology tends to be subjected to moderate
rigor and moderate rates of approval. As a consequence, poor
quality research is approved and produced by anthropologists
who tend to be handsomely funded; less research is undertaken
by the applied disciplines of social work, often only modestly
funded but of a higher quality; and the highest quality research of all is produced by psychology.*

He recognized the "disparate and unintegrated, non-cumulative"
character of much of the research generated by unsolicited proposals and asked whether " 'commissioning' of needed research
should not be undertaken on both theoretic and problem oriented
issues" (II, 396).

From the foregoing evidence, it appears that: qualified observers can hold pronouncedly different views of the quality of the
same research program; quality can vary considerably in different
parts of a program; and quality judgments are related to larger
judgments about the purpose of a program and how it should be
administered—particularly, about its reliance on unsolicited proposals or on projects commissioned by agency officials. One cannot
decide how good a program is without deciding *what* it is good *for*.

In respondents' evaluation of the quality of research sponsored by the Office of Education, a similar cleavage was evident
between advocates of unsolicited proposals and proponents of "directed" projects. The former criticized the growing OE trend toward
directed research as "somewhat authoritarian," unsuited to the state
of basic knowledge in the field, not "the way scientific inquiry pro-
ceeds most fruitfully," and unlikely "to attract the best minds to the
field" (II, 138–139, 141). The latter argued, contrariwise, that the
trend was "desirable . . . for improving the quality and usefulness
of research" and that, as small investigations had "relatively little
impact on national understanding. . . . it would be wiser to mount
larger scale attacks" which could better attract able and experienced
investigators (II, 113, 127).

Plainly, one factor affecting these opinions was the degree to which research quality was equated with scientific merit (as academic men define it) or with practical usefulness and influence (as defined by administrators and applied social scientists).

Despite the criticism I have noted, it seems fair to say that respondents had a better opinion of the quality of research in the area of health and medicine than in the five other domestic areas examined.[2]

The only direct evaluation offered of criminological research was that it was "surprisingly good," a not unequivocal expression; respondents were more concerned about the absence than the quality of research in this area. But silence can speak as loudly as words, and even a casual foray into the professional literature reveals a body of highly critical opinion of a kind not expressed to the committee. For example, Howton finds that "while the scale of the research effort [into the causes of juvenile delinquency] is impressive, the findings are not. Too often they are so inconsistent as to nullify each other and bring us back practically to the zero point. . . . [The] escalation of error damages both the rationality of practice and the prestige of science" (1964, pp. 154–156). After reviewing the research literature on the prevention of delinquency, Rosenfeld concludes, "Not only have we not learned anything in the past thirty years, but we seem to have proceeded on premises which common sense, logic, and available knowledge would declare to be most naive" (1965, pp. 367–380). As "a middle-aged 'new boy' " not long arrived at the University of Chicago from overseas, Norval Morris thought "it would be misguided" to comment about research quality; but elsewhere (1965) he has written that much research into the effects of correctional practices "is pursued by

---

[2] The questions were: "What is your opinion of the general quality, scope, and nature of the research now being sponsored by the federal government into the causes, characteristics, and control of crime, delinquency, and violence? Have you any suggestions for improving the quality and usefulness of this research?" Alternative forms of the questions ran: ". . . of the educational research now being sponsored by the federal government—particularly the U. S. Office of Education?" ". . . of the research on problems of poverty now being sponsored by the federal government—particularly the Office of Economic Opportunity?" " . . . of the research now being sponsored by federal agencies in the field of social insurance and welfare assistance?" ". . . of the research on urban problems now being sponsored by the federal government?"

research methods of such naivete that valid results rarely emerge." True, the foregoing judgments pertain to the general professional literature rather than to that portion of it financed by the government; but the judgments given below do not suggest that the quality of research in a field is immediately transformed by the infusion of federal funds.

OEO-sponsored research, Joseph Kershaw said, "is generally good. It should improve in time, since some of it was contracted for under considerable pressure" (II, 251). Harold Watts's appraisal was perhaps a shade more critical: "the poverty-oriented research generated in the last two years by federal agencies, and OEO in particular, is generally lower on any scale—quality, scope, or relevance—than that directed toward areas which have received equal attention for a longer period of time. But it . . . is as good as if not better than [what] we should expect from a relatively rapid mobilization of research resources" (II, 267).

The few appraisals of research on social insurance and welfare assistance ranged across the spectrum of quality. Margaret Gordon considered the "general quality, scope, and nature" of the research sponsored by the Social Security Administration to be "very good" (II, 447). Of the federal program in this area, Robert Morris said that "a promising start has been made, but only that" (II, 455). Criticism of "the low quality and small amount of research now being done in the social welfare field," Charles Lebeaux wrote, was due to the "lack of research in this field" and "the shortage of qualified people" (II, 453–454). Winifred Bell was more devastating:

> . . . I had occasion several years back to review every progress report so far submitted in response to grants made under the Cooperative Research and Demonstration Grants program . . . of the Social Security Act. The search was for methods of intervention that worked to cure poverty or to mitigate its consequences. . . . my review revealed that unpromising projects continued to be funded year after year, most studies were inconsequential, hard facts were difficult to locate and when located were rarely useful. . . . In the intervening years, attempts have been made to improve the quality

of projects and to encourage projects of greater significance, but in my judgment the effort has met with indifferent success, so far as the area of welfare assistance is concerned [II, 442].

Those who commented on quality of research in the ill-defined field of "urban problems" were not ecstatic. "There is, of course, a range of quality in urban research," Aschman observed, "but we would say that on the whole, quality is reasonably high" (II, 499). That assessment was the most glowing. Scott Keyes said merely that quality "obviously varies both within the same program and among different programs" (II, 512); F. Stuart Chapin, Jr., that it was "uneven" (II, 501); Robert Charpie, that it was "no better than average" (II, 506); and Robert Jones, that most urban research was "of rather limited usefulness" (II, 507). William Wheaton declared that, because the government had "shamefully neglected" urban research, "most talented researchers have gone into other fields" (II, 525); and Lloyd Rodwin, that "I know no responsible urbanist or official . . . who is not seriously concerned about the dearth of the intellectual capital in the field of urbanism" (II, 519).

Whereas the less-than-uniformly-outstanding quality of government-sponsored research in criminology, poverty, welfare, and urban affairs was often attributed to the dearth of money and of the talent that money attracted, in education it was attributed to the recent glut of money and the difficulty of attracting enough high-quality talent to use it. (Was the ideal situation a high level of funding maintained over a substantial period?)

Obviously, expenditures running at an annual level of from $80 million to $100 million (which would command the services of about three thousand persons at $30,000 a head, including supporting services and expenses), dispersed across the nation, cannot support research of uniformly high quality. The more sanguine opinion was that quality "has improved markedly since OE research expenditures began to rise (II, 141); that "educational research is a much more vigorous field of inquiry because of federal funding" (II, 117); or that the quality of educational research sponsored by the government "is as high as it has ever been" (II, 122). But others gave more austere judgments: quality was "generally poor"

(II, 109); it is "not as high . . . [as] in other fields of psychology" (II, 138); and, in the opinion of former education commissioner Sterling McMurrin, education research "lags behind most scientific and industrial research . . . in quality and effectiveness. Certainly much educational research has been trivial, irrelevant, or incompetent" (II, 129).

The most damning evaluation of educational research that I have encountered was also one of the most careful, and the only comfort is that, as it concerned educational research articles published in 1962, their general quality *may* since have improved and those financed by the government *may* be better than others (both opinions are held by OE staff). Under the direction of a committee of the American Educational Research Association, 125 judges (mainly educational psychologists) each assessed one research article (sampled from 827 published in forty-one journals in 1962) on twenty-five characteristics. The main conclusion reached was that "A majority of educational research articles published in 1962 were defective; a large proportion of the articles contained unsubstantiated conclusions." The committee compounded this cruel verdict with the opinion that "no significant change has occurred [between 1962 and 1967] in the quality of educational research published in journals" (Wandt and others, 1967).

It takes little effort to collect similar verdicts, though few are based on such methodical procedures, about the average quality of the research literature in many social science fields. For example, Crick (1954) writes of the "proliferation of quite trivial and uneducative research" in political science, an opinion shared by two-thirds of a random sample of political scientists who agreed that "Much that passes for scholarship in political science is superficial or trivial" (Somit and Tanenhaus, 1964, pp. 14–15). Fully 70 percent of a sample of sociologists believed that "pressure to publish has usually resulted in a flooding of the journals with inferior work" (Gouldner and Sprehe, 1965). Hexter (1967) speaks of "the low yield of intellectual nourishment provided by much of the enormous output of historical writing," which he attributes to "an explosion of demand so powerful as to set at naught the feeble attempts to maintain quality control over supply." Gordon (1968) observes that "the incidence of poor research . . . [is] distressingly high in the social sciences. . . . one all too frequently encounters social science research which builds uncritically on data of questionable accuracy, which is slipshod in method, or which is simply discursive and unfocused." Summarizing "hundreds of research studies on the discovery and application of social-science knowledge relevant to public health education programs," Edward Suchman (1967b p. 576) says, "The quantity of activity in this area is overwhelming; unfortunately, the quality is not. The research studies are apt to be poorly designed, the execution haphazard, and the analysis over-simplified. The result is a vast array of disconnected, dubious findings." Of welfare agency research, Ruderman writes, "much . . . is poor or at best mediocre. . . . It is frequently wasted effort, and wasted money" (1968, p. 62).

In fact, so many brutal judgments of their colleagues' work are made so often in professional circles that we must infer that no social research has the unqualified praise of all social scientists; that many respondents took an unduly rosy view of the facts; or that, despite innumerable defects, government-sponsored research has generally been of better quality than comparable unsponsored research. Very likely all three inferences are true. Government-sponsored social research may ask small rather than large questions; it may be informative rather than inspired, conventional rather than original, and respectful rather than critical. But, being relatively well financed and having to pass some methodological scrutiny, it is likely to be technically sounder than the self-generated and self-scrutinized work of scholars. This point was made forcefully by the head of a government research unit with a deserved reputation for rigorous statistical work. He was appalled at the slapdash procedures often employed by eminent professors which contrasted so markedly with the painstaking attention to detail (by numerous clerks and professional assistants) to which he was accustomed. Yet the professors had a greater reputation and influence than the official—deservedly, if outspokenness warrants influence, or not, if influence should be proportionate to the quality of knowledge imparted to the public.

That is an anecdote and an anecdote proves nothing. Nor can I prove that at least some respondents gave a rosier picture to the Congress than they might to professional circles, but this conclusion seems likely. Frank criticism helps to maintain the standards of a profession and to clarify schools of thought, but it is not the customary way to bolster public confidence in, and to increase appropriations for, the social sciences.

I have elsewhere discussed the quality of the research supported by the National Science Foundation and the National Institutes of Health, scientists' "model" agencies, concluding that their primary objective was "*not* to encourage and support high quality science wherever it may be found, but rather to encourage and support *more* science (of ordinary as well as high quality) at *universities,* which constitute the principal constituency of these programs just as farmers are the constituency of the Department of Agriculture" (II, 630). This general objective of basic research programs has confounded any more selective goal they may also hold of sponsoring research of high quality. In such programs as NSF and NIH have administered, less-than-high-quality research serves many functions, including routine mapping of new lands discovered by notable scientists and strengthening the scientific and political foundation for their work.

The self-directed, self-appraised, and in good measure self-allocated administration of government appropriations by university scientists has worked well in basic research programs. But it is a mistake to imagine that this method can work equally well to meet the practical needs of government officials for timely and relevant information on designated national problems. Even NIH and NSF are now forsaking it in their recent programs directed to defined social objectives. For that purpose, the "laissez-faire proposal system is probably obsolete," as Robert Wood remarked.[3]

Improving Research Programs

Dismissing that alternative, what can be done to improve the quality of domestic research programs that so palpably need improvement? An ideal set of prescriptions can be advanced, but it will not be easy to implement them all. Washington is a turbulent

[3] At a September 6, 1958, panel discussion of the behavioral sciences and the federal government at the American Political Science Association meeting in Washington, D.C.

place, and domestic research programs are close enough to the center of that turbulence so that one catastrophe or another—a congressional hearing, an executive reorganization, a financial crisis, a resignation, the eruption of a new social problem—is bound to disturb the best-laid plan of the best-managed program. One cannot expect research into vexatious social issues on which power, passion, and money hinge to run as serenely as research on white mice and college freshmen. With luck, courage, and skill, it can enjoy periods of marked achievement.

One common prescription is to improve the quality of the staff administering research programs. Better people should be able to prepare better plans, to make better awards, and to make more perceptive use of findings. And the number of high-salaried positions available to research agencies has usually been limited. But too much can be made of government salaries, which are no longer as low as they once were, and not enough of other conditions less readily changed, which can drive the highest salaried men from public service. The red tape, the circumspection required in public remarks, the need for loyalty to superiors, the obligation to implement and justify unwelcome policies, the exposure to congressional harassment, the constant pressures that reduce operational freedom without reducing personal responsibility can reduce the time that able men, particularly those accustomed to the freedom of academic life, will devote to public service.

Can these enduring conditions of government employment be changed? Relative immunity from political pressures and professional freedom may be maintained in basic research and "old-line" programs, but new social programs at the front of the political stage cannot expect the same insulation from critical scrutiny. The research director of an agency such as the Office of Economic Opportunity or the revitalized Office of Education must be prepared to tack with the political winds and to work closely with the head of his agency as well as with leading social scientists in his field. His work will be significant and exciting, but it cannot all go according to the neat plans and methodologies of the academy.

The second half of the personnel prescription is to improve the quality of the social scientists conducting sponsored research. Initially, the prospects appear good, since, in principle, a research director is free to enlist the help of any intellectual in the nation or abroad. But the best people are also the busiest and may not be interested in his problems. He must settle for the people he can get right away, while continuing his efforts to attract the best by (among other strategies) broadening and modifying his objectives to suit their interests. If he is persistent and flexible, he may eventually succeed; but the resultant research will not be what he originally sought.

If you have to wait, let us say, two years to get the right person and another two to get his report, the world will have changed considerably. A research program should be sufficiently flexible to allow for such changes, though their exact nature cannot be foretold. But a research plan which is too flexible is no plan at all and offers little guidance to the professional community and little hope for cumulative results. Richard Dershimer has, with warrant, criticized the Office of Education for too frequent changes of plan: "Programs come and go and the Office has had wide swings in the priorities it sets even from year to year. Project English and Project Social Studies, and the media research program are only three that have evaporated as formal programs (not as areas of interest) in recent years. A more recent illustration of how priorities can shift rapidly is the announcement that the funds for unsolicited projects that could be initiated in FY 1967 would be reduced to one-fourth of what they had been in 1966. The researcher in the field is hard-pressed to understand what will be funded from year to year" (II, 118).

The ideal objectives of a good research plan should fall between the extremes of doctrinaire rigidity and infinite adaptability, with its immediate capitulation to every academic fad and Congressional whim. These goals should consistently delimit a set of questions which are narrow enough for a period long enough to compile answers and yet are broad or insightful enough to remain applicable to policy issues that are alive and not historic at the conclusion of the research. In practice, not one but two sets of objectives are needed: one geared to long-term and the other to short-term goals, collating the findings of brief studies and such interim information as can be siphoned from continuing research.

The critics of planless and scattered projects could err in the opposite direction of imposing a too comprehensive plan on a large sector of the professional community. Such a plan could be as unproductive as the planless projects it seeks to replace, for it would coat the diverse interests of able individuals with a varnish of words or else enroll such pedestrian talents as devote themselves to routinized activity; while emergent problems and the live issues falling in the interstices of any methodical plan would be disregarded. Accordingly, a partial plan is wiser than a whole one and a short list of priorities more realistic than a long list. One can reasonably attempt to give some order and some direction to a program, but too much order and direction is stultifying.

Summary

A type of evaluation that has been singularly lacking has been the evaluation of the quality and effectiveness of social research programs themselves. The replies of most government officials to our inquiry about this type of evaluation were nonresponsive, evasive, or unsatisfactory. However, the few efforts at genuine evaluation demonstrate that it is feasible. One must suspect that its rarity is due to the embarrassment that might ensue from applying the tools of social science to the work of social scientists. And a social scientist who concluded that expenditures should be reduced in a particular program might well fear a trial for treason and summary execution by a rump court of his colleagues.

10

"Utilizing" Social Research

The growing interest in the uses of social science knowledge has multiple causes. As social science expenditures grow, questions naturally arise about their value, and one measure of that value is the degree to which the results have a discernible use that is beneficial to society and not merely to the scholarly community. The exacerbation of long-standing social problems such as inflation, urban services, civil disobedience, racial conflict, and crime puts increased demands for information, explanation, and advice on those who profess to understand these problems—demands not only from established authority but from every special interest which would divest that authority of some power. And as their numbers grow and their confidence in some of their knowledge also grows (justified by objective tests of reliability or subjective tests of agreement), social scientists are not all content to remain scholars; some seek and obtain positions of influence behind or on the seats of power.

In this situation, even the National Science Foundation, which had supported only social research which was "scientific" and "basic," specifically excluding research into public policy issues, in 1968 appointed a special commission to offer recommendations "for increasing the useful application of the social sciences in the solution of contemporary social problems" (Brim, 1969, p. 1).[1] Most of the programs examined in the Reuss inquiry sought to increase the usefulness of their sponsored research. Nonetheless, the dominant opinion of our respondents and other observers was that social science knowledge was inadequately utilized.

Is Knowledge Well Used?

The subcommittee inquired about six major areas of sponsored social research: law enforcement, education, poverty, health care, welfare, and urban problems.[2] Characteristic comments in the area of law enforcement were that "existing knowledge is not well utilized by the courts, police, [and] prison officials" and that "research data . . . are [not] put to good use by practical law enforcement. . . . there is an enormous gap between research and practice and so far nobody has found an effective way to bridge the gap" (II, 29, 35).

In education, respondents were somewhat more optimistic. Information developed by the Office of Education research bureau "played an essential part" in shaping OE legislative proposals, Frances Keppel stated, and the "advice of private scholars has certainly been used by both the Office . . . and local educational

[1] The appointment of the commission by the National Science Board was announced in February 1968; in July, the National Science Foundation Act was amended to authorize support for applied as well as basic research and to designate the social sciences explicitly as disciplines in which research was to be supported.

[2] The following questions were asked: "Is existing knowledge well utilized by the courts, police, prison officials, and others most responsible for dealing with law enforcement and crime reduction? Is the advice of private scholars utilized to evaluate the effectiveness of law enforcement?" (II, 26–27). "Is existing knowledge well utilized in shaping national and local educational programs? Is the advice of private scholars utilized to evaluate the effectiveness of these programs?" (II, 108). Similar questions were asked about programs dealing with poverty (II, 250), health care (II, 377), welfare (II, 441), and housing and urban development (II, 498).

groups in evaluation" (II, 127). "Existing knowledge is never utilized well enough in shaping national and local educational programs," Julian Stanley said, "but such utilization seems to have been increased and hastened during the past several years" (II, 142), and many observers would agree. The establishment of educational "laboratories" across the nation, in large measure to encourage educational innovation, alone supports that opinion.

However, contrary opinion can also be marshaled. For example, a 1967 study found that, though research on learning processes represents "perhaps the largest single area of investigation presently being pursued by experimental psychologists. . . . there has been no systematic effort directed toward practical application of the findings. . . . modern learning research is producing very little impact on educational technology or training practice."

> *Noble . . . has pointed out that not only is the absolute level of effort in learning research very large but there is an increasing trend in the percentage of articles devoted to studies of human learning. In psychological journals, in general, the percentage increased from about 15% (1940) to about 30% in 1962. In the* Journal of Experimental Psychology *. . . from about 30% in 1940 to about 60% in 1962. . . . In spite of the level of research effort and obvious interest in learning processes, it is difficult to find even isolated, much less systematic, applications of modern psychological research on learning to educational technology. . . . In a round-table discussion at the 1966 APA meeting devoted to the question "How can psychologists contribute effectively to education?," it was evident that the participants saw no clear or obvious ways in which this could be done [Mackie and Christensen, 1967].*

When a national sample of school superintendents was asked, in 1968–1969, to identify the results of educational research and development having widespread influence on school practices, 64 percent of those replying gave no response at all (Office of Education, 1969, pp. 146ff). Although the superintendents might simply have been unaware of the research sources of new practices, this finding was taken by Commissioner of Education James Allen as evidence that "Current research activities have had little impact on classroom teaching" (Feinberg, 1969).

The mental health field is often cited as one in which research results have been applied well, the classic example being the influential 1961 report of the Joint Commission on Mental Illness and Health which was followed (and also accompanied and preceded) by important changes in the system of mental health care and a reduction in the number of patients in mental hospitals. Ewalt, director of that commission, understandably felt that knowledge was generally "well used in the mental health field" (II, 382). Robin Williams felt the same about national programs: "At state and local levels, the record is very spotty" (II, 406).

Of the utility and utilization of social and economic knowledge to improve other health services our respondents had less good to say. Fuchs believed that "very little use is made of economic knowledge in shaping . . . health programs" (II, 385); Visotsky, that "economic, social and psychological data is rarely utilized in shaping . . . health programs" (II, 402); the anonymous sociologist, that the "question of 'usefulness' . . . is almost never asked anywhere" in the process of awarding Public Health Service research grants; PHS and NSF "don't have any mechanism for bringing this knowledge to bear on . . . health programs" (II, 396).

With regard to antipoverty programs, Seymour Miller wrote, "In some cases there has been important utilization, e.g. the research on large families . . . encouraged the development of population control measures. But my impression is generally of low utilization." He blamed "the Congressional mandates which structure programs on the basis of frequently inadequate formulation of the issues" (II, 262–3). Moynihan (1966b) placed more blame on social scientists: "Of all the major social initiatives of recent times, none, I think, arose more directly from academic research and evaluation than did the War on Poverty." Miller believed that evaluations "frequently have little impact on local operations," and Oscar Ornati, who examined three program evaluations with some care, also concluded that their effect on OEO was "minor" (II, 310)—a judgment which OEO's Robert Levine rejected. The facts about the degree of utilization of OEO research are really in less dispute than whether one should commend or criticize these facts.

There is ample ground for either position, as Harold Watts demonstrated by subscribing to both: "By any absolute standard existing
knowledge is probably not well utilized in shaping antipoverty
programs. However, existing knowledge on any subject leaves many
gaps and is rarely so unequivocal in its implications for policy that
one can confidently determine whether it has been given due weight.
. . . Compared to [the utilization of knowledge to implement the
Full Employment Act since 1946], the utilization of existing knowledge for antipoverty efforts is remarkably efficient" (II, 268).

"The extent to which existing knowledge is utilized in shaping . . . welfare programs," Margaret Gordon wrote, "leaves a
good deal to be desired" (II, 449). While Daniel Price viewed the
situation tolerantly—"no matter what sort of program is developed,
it is possible to find some private scholar who would recommend it"
(II, 460)—Winifred Bell did not: "The most discouraging fact . . .
about . . . welfare programs is their lack of responsiveness to new
knowledge. The remarkable fact about public welfare is not how
much it has improved in ten years but how little it has changed in
four hundred years. . . . I know of no evidence that suggests that
new knowledge is systematically brought to bear in shaping the
nation's welfare programs" (II, 445).

Comments on the application of knowledge in urban programs were generally favorable but, in the manner with which we
are now familiar, ran the spectrum from "yes" to "no." Among
those responding "yes" was Morton Schussheim. "The present
Secretary [of Housing and Urban Development] and his top assistants are . . . close students of urban problems. . . . Increasingly . . . private scholars have been called upon to review policy
questions and help shape programs" (II, 523). Scott Keyes agreed:
"One thinks of the rapid growth of metropolitan planning; of . . .
metropolitan councils, and now the Federal metropolitan expediters
. . . ; of the growth and development of comprehensive land use
and transportation planning . . . comprehensively planned new
towns . . . community renewal planning . . . demonstration cities.
. . . to argue that on the whole we are not making use of our social
and economic knowledge in sharpening programs would be, I
think, a misinterpretation of the record" (II, 514–515). To Robert
Jones, existing knowledge was not yet well used, but the situation

was improving. F. Stuart Chapin and William Wheaton took the unexceptionable position that in some areas information was utilized and in others it was not. Lloyd Rodwin was most firm that "there is a serious gap between what we know and what we do . . . major improvements are feasible if we bring average practice closer to best practice" (II, 519).

If the foregoing opinions do not demonstrate how well social science knowledge has been used in domestic social programs, they do indicate what evidence can lead an observer to believe that it has, or has not, been well utilized.

Utilization as Change

Thus, the introduction of significant new domestic programs or program alterations; new social or administrative policies, methods, or arrangements; and even technical innovations (as in educational paraphernalia or urban planning) whose origin can be at least partly traced to the social sciences are taken as signs of utilization, whereas the mere continuance of existing programs, policies, methods, and technologies betokens nonuse. Thus it would seem that one necessary element of utilization is visible change. Thinking of the many new programs and appropriations he helped secure, former education commissioner Keppel believed that social science knowledge was well utilized; thinking of the many dilapidated schools and ossified classroom methods, Commissioner Allen believed that it had not been.

The change is, of course, equated with progress or social betterment. Here we come to a deeply utopian aspect of social science thinking and also one in which there may be cause to distinguish economics from the other social sciences. Presumably, certain kinds of change—perhaps increases in crime, unemployment, insanity—are retrogressive. But who is to say? Social scientists studying crime are generally more sympathetic to the criminals and more critical of the society which breeds them than are (for example) the police. Hence, if social science knowledge is to be properly used, its utilization must be in the direction that the social scientist advocates—which is to say, usually in a liberal direction or one which, in his view, serves to better the human lot (though, more likely, it merely alters the manifestation of an unalterable vice or exchanges one problem for another).

Economics differs from the other social sciences, especially sociology, in several respects. Since it has a corps of members in business schools and in business and financial institutions, the profession can sound a conservative note as well as a liberal one. Reputable economists at times advocate increased unemployment and reduced government spending, but are there reputable sociologists who advocate police violence and a reduction in welfare expenditures?

Since economics deals with material matters—work, money, and goods—its data are relatively uncontaminated by subjective considerations. Those who favor and oppose a particular income distribution, budget, tax, or unemployment level can accept the same statistics as accurately describing economic conditions. But we are not inclined to accept social statistics—of crime, education, divorce, or illegitimacy—as adequately depicting the nation's social condition because a solely objective description of the human condition is less adequate and humane than one which recognizes subjective elements. But when subjective elements intrude, the meaning of even the most reliable statistics becomes debatable. Divorce rates rise—but if unhappy couples separate, may that action not add to human happiness? Cannot social protests lead to social reform? If drug arrests increase, should not drug abuse be legalized? Does the increase of car thefts not reflect the growing number of cars? Does not the stigmatization of illegitimacy represent a failure of bourgeois charity rather than of individual morality? Such inverse sociological logic can add to the interpretation of social statistics a critical dimension that is not present in economics or the natural sciences.

The comparability and aggregability of dollars gives economics a notion of limit, of trade-off, and a basis of comparison that other social sciences lack. If N billion dollars are allocated to program Y, there will be that many fewer for other programs; but advancing the welfare of a million persons does not necessarily reduce the welfare of anyone else. The lack of aggregable measures of national welfare gives to the other social sciences the air of being utopian or oblivious of harsher realities. Either they are constantly improving the welfare of everyone so that the nation is getting unbearably happy; or they have neglected the less happy consequences of social benevolence; or the human condition cannot, in fundamental respects, be changed by human action.

Changes in economic policy—in taxes, prices, interest rates, or wages—can be made without major administrative or social changes, merely by preparing a new computer program, price list, or tax table. Hence, most of the problems in using economic knowledge occur before the act: once the decision to change an economic policy is made, its implementation can be routine. In contrast, the adoption of a new social policy is merely the beginning of a long process of implementation, which may require the formation of new organizations, the recruitment of new personnel, extensive communication, learning, and accommodation between the administering organizations and their client populations, and the adaptation of the initial policy to practical realities. The implementation of a new social policy requires the persistent application of political, administrative, and educational efforts until the policy becomes institutionalized.

If this analysis is correct, what is regarded as the utilization of sociological knowledge commonly requires manifest social or institutional change, whereas the application of economic knowledge does not. Were sociology again to acquire an influential body of conservative doctrine and practitioners whose efforts to preserve existing institutions were deemed intellectually legitimate, the utilization of its knowledge might become more simple and conventional.

Utilization as Use of Social Scientists

Another way to define utilization was to estimate the number, quality, and rank of the social scientists engaged on extramural research, used as consultants, or employed directly by the agency to administer extramural research, monitor the findings, and bring them to the attention of government officials. As federal agencies sponsored more research and employed more social scientists than local agencies, they were said to utilize the social sciences better. However, the presence of social scientists in high positions and a sympathetic attitude to social research could be accorded more importance than either large extramural expenditures or a large staff of social scientists. Thus, the Department of Housing and Urban Development received tolerably good marks for research utilization, despite a negligible research budget, because of the interest of senior officials in the social sciences and their efforts to expand the department research program, which had been repeatedly blocked by the Congress. On the other hand State Department use of social research was excoriated, despite the occasional appointment of a prominent social scientist as an ambassador or assistant secretary and the employment of many social scientists in research and intelligence activities. Indeed, according to the best available but nonetheless incredible statistics, in 1966 State employed more economists than any other department (National Science Foundation, 1968a). The low standing of the State Department was due, among other causes, to its reputation for preferring traditional forms of scholarship to the empirical social sciences; its miniscule extramural expenditures, which it had not made noteworthy efforts to increase; and the fact that it had not moved to pick up the support of overseas research whose sponsorship by Defense agencies had been repeatedly attacked.

Private social scientists do not usually like a large intramural research staff, which can compete with an extramural program, so much as a smaller staff which administers contracts with a light hand and can bring the results to the attention of the right people. The collection of statistics may be delegated to government staff, but not original research requiring an independent outlook and leading to independent publication. In addition, at many of the departments with large social science staffs—such as Agriculture, Labor, and Commerce—what may once have been a genuine research function has become so routinized that it no longer excites the research community. Concerned with the frontiers of knowledge, that community is interested in the use of new, not old, knowledge. So, asked "Which one or more federal agencies would you cite as making exceptionally good use of the findings of social research grants and/or contracts in formulating, evaluating, and improving their domestic social programs and/or policies?" private social scientists notably disregarded most of the departments with the largest number of social scientists. Defense and HEW (which employed the largest numbers of social scientists outside of the older civil service classifications of "economist" and "psychologist") and the Office of Economic Opportunity were cited, but not the Veterans Administration, Agriculture, or other old-line agencies.[3] These citations were consistent with the prevailing distribution of agency obligations, for in 1966, DOD, HEW, and OEO allocated to extramural programs more than 90 percent of their total social research obligations, whereas State, Agriculture, Labor, Interior, and Commerce allocated from 42 to 66 percent, and the Veterans Administration no funds at all (I, 22–23). Plainly, the newer programs, using extramural research more than the older programs, have been welcomed by the social science community. It may be that social research is most fully utilized when it becomes routinized and incorporated in normal agency operations, ideas which were once speculative and distrusted having (despite continuing ambiguities) become crystalized into statistics and accepted as conventional facts with which the national economic and social machinery functions. But contemporary social scientists are more preoccupied with their own struggles than with their predecessors' achievements.

Utilization as Influence

The third inference that can be drawn from respondents' comments is implicit in the other two: the meaning of utilization which is dearest to social scientists is intellectual, public, and political influence and recognition. The cases in which a research report

[3] Of the 53 private social scientists to whom the foregoing question was put, only 20 answered it by naming one or more agencies. Nine named the Department of Defense or some branch thereof; 7 the Department of Health, Education, and Welfare, or some subdivision; 4 the Office of Economic Opportunity; 4 the Federal Reserve Board; 2 each the Treasury and Interior Departments, Council of Economic Advisers, Agency for International Development, and Peace Corps (demonstrating that the failure of anyone to mention the State Department was not due to a scrupulous regard for the question's reference to "domestic social programs"), and 1 each, the Departments of Agriculture and Commerce, National Aeronautics and Space Administration, Atomic Energy Commission, National Science Foundation, and Bureau of the Budget.

has had palpable practical consequences that can honestly be attributed to that report are far fewer than those in which it has not;
yet invariably they are seized on to demonstrate that research is
being utilized, though their rarity might better demonstrate the
precise opposite. However, these cases are gratifying, and that sense
of gratification and usefulness can overflow on an entire program or
discipline. How many sociologists were gratified by the Supreme
Court's reference to Myrdal in its 1954 decision outlawing school
segregation—and chagrined by President Johnson's 1968 reference
to "kooks and sociologists"? How many economists feel that their
work is more important and better utilized since economists began
to litter the corridors of power?

    Influence operates at many levels, and men of different
degree are satisfied with different signs: many are pleased with a
footnote; others can be displeased with the President's conduct in
repeated discussions.[4] Moderate and experienced men know that, at
best, social science knowledge can provide only one of many ingredi-
ents on which action rests; for fair work they may reasonably expect
a fair hearing—and that is all, unless more can be extracted by
strictly nonintellectual means. More than one social scientist or
institute director has become astute at courting attention for his
views in the press, in the Congress, in the parlors of the Executive,
and with whatever groups he may cast his lot. The potential influence of a report depends on who within an agency will read or
endorse it; different institutes are known to have special entree at
different agencies and certain scholars to have the confidence of
certain officials. Neither in public nor private affairs will a sensible
man make important decisions on the basis of faceless information

    [4] See the account by Edwin Nourse, first chairman of the Council of
Economic Advisers, of his meetings with President Truman. "Of course, I
wasn't completely happy with the relations we did have with the President.
There was never a time when I called Matt Connally, the President's appointment secretary, when there was the slightest difficulty in getting an appointment. . . . But when I got there, the President was always very gracious,
friendly and nice—too nice, in fact. He wasn't business-like enough. He'd tell
me what happened on his walk that morning, or tell me chit-chat about his
family—wasting minutes of this precious appointment. As I think back, I
can honestly say that I think I never had a real intellectual exchange with
the President, that I was opening my mind to analysis with him, that he was
following me" (Silverman, 1959).

and advice inscribed on paper, without evaluating the processes by which and the persons from whom it was obtained.

All of which is merely to point out that the influence which a social scientist may exert in a school, a mental hospital, or the White House depends on personal factors as well as on impersonal knowledge; and the person being influenced plays a large part in deciding whom he will listen to and what he will hear. Or: influence depends as much on perception, character, opportunity, acquaintanceship, persuasiveness, and power as on the truth. When a scholar sets out to win friends and influence public affairs, he must pay as much attention to these factors as to the truth; and he may readily pay too much attention to them to retain his status as a scholar.

Lee Cronbach has bitterly described how, helping educators to understand and utilize his ideas, the gifted researcher, "the eternal skeptic," can be transformed into an evangelist or a huckster. "After an idea is sold in one town, there is always another town down the road. . . . To get school people to discard the familiar and take on the insecurities of the novel, one must be persuasive, and persuaded. . . . His conscience may prompt him to say that his studies are preliminary—but no one listens, and the escape clause is soon crowded out. . . . Our young man has made the full descent from inquirer about education to peddlar of an untested nostrum" (II, 223–224).

That is a harsh judgment of a middle-aged scholar about a fictitious young man who forsook the scholarly calling. Must—can —every intellectual always remain an intellectual to preserve his immortal soul? Must every evangelist and every salesman be indicted on intellectual grounds? There is truth in Cronbach's indictment, but not the additional truth that would permit a more charitable assessment of the young man's activity.

At the highest level at which social science advice had been institutionalized in government, the Council of Economic Advisers, a similar issue has been posed. The chairmen of the council have repeatedly been accused of dishonestly advocating policies of which they disapproved in order to maintain their influence with the president. An adviser does not gain influence by disagreeing with the president in public, and (agreement, respect, and confidence being closely linked) few can do so too strongly and too often in private while yet maintaining his confidence: ". . . there is no other way of guarding oneself from flatterers except letting men understand that to tell you the truth does not offend you; but when every one may tell you the truth, respect for you abates," wrote Machiavelli. "Therefore a wise prince ought to hold a third course by choosing the wise men in his state, and giving to them only the liberty of speaking the truth to him, and then only of those things of which he inquires, and of none others; but he ought to question them upon everything, and listen to their opinions, and afterwards form his own conclusions" (1938, p. 191).

The first council chairman, Nourse, shunned the advocacy role, confining himself to scholarly analyses of the economy and private advice to the President without publicly endorsing or defending presidential policies. Though sometimes criticizing presidential policies at professional meetings, he declined to appear before congressional committees, fearing that their politically motivated questions might prove too embarrassing. Nourse (1950) rejected the course other council members have adopted. "The suggestion that one should not be appointed to the Council unless his economic views are essentially in accord with those of the President . . . is no solution. . . . it would mean that no one could survive in the Executive Office to give the President objective reactions. . . . I myself am one of those old-fashioned girls who has no liking for the idea of being a 'kept' economist." That sounds the same scornful note as Cronbach's; and the note of hostile scorn or friendly commiseration is heard often enough in Washington as council members are forced to tack with each political breeze.

Nourse's disagreements with Truman's policies were evidently minor or were so regarded by others; but he was as much exercised over hypothetical as actual disagreement, for he knew that he could not deal with it by silence, guile, the hearty defense of a second-best policy, or similar strategems that other council members have employed. The effect of his refusal to advocate the President's policies was simply that others did so—in this case, the two other members of the original council, Leon Keyserling and John Clark.

Burns, council chairman under President Eisenhower, sought

to establish a congressional role midway between Nourse's withdrawal and Keyserling's responsiveness. "My own . . . inclination would be to stay out of the limelight, make my recommendations to the President . . . and then . . . remain eternally quiet." However, he recognized that the council had statutory obligations to inform the Congress and that there were technical matters about which he could testify without breaching his private advice to the president. Yet, no more than his predecessors could he escape the dilemmas of the job. ". . . how could I criticize the President publicly and still remain a useful member of his administration?" he asked. "On the other hand, how could I say to a congressional committee that something is sound when I believed otherwise?" (Silverman, 1959).

The final remarks I cite are those of Blough (1950), who came to Keyserling's council from the University of Chicago. As Blough saw it, difficulties arising between council members and the President depended "perhaps as much on the individual as on the inherent conflict of roles." He recommended selective silence as the principal anodyne: "There are many inconsistent positions in this world. . . . What the individual in an inconsistent position like that facing the Council may do is to carry on as well as he can, thinking and speaking as independently as possible but being discreet and cautious, never abandoning his standards of integrity by saying what he does not believe to be true, but not trying to say all that he believes to be true." Beginning on a hopeful vein, Blough ended more pessimistically, suggesting that there was just that much which an intellectual of integrity could accomplish in government, and when the strains of office became too great, he should depart. "Perhaps we should look on Council members as expendable, each carrying forward the work as far as he individually can and then retiring in favor of others who can carry it farther before they, too, drop by the wayside."

Just what influence have economists and the Council of Economic Advisers actually had on government policy? Many recent assertions are prideful. ". . . as the economist contemplates the increasing role which he and his confreres play in government," Boulding writes, "he may be allowed perhaps a thimbleful of pardonable pride. No more than a thimbleful—for there is a sad record of mistakes" (1958, p. 129). After the Kennedy era, his thimble becomes a cup. "It is clear that economics as a social science has now reached a degree of sophistication where its impact on the economy is very substantial and is likely to be even greater in the future. It can hardly be denied as far as economics is concerned that we now know something and that this knowledge can be applied" (1966, p. 44).

His "now" represented a conviction, bred by the fortunate experience a younger generation now shares with the old, that the nation had gone many years without a major depression and that economics should be given some credit for this fact. "One has only to compare the miserable failure of the twenty years after World War I with the at least moderate success of the twenty years after World War II to see what difference a more sophisticated approach to economics and to economic policy has been able to make. Judged by their impact on society, the other social sciences do not look so good" (Boulding, 1967, p. 14).

Boulding's opinion, which was surely held by much of the profession, was echoed by Calkins and Mosak in their discussion of "The Production and Use of Economic Knowledge" at the 1965 meeting of the American Economic Association. Calkins states that "the ideas of economists have had a vast and increasing influence on public affairs. That influence, often with a notable lag, has been felt on central banking, monetary policy, fiscal policy, international monetary policies, defense policies, defense management, foreign aid, economic development, and countless other programs. Both economists and their theory have gained in influence since the 1930's, especially since 1941, and even more since 1961" (1966, p. 530). Mosak concurs and adds that the growing influence of economists was a worldwide phenomenon. ". . . the expanding role of the economist in influencing major economic policy. . . . has been unmistakable in the United States since the New Deal period, in Western Europe since the Marshall Plan and the formation of the Common Market, and in the last five to ten years it has also become clearly evident in the centrally planned economies" (1966, p. 557).

Many would agree with the foregoing economists, with Wilensky's opinion that "As an example of success in the application of reason to public affairs, economics stands alone among the social sciences" (1967, p. 106), and with Sherwin's opinion that "If the era of the 40's and 50's was the era of the scientists in Washington, the 60's is the era of the economist" (1967). Nonetheless, reservations are in order about the nature of economists' influence and the advice on which it is based. These may appropriately start with the testimony of Heller, who as chairman of President Kennedy's and President Johnson's council from 1961 to 1964 was intimately involved in whatever influence economists then exercised in government: "Two Presidents [Kennedy and Johnson] have recognized and drawn on modern economics as a source of national strength and Presidential power. Their willingness to use, for the first time, the full range of modern economic tools underlies the unbroken U. S. [economic] expansion since early 1961. . . . one finds it hard to imagine a future President spurning professional economic advice and playing a passive economic role" (1966, pp. 13–14).

That statement appears to be a strong confirmation of the influence of economists on two presidents, but on further reflection some questions arise. As has been noted, there was relatively little divergence between Nourse's views and Truman's policies; nonetheless, Nourse felt that his influence was slight and that the President did not really understand and was not even much interested in his recommendations. Either Burns had more influence than Nourse or he was more content with the influence that he had. At times Eisenhower's policies diverged markedly from Burns's preferences, but Burns did not hold these differences against him since they enjoyed a good relationship and Burns appreciated the political obstacles to implementing his recommendations. ". . . in some cases the President had to adopt policies that he didn't like and that I didn't like," Burns wrote. "He had to do it for reasons of overall political policy, but his heart was bleeding over it" (Silverman, 1959, p. 16).

Kennedy's understanding was sharp, but if his "willingness to use . . . the full range of modern economic tools" means full and prompt acceptance of council recommendations, or that never before had there been five years "of unbroken . . . expansion," or that government economic policies and the national economic condition during those years were as satisfactory to Republican as to Democratic economists, Heller's statement is simply not true. Saulnier, Eisenhower's council chairman from 1956 to 1961, expresses decidedly less contentment than do most "new economists" with the state of the economy and government policies during this period: "fiscal policies which were the principal cause of (1) 4 percent a year cost-of-living inflation; (2) 6 percent a year wage inflation; (3) 5 percent a year labor cost inflation; (4) a budget deficit of $25 billion; (5) federal financing requirements that siphoned off 25 percent of funds raised in capital markets; (6) century-high interest rates; (7) a seriously eroded gold supply; (8) a greatly weakened international position of the dollar; and (9) the danger of financial crisis, domestic and international, must be regarded as a failure" (1968, p. 70). Criticizing economists' hubris, Spengler writes that the American economy has performed little better after the establishment of the Council of Economic Advisers than before. "Crude comparison of the period 1904–1929 with 1945–1970 indicates little improvement in the overall level of employment and a not much higher rate of increase in average output. The most striking difference is the increasing tendency . . . to inflation" (1972, p. 16).

Heller's glowing account of economists' influence may more soberly be set down not to any special magic of the profession but to his satisfaction with his relations with the President, his adeptness at White House maneuvering,[5] a few signal policies (particularly

---

[5] ". . . in the early months of the Kennedy Administration," Heller writes, ". . . the policy train often flashed past before we could get out the flag to stop it. One of our major tasks was to establish constructive relationships with the men around the President to help insure that the Council's voice would be heard before the final decisions were made" (1966, p. 54).

Contrast this move toward the center of the stage with Nourse's more passive and peripheral position. The Truman council "was not part of a regular flow of procedures and documents. The Council had to make new connections or else wait until people came to consult it—things did not flow across its path," an observer noted (Silverman, 1959).

See also the exchange between the skeptical Herbert Stein and the cautiously optimistic Arthur Burns about the progress of economic knowledge:

Stein: ". . . you seemed quite optimistic about our learning from experience and complimentary about what had been learned . . . [between 1961 and 1967]. But . . . I am not sure that this learning process has been a secular trend rather than a cyclical trend."

the wage-price guideposts and the 1964 tax cut) for which he received credit, and a good run of prosperity for which no man or profession should take credit before history assigns it. Nourse (1969) is not alone in asking whether, in its larger pretensions, the "new economics" has been right or lucky. "Is the pleasant conclusion that we now have put the cycle of boom and depression permanently behind us demonstrably valid or perhaps still premature? Or have we, perchance, been riding (with greatly improved seamanship) a particularly long wave in the endless stream of economic life, in which the conjunction of technological, sociopsychological, and demographic factors was extraordinarily favorable?" Before long, Heller himself answered that question by withdrawing his 1966 book *New Dimensions of Political Economy* from the reading list of the introductory economics course at the University of Minnesota, because its "optimistic tone . . . does not hold up well in light of what has happened to the country since" (*Economists . . . ,* 1972). Silk (1970) detects a "new modesty of economists. . . . Economists are modest today because they have much to be modest about." How long will this unaccustomed mood last?

Ackley (1966) has commented wisely on the element of political realism that must be present if professional advice is to be influential or, as he and other council chairmen have put it, that second-best advice must often be given. Thus, professional advice becomes influential when it is not purely professional but is adulterated with practical considerations. "An adviser who . . . refuses to consider second-best alternatives that have greater feasibility is not . . . likely to remain an effective adviser for long. . . . not all courses of action are equally feasible, and often . . . the ideal course of action must be compromised in favor of a good course."

This discussion of the nature of social scientists' influence and the degree to which it is founded not only on knowledge but on additional—especially personal and political—factors may suitably close with Samuelson's (1962) reflections on the influence of

Burns: "I agree with much of your comment . . . what we learn from experience, we remember for a time and then, not infrequently, we forget again and repeat the old mistake. . . . And yet I see, or think I see, a gradual secular improvement in policymaking" (Burns and Samuelson, 1967, pp. 112–113).

economists' ideas. He observes that the profession assigns an order
of importance to many economists which is different from that accepted by the public. Karl Marx affords an outstanding example.
Though the typical judgment of (non-Marxian) economists was
expressed by Keynes, who considered Marx's work " 'turbid' non-
sense," that has not kept it from having a huge influence. ". . .
one must never make the fatal mistake in the history of ideas of
requiring of a notion that it be 'true.' For that discipline, the slogan
must be, 'The customer is always right.' Its objects are what men
have believed; and if truth has been left out, so much the worse for
truth." From the cases of Marx and David Ricardo, he infers that
"obscurity . . . has often been a contributory ingredient to fame"
among scholars who imagine that there must be something profound
in writing they cannot understand. J. K. Galbraith's popular fame
he credits to clarity of expression and ability at popularization—
"vulgarization" is the term of detractors.

Turning from the subject of economists' influence on the
history of scholarly and popular ideas to their influence on government, Samuelson quotes Keynes's famous passage: "the ideas of
economists and political philosophers, both when they are right and
when they are wrong, are more powerful than is commonly understood. Indeed the world is ruled by little else. Practical men, who
believe themselves to be quite exempt from any intellectual influence, are usually the slaves of some defunct economist. Madmen in
authority, who hear voices in the air, are distilling their frenzy from
some academic scribbler of a few years back. I am sure that the
power of vested interests is vastly exaggerated compared with the
gradual encroachment of ideas. . . . soon or late, it is ideas, not
vested interests, which are dangerous for good or evil" (1936, pp.
383–384). This cerebral view of history fails to explain how madmen and statesmen come to seize, and to act, on particular ideas.
Samuelson does not explain how either, but at least he recognizes
the problem. "This is fine writing. And no doubt it is flattering to
our egos. But is it really true? . . . The leaders of this world may
seem to be led around through the nose by their economist advisers.
But who is pulling and who is pushing? . . . he who picks his
doctor from an array of competing doctors is in a real sense

his own doctor. The Prince often gets to hear what he wants to hear."

Concluding, Samuelson adjures economists to "call . . . shots as they really appear to be . . . even when this means losing popularity with the great audience of men and running against 'the spirit of the times.' " He quotes Blake, "Truth can never be told so as to be understood and not be believed"—presumably, by men professionally qualified to understand it, since he had just emphasized how easily ordinary men fall for economic error and vulgarization and how they neither understand nor are interested in the finer points of economics.

This beautiful professional conceit may be set beside Robert Brookings' remark that "Good economics cannot but be good ethics." If what is true is understood and, thus, believed and, being believed, influences the lives of men; if ordinary men who cannot understand subtler truths relinquish the requisite power to professional men who can; and if what is true is also good, then truly the social sciences will make this the best of all possible worlds.

That chain of "ifs" is too tenuous to hold at every link of truth, virtue, and power. Nor is Samuelson so naive as to imagine that citizens, businessmen, and politicians will relinquish their power to economists. Rather, he suggests, though quite ambivalently, that economists should relinquish theirs. "Not for us is the limelight and the applause. . . . In the long run, the economic scholar works for the only coin worth having—our own applause." Did he really mean thus to frustrate economists' aspirations for fame, fortune, and reform or merely to give a commendable explanation of why he declined to become President Kennedy's official economic adviser?

Summary

The general judgment of our respondents as well as of others who have studied the question was that social science techniques and knowledge have not been utilized as well as they should and could be in domestic social programs. There are managerial and economic tests of program effectiveness, but these are not all that is meant by the effective use of social science. Often such use implies the adoption of changes recommended by social scientists or, more broadly, a growth in their public influence. However, influence is not merely an intellectual but also a personal and political thing, so that a gain in influence does not necessarily represent a gain in the public acceptance of what is true. On the contrary, ideas can become influential because they are congenial, convenient, or practicable; historically, some of the most influential ideas have been dead wrong. There is substance to the academic man's fear that a gain in influence involves some compromise with the truth.

11

Organizing Knowledge and Advice

Setting aside questions about the relevance of much research to practical problems and the quality of much knowledge that is relevant—the degree to which a scholar would stake his child's life or even his wife's wardrobe on it—the impression remains that available knowledge is inadequately used; that it is folly to spend large sums on the production of reports which no one reads; and, hence, that greater attention to the matter of utilization is called for. One institute director has dramatized this need by proposing that a particular government program suspend all research expenditures for a year and devote its resources to applying existing knowledge.

The increasing concern about the utilization of knowledge is salutory—to a degree. The nation has every right to expect demonstrable benefits from large research expenditures and, if they are not forthcoming, to try to improve the situation or reduce the expenditures. In turn, the demand for practical consequences imposes a sense of responsibility that may impel the scholar to unaccustomed silence or to work that is closer to the needs of his fellow citizens. After all, the concern about utilization indicates that research is being taken seriously, which should either please or alarm the serious scholar.

The alarm reflects the trepidation and uncertainty about the quality of human knowledge and intellect that many of the best scholars rightly feel. No matter how important reliable knowledge could be, it cannot be summoned up on command out of ignorance or mere information. ("You know," Keynes remarked, "we can promise to be good, but we cannot promise to be clever.") The alarm also reflects a state of mind characteristic of the man of inaction, unlike that of those gamblers, playboys, fools, and politicians who prosper on uncertainty.

Curiously, one kind of social knowledge which is reliable, widely used, and indeed indispensable to modern society—"hard" social and economic data—is not usually considered a product of "research" or, hence, a central subject of efforts to improve the utilization of research. In many developing countries laboring to establish the statistical underpinnings of industrialization and national planning, the collection of such data commands the services of leading scholars, whereas in the United States it has long been delegated to statisticians and clerks while scholars occupy themselves with loftier matters. Thus, a recent massive tome on *The Uses of Sociology* (Lazarsfeld and others, 1967) devotes relatively little attention to the data without which the nation might well collapse and much attention to the fate of sociological ideas about which the nation is indifferent.[1]

---

[1] "Evidently, many sociologists who regard themselves as men of ideas find the supply of mere data too pedestrian to warrant much attention. . . . While dealing with hard data is both necessary and useful, softer and more ambiguous data are more characteristically human and hence retain a special fascination and challenge. In any event, they receive the special attention of most contributors. . . . Certainly an idea, which can lead somewhere, can be more *influential* than a fact, which by itself leads nowhere at all; and contributors may concentrate upon ideas that have gained favor because the usage of 'use' which interests them most is 'influence'" (Orlans, 1968a).

"The principal quality of ideas as affecting action is the relative amount of truth and error that they embody. . . . The natural tendency of truth is to cause progressive action," wrote Ward (1906, p. 82) with an optimism typical of American social scientists—and quite opposed to the view presented in the preceding chapter that the influence of ideas bears an erratic relation to their truth. Marxism may be bad economics and racism bad anthropology, but they have nonetheless been enormously influential doctrines. The historical viability of an idea bears little necessary relation to its truth or academic respectability. Insofar as the social sciences progress toward more refined and valid truths, the society they leave behind must have functioned with progressively coarser error—but function it did; and it also follows that the ideas which the social sciences offer society today are the errors they will correct tomorrow. However, it is a form of vanity to deem the intellect and social knowledge of earlier times—of our parents, of Jefferson, Voltaire, Montaigne, Aristotle—any less adequate to their needs than is ours. That part of social science in which knowledge cumulates into laws and not libraries must be far smaller, and that which is timebound and historical far larger, than is commonly supposed. Overall, social knowledge[2] remains on an eternal treadmill: "of making many books there is no end."

In public office men have a responsibility to inform themselves of the available facts before they act; any gross failure to do so is a mark of negligence or incompetence. To justify their usefulness, the social sciences need make no greater claim than that they are helpful in the compilation and interpretation of some (but very far from all)[3] of the knowledge which should be taken into account in public affairs. However, even the largest research programs cannot generate all the knowledge that might prove useful to government, and the solution to this problem, insofar as there is any

[2] Here, *social knowledge* may be defined as a society's information about, and understanding of, its own workings, the conscious and unconscious purpose and functions of different groups, and the net consequences of their actions.

[3] Room must obviously be left for the knowledge imparted by every other relevant discipline and profession (particularly the sciences, engineering, history, law, and journalism) and the copious knowledge of administrative, political, and personal intelligence.

solution, cannot be simply to conduct more research. The contingencies for which knowledge may be needed can never be wholly foreseen, and research produces at least as many fresh questions as answers. The solution must be found in two ways: by mastering—encompassing, organizing, synthesizing, distilling, indexing, and disseminating—available knowledge better, so that it can be searched and seized more quickly; and by shortcutting the research process by various means so that probable, approximate, or plausible answers can be obtained quickly when better information is not available.

Since the physical and administrative arrangements for organizing and transmitting knowledge are readily alterable, they tend to occupy a major place in discussions of its utilization. Unfortunately, the arrangements for the intellectual and emotional digestion of knowledge are far less alterable, and the entire process by which knowledge registers and induces action takes place in the utterly unalterable, iron framework of time.

Scholarship and Parascholarship

To an extent, the physical mastery of available knowledge is a problem in librarianship, and libraries remain an important place to which some social scientists still resort. Much can be deduced about the intellectual depth or ephemerality of a research institute from an inspection of its library, and despite the saving grace of the Library of Congress, the same is true of government agencies. Here, if not in other resources, the academic social scientist usually has a decided advantage over his colleagues off campus. Good librarians, who put the active use of a collection above its immaculate preservation and special services above uniform regulations, are too rare and undervalued and very helpful to the utilization of available knowledge.

However, if most true scholars gather their facts in orderly libraries rather than in the disorderly world, the empirical social sciences have produced numerous parascholars who rarely enter a library. The topical nature of much contract research, the faddishness of much academic research, and the dominant scientific posture of the social sciences all dispose researchers to neglect historical materials. To students of the contemporary, the eternal present, less scholarly but more timely sources of information have become important. The parascholar subsists on a paraliterature of newspapers, newsletters, magazines, government reports, and multilithed, mimeographed, xeroxed, and offset documents of all kinds. Because this near-print material assumes special importance to nonacademic social scientists, they probably know more about it and have better channels for obtaining it than their academic colleagues.

A new profession of documentalists and information specialists has arisen to monitor and distribute such topical materials and the large body of research reports produced for the government. A goodly portion of recent efforts to improve the utilization of social science knowledge consists of establishing more efficient and comprehensive information systems about research projects and reports. The difficulty of getting adequate information about much federally sponsored social research cannot be fully ascribed to the diffuseness, ambiguities, and complexities of social facts. The point was noted by Senator Hubert Humphrey (1962), a staunch protagonist of social research, whose subcommittee conducted a considerable investigation of information management in the natural and social sciences: "in the judgment of our staff, information management in the social and behavioral sciences appears far less advanced than in other sciences. To some extent, this is due to the . . . relatively "soft" nature of the social science information with its infinitely subtle and difficult to quantify variables as to human conduct. But some of the management lag is due to the fact that the social and behavioral science professions do not appear to have devoted enough of their energies toward coming to grips with the information problem, per se."

Other factors than the purported disinterest of the profession have contributed to the weakness of the government information system. The National Institutes of Health and National Science Foundation do not disseminate the results of research which they finance, expecting investigators to rely on normal professional publication channels; they do not even require the submission of a technical report at the conclusion of a grant.[4] Contracting agencies

---

[4] At NIH, which awards annual grants, a progress report is required

require such reports and often attempt to make them available at least to their own contractors, but their research in the social sciences may be less widely indexed and circulated than is natural sciences research. Work conducted at contract research centers, such as those of the Department of Defense and the Office of Education, is more difficult to identify and monitor than that conducted under discrete projects. The possible political sensitivity of social research often leads to controls over the release of reports, as has been documented. Social research has also suffered from being a latecomer to information systems established for the natural sciences, systems which have only slowly been expanded to incorporate these less disciplined disciplines.

NSF and NIH can be criticized for not ensuring that the public receives *something* from the expenditure of public funds. But a policy of full and free distribution of all contractor reports would be no more satisfactory, since the mass distribution of reports subjected to no professional review would undercut the economic structure and technical standards of normal professional publication. A reasonable compromise is the practice of some agencies of making reports publicly available at depository libraries across the nation and providing (free or for a charge) a limited number of copies on request. While the public accessibility of reports is necessary to guard against the suppression, neglect, or excessive duplication of significant truths, it also enhances the danger that these truths will be lost in an ocean of verbiage.

The traditional system of professional review may or may not reduce the quantity of useless publication. One careful study (Garvey and Griffith, 1964) concluded that, in psychology, "few rejected articles fail to appear in one journal or another. . . . rejection keeps an article out of a particular journal—not out of the literature." Furthermore, "increasing the rejection rates of manuscripts submitted to journals almost automatically increases the birth rate of new journals." If this conclusion is generally true

---

at each yearly application for renewal. Similarly, NSF, which grants for longer periods, requires a short annual report and a more comprehensive final report. These are for internal agency use and, occasionally, publicity purposes; they do not routinely enter a public channel of professional communication.

in the social sciences, then editorial review serves not to prevent the publication of inferior work but to striate journals and publishers into broad quality strata, providing a rough classification that simplifies the problem of sifting the literature. Unfortunately, this type of quality classification is lost in government information services which indiscriminately index and distribute work of much and little merit.

The information services publicize work in progress that is never completed and reports which would otherwise not enter the professional literature. And they help to persuade the Congress and the public that research programs are being well managed. The question nonetheless arises whether their value justifies their large cost. Different answers are warranted for different services: in one, the budget should be pared; in another, reallocated; and in a third, raised.

Some enthusiasts seem to believe that the physical availability of knowledge together, perhaps, with enough publicity to make its existence known—cries of naked, infant truth—suffice to stimulate its use. What other belief underlay the episode in which 1740 documents on education for the "disadvantaged" were "processed" (granulated?) by ERIC and "disseminated" (sown?) to "500 randomly selected medium sized city school systems, to 100 large-city school systems, and to the 50 state departments of education"?[5] Even here, the promotional element appears, but it is a general promotion of knowledge or of change for the sake of change and the hope of progress rather than an advocacy of specific educational doctrine. The saving political feature is precisely the incombustible mass of the documents and the number of school systems and state superintendents, each of whom is free to peck from that mass whatever grains of truth suit his needs and taste.

Special and Common Truths

Again, we return to the inescapable problem of selection, of sifting the imponderable hoard of recorded knowledge for what is pertinent to the purpose at hand. The problem recalls Rabindranath Tagore's story of the holy man who wandered the roads,

[5] As reported in *Educational Researcher*, December 1966, p. 6.

searching for the touchstone of truth. At first, he would examine each pebble with care, then more perfunctorily, until, as the years passed, he could pick a pebble up, touch it to his waist-chain, and discard it without a glance. One day he realized that the chain had turned to gold. So he must have held the touchstone in his hand, but when and where he did not know.

The story has a hopeful as well as a cautionary moral. On the cautionary side: the final full and certain truth that would strip life of its hazards and contingencies is God's, not man's. Should he ever chance upon it, how could a fallible man infallibly distinguish the pure truth from its infinite impure semblances? Even in great crises when the fate of nations can hinge on elusive facts and every possible resource is marshaled to find them, they may not be forthcoming, the seconds tick by imperturbably, and decisions must be made in an uncomfortable degree of uncertainty. How can it be otherwise? The past is not fully recorded, and the available record, which is daily diminished, augmented, and reinterpreted, is not fully accessible in any one place; allowance must also be made for additions and corrections living witnesses can still make to the record as well as for errors present on such good authority and repeated so often that they never will be eradicated. Even were the record complete, authentic, perfectly indexed, and instantly searchable, it could not suffice to forecast the future or to dictate the choices that every man and nation must make at every moment, if for no other reason than that the processes of growth and attrition, creation and obliteration, daily reconstitute the human community.

On the more hopeful side, there is much redundancy in social information. Most of the facts that administrators seek and social scientists provide are run-of-the-mill pebbles on the holy man's road. Government cannot be administered nor society function on transcendent truth; a grosser and simpler order of knowledge must suffice. This is not to say that there is no sophisticated or subtle social truth, but it must be put in its place, which is *not* at the operating center of national affairs. The simplification and even vulgarization of scholarly ideas, which Samuelson rightly perceived as part of the process by which they acquire influence, is essential to practical politics and to the development of realistic, administrable programs.

If this process deprives the social sciences of some enchant-ment, it also renders their stock of information and ideas more manageable, since none of it will be indispensable, repetitious work need merely be sampled, and in no event should large decisions rest on a single observation. Whether the massive, unique, and "defini-tive" study should be considered as a singular or multiple observa-tion is a nice point. The problem is similar to that of archeologists who, having prepared neat statistics of shards, do not quite know how to count a whole pot. Let me merely say that the large study should be examined with special care: no social study is "defini-tive" in the sense of being faultless and unambiguous.

National Data Center

Special mention should be made of one noteworthy attempt to cope with the proliferation of information: the central bank of data available for scholarly analysis. The principle is exemplified by the Roper Public Opinion Research Center at Williams and the Human Relations Area Files at Yale, both founded in the 1940s and now linked with a network of affiliated universities. It has as-sumed increased importance since high-speed computers have facilitated the storage, search, and regurgitation of vast quantities of data. Some government agencies—notably the Bureau of the Census, the Internal Revenue Service, and the Bureau of Labor Statistics—hold monumental quantities of social and economic data significant for both academic and policy research.

In 1965 and 1966, several committees of economists pro-posed the establishment of a national data center to improve the usefulness of government statistical collections and make them more accessible to scholars. Congressional hearings raised the specter that such a center could be used by the government to compile damaging personal dossiers by collating information now widely compart-mentalized. Since such use was the last thing those promoting the idea had in mind, they were initially insensitive to the issue and not fully convincing in their attempts to dispose of it. Various measures can be taken to protect the confidentiality of data on individuals, but to every measure there is a countermeasure, and in the end a choice will have to be made between the possible infringement of individual rights (which can be made illegal but not impossible) and the value of a central data facility to scholarship and to public policy. I agree with the several committees of social scientists who have examined the question that, on balance, the value of such a data center should outweigh the occasional dangers it may pose. However, these dangers will not be dispelled by being disregarded. They may be reduced by careful study and the adoption of protective measures by industry, government, research institutions, and professional associations.

A center that can facilitate access to raw survey data can enable scholars and private interest groups to conduct timely analyses of the same data on which government policy is partly founded. For example, the Internal Revenue Service sample of one hundred thousand income tax returns can be used to project the effect of alternative tax policies on national revenue and the net income of different classes. With these tapes, a private witness can testify before the Congress on proposed tax legislation, in some ways as knowledgeably as the Secretary of the Treasury.

The publication of summary statistics can lag months or years behind their collection, and the selection and format of tables can conceal information that might embarrass government policy. Such awkward information is less readily cleansed from a magnetic tape. Nonetheless, it is not difficult to imagine situations in which an agency would deliberately delay completing a tape or delete selected data before releasing it to the scholarly public.

In sum, a central data bank should increase the usefulness of government data and the relevance of social and economic research to current policy issues. It should also serve an important educational function, increasing the number of persons throughout the nation who are able to follow current economic and social trends closely and who may be drawn into practical research on these trends as protagonists or critics of government policy.

Private Judgment

It may be said that I have made too heavy weather of the problem of selecting the "right" knowledge, since this is not just an intellectual but a practical problem, which is dealt with pragmatically by the personal judgment of political appointees, their staff, and private advisers. When there is plenty of time, special research can be commissioned; but when time is pressing, an estimate must replace a count, the telephone replaces correspondence, and long hours under pressure replace more careful and leisurely work. In both the careful and the hectic process, available knowledge and personal judgment prevail.

Unfortunately, personal judgment covers as many political and intellectual frailties and sins as strengths and virtues, and there is no evident way to increase the quantum of virtue in the judgment of either public officials or social scientists. Programs for improving the quality of the public service generally consist of improving educational qualifications, selection methods, and employment conditions. Those who have considered how social science might be better used by government advance similar recommendations: increase the number, status, quality, and salaries of social scientists in government; encourage officials to return to university for a period of study in the social sciences; and include more social science in curricula preparing graduates for public service.

The tides have been running for the social sciences in this century (as they have been running against the humanities, judging by the relative proportion of degrees awarded in the two areas). If the social sciences are increasingly to be used by society, a growing number of social scientists will be employed to use them. Certain educational problems remain, such as improving the training of social scientists, enhancing their administrative sophistication, and, in general, reducing their intellectual parochialism, their painful scholasticism, their scientific pretentiousness, and their historical obliviousness. But because these *are* practical problems, they can in principle be dealt with (which does not mean that in practice they will be).

Yet when all of this has been done, what confidence can we have that the social scientists selected for key positions will select the "right" knowledge and exercise wise judgment? From the full circle of knowledge, facts can readily be selected that point in almost any direction an administration wants to go, and only a modicum of professional competence is required to find such facts.

Professional advice, conveying selected facts, that is rendered in private cannot be subjected to the normal processes of professional publication, discussion, criticism, and assessment. The sciences are founded on the public scrutiny of published evidence, but much of government involves the (in both senses) *partial* utilization of such evidence and confidential intelligence and opinion. Partisanship is an inescapable aspect of the partly rational and partly accidental process by which certain facts, ideas, and opinions are reckoned with by government while others are not.

Public Discussion

Nonetheless, there are aspects of the system by which social science advice is conveyed to the government which can fruitfully receive more public discussion. When consultants acquire a formal status by appointment to advisory panels, their qualifications can become a fair subject for professional discussion. However, such discussion is all too rare. A detailed public evaluation of the professional views and reputation of, for example, social science members of the National Academy of Sciences or of government advisory committees has not, to my knowledge, been undertaken. Admittedly, such an analysis is difficult to conduct in a way that is informed, responsible, and enlightening and yet within accepted bounds of professional decorum.

Professional journals could also usefully encourage critical evaluation of significant reports, policy recommendations by eminent social scientists, and even, occasionally, significant testimony at public hearings. Several journals have been established to deal with aspects of social science involvement in public affairs (such as, *The Public Interest, Society* [formerly *Trans-Action*], and the *Journal of Human Resources*), but their number is trifling compared to the prodigious volume of journals devoted to academic matters. The recent addition of several journals is most welcome: *Policy Sciences,* a quarterly to which RAND staff made a substantial contribution; *Social Policy,* a monthly seeking to define a position to the left of *The Public Interest;* and *Behavior Today,* an overpriced commercial newsletter.

A searching professional scrutiny is particularly important in the case of work which, because of its scale, cost, and auspices, is relatively unique and cannot easily be duplicated. Examples are the Myrdal and Coleman studies and the reports of the Behavioral and Social Sciences Survey Committee and of the presidential commissions on automation, crime, riots, violence, and pornography. Here, the professional community is improving. The Coleman report has been discussed extensively, and the original data have been made available for additional scholarly analysis; so have the data of the BASS committee and of most presidential commissions. Still, it cannot be said that adequate machinery yet exists to give material of this kind—the empirical foundation of important public policies—the systematic professional review which its social importance warrants.

The slow pace of academic work is fatal neither to the academy nor to Washington. Our government has survived the disdain or disinterest of many social scientists as successfully as have foreign governments with few social scientists to draw on. Conversely, many public issues have been with us long enough to be examined by the most painstaking scholar; many issues undergo long cycles of recurrent attention in which even the slowest scholar's work can prove surprisingly relevant.

However, the social sciences are not well prepared to supply the quick response often needed in public affairs. Current policy discussions are seldom adequately reported in professional journals except for the few, such as the *American Economic Review* and the Social Statistics Section of the American Statistical Association, which publish a proceedings issue. The monthly newsletters of the anthropological and psychological associations do not provide a medium of professional analysis and discussion. Though the quarterly publications of the political science and sociological associations, *P. S.* and the *American Sociologist* (now a monthly tabloid), allow for some articles, communications, and correspondence, the level of many contributions has been embarrasingly low as normal review procedures have been sacrificed to the freedom of discussion and speed of publication. Perhaps the best publication of this type has been the monthly *American Psychologist,* which presents good papers, contains meaningful and not intemperate or naive correspondence, and occasionally devotes an entire issue to a subject of both professional and public importance. A similar publication catering in a mature and informed manner to the common policy interests of all the social sciences would be most useful. However, by present appearances, the social sciences have a good way to go before they can sustain a journal of news and discussion comparable in timeliness and quality to *Science*.

A Professional Truth Squad?

Davis (1967) proposes that each association set up something like a truth squad which would issue public statements to correct flagrant and significant misuse of social science knowledge:

> . . . *the social sciences need to have, in each field, mechanisms set up for instant refutation of deliberately false or foolish interpretations that may have important consequences. We have some defense against medical quackery, but we have none at present against social-science quackery. . . . occasionally the newspapers, public officials, and leaders generally seize, as a basis of policy, an interpretation that the social scientists working in that field know is stupid and unworkable. In such cases, at present, nothing can be done. An individual social scientist may protest, but his voice is drowned by the sheer repetition of the popular interpretation. An organized official means of meeting such crises would be highly desirable.*

Yet further reflection will indicate the difficulties and dangers of such action. Perhaps 99 or 91.3 percent of social scientists would disagree with certain fancies, illusions, and errors retained in one or another market of ideas. But can an academic profession expropriate a body of social knowledge and then regulate and police the national traffic in "its" ideas and information—including that emanating from the government? Presumably, the profession has more ability and right than any other agency to police its own members; but, as has been noted, psychology is the only major social science field which can yet make that claim and the regulation of a member's misconduct by the American Psychological Association requires a protracted process approximating the due process of law, which is not compatible with the instant correction of a grievous error.

What are the dangerous errors plain to all social scientists but not to a gullible nation, and how can the pronouncement of an association undo them? Is racism an example? The pronouncements of many professional associations have not destroyed that doctrine or its hold on the history of many peoples. Hitler was also much influenced by astrology; why are astronomers not impelled to correct that doctrine?

The unanimity of a profession is no assurance that it is right, since truth is not determined by plebiscite. And on most important issues which they have any competence to judge, social scientists are politically divided; even a quiet minority of Republicans or a loud minority of radicals can stir up significant professional dissent. To guard against the suppression of dissident opinion, many thoughtful social scientists have opposed the professionalization of their disciplines, fearing that only conventional truths will be licensed. "Since no valid consensus exists as yet among social scientists, any system of licensing would be damaging," Shils (1949) warns. "The bureaucratization of science is to be feared at all times but especially is it to be feared in a science which is still in a formative state."

Such opposition to professionalization militates against the truth-squadding advocated by Davis. One can imagine the social science associations sponsoring publications and meetings at which policy issues are discussed in a format that permits the expression of divergent opinion. As has been seen, they have periodically endorsed (but seldom vigorously pursued) policies which are in the self-interest of members or which command their political and human sympathies. But their assumption of a more active role in policy deliberations by public or private agencies has encountered so many obstacles that the agencies have generally obtained advice through other channels. The mass membership professional association has simply not proven an effective agent for promoting the utilization of social science in public affairs.

Institutionalizing Advice: The National Academy of Sciences

In the absence of participation by the major associations in the policy advisory business, a place has been opened up for less representative professional groups, among which the long dormant but now budding social science components of the National Academy of Sciences (NAS) complex are active. In recent years, they have undertaken new social science assignments for government agencies in such areas as defense, education, foreign research, urban problems, information systems, arms control and disarmament, rural social change and poverty, and outdoor recreation. The academy and its staff arm, the National Research Council, have broadened their membership in the social sciences; since its formation in 1962, the NAS Committee on Science and Public Policy has included social scientists among its members, coopted others for special purposes, and, with the Social Science Research Council, sponsored a major inquiry by the Behavioral and Social Sciences Survey Committee. All told, the academy must now be reckoned a principal institutionalized source of policy advice in the social sciences as well as the natural sciences and engineering. Evidently the rising national expenditures on the social sciences, the rising student interest in these fields, the growing strain on the status and budgets of the natural sciences, the increased influence especially of economists, and the increasing concern with harmful social consequences of scientific and technological developments have fostered an accord among disciplines which have often fought for influence and money in government.

Plainly, an academy, a self-designated elite, is a less democratic body than a professional association. Officers are not compelled to account to professional colleagues, graduate students, or the press for their selection of committee members, and they have no obligation to publish their reports. *Science* reporter Nelson (1968) did not like this attitude which he encountered at the National Academy of Sciences. ". . . the question of how the Academy has been governed, as well as most other questions affecting this august body, remain shrouded in a self-imposed air of mystery and obfuscation." As the NAS is a quasi-governmental organization, most of whose budget comes from the government and whose reports are printed by the Government Printing Office, such an attitude is impolitic, if not improper, but—there it is.

Whatever may be the level of internal academy discord, it

need not, like the furious dissensions within the social science associations, be aired at public meetings. The academy has also escaped some aggravating debates about professional responsibility by formally absolving itself of responsibility for the recommendations of its committees. ". . . the Academy rigidly holds to the position that, as an institution, it takes no stand on any issue. All that it assumes responsibility for, it contends, is selecting qualified committeemen . . . to study the problems of its clients" (Greenberg, 1967). This course has certain ambiguities. For, from the choice of committee members and, especially, of the committee chairman, one can usually anticipate the general political tenor of a report.

It is hard to fault the principle that the scholars who actually examine a problem and reach certain conclusions about it should themselves be responsible for those conclusions. The more that responsibility is shared with colleagues who have not themselves examined the same facts in the same detail the more attenuated is the responsibility of any individual and the more is their collective responsibility liable to become an expression of personal or political conviction. On the other hand, the men who select the members of a committee are responsible for *that* choice; and unless they are unbelievably obtuse, the political nature of their choice (be it left, right, or dead center) will be evident. Almost by definition, advice emanating from the academy combines technical competence with political sobriety if not soporiferousness.

The rising importance of the academy in social science affairs is attributable to political arrangements which some leading natural scientists and social scientists have made to work together under the academy umbrellas. In the 1930s, influential social scientists helped to defeat scientists' requests for government research funds;[6] and for many years in the 1950s, influential scientists responded in kind to social scientists' requests for funds from the National Science Foundation. During the latter 1960s, a rapproche-

[6] Notably MIT President Karl Compton's 1934 proposal of a National Program for Putting Science to Work for the National Welfare, under which the government would appropriate funds to the National Academy of Sciences for research grants in the natural sciences (Lyons, 1969, pp. 68–70).

ment developed between the fields. But alliances of fields resemble those of nations: they will continue as long as they serve the signators' interests.

Getting Social Science into the Executive Office

A number of proposals have been advanced to institutionalize the means by which social science advice is conveyed to the President—or, since he is not physically able to assume responsibility for everything done in his name, to the staff in the White House and the Executive Office of the President. The proposals are not all mutually exclusive and, as matters often work out in Washington, several may ultimately be adopted regardless of the apparent conflict of function that may ensue. These can be divided into two types: proposals which would assign to a body of social scientists explicit responsibilities with regard to national social problems or policies, and proposals to absorb the social science element in a broader function. Among the former are proposals to establish a Council of Social Advisers and an Office of Behavioral Sciences; among the latter, proposals to enlarge the participation of social scientists in such bodies as the Office of Science and Technology and the Council of Economic Advisers or a new entity with broad planning functions.

The establishment of an Office of the Behavioral Sciences Adviser to the President was recommended in 1965 by a House subcommittee chaired by Dante Fascell (1966), following hearings on Project Camelot. Such an office, the subcommittee hoped, would forestall additional Camelots; improve the planning, coordination, and utilization of foreign affairs research; and "provide the direction essential to an effective Government-wide effort in the . . . behavioral sciences." Most of our respondents received this proposal coolly. Those who liked the idea were dissatisfied with the representation and utilization of the social sciences in the existing science policy machinery. ". . . the science policy agencies. . . . impose a disfunctional filter of natural scientists between social scientists and policy-makers," Davis Bobrow wrote (III, 37). If the social sciences are to prosper, Anatol Rapoport reasoned, they must develop their own approaches and not be confined to those of the natural sciences; therefore social science research policies and standards should be set by other social scientists and not be subject to review or approval by natural scientists (III, 165).

Respondents who rejected the proposal of a separate office agreed that natural scientists were not competent to legislate for the social sciences, but their solution was to add social scientists to the science policy bodies: "The only thing wrong with the present structure of the Office of Science and Technology [OST] and the President's Science Advisory Committee [PSAC] is that it does not have the technical competence to deal with problems for which it has a stated responsibility. It is difficult to understand how competent and esteemed men on these bodies feel qualified to direct policies in areas to which their competence does not extend. This limitation can be eliminated by the simple procedure of adding several social scientists to these agencies" (III, 146–147). Derek de Solla Price suggested that as the science agencies were not even "particularly competent" to formulate and review policies for the sciences, they should be strengthened with social scientists (III, 157). The science agencies "are up to their necks in social science questions—and either forced to handle them on an amateur do-it-yourself basis, or to call for outside help" said Herbert Simon (III, 193).

These latter positions do not confront the argument that the social sciences can be better cultivated independently than under the domination of the natural sciences; but those who prefer to work within existing science agencies anticipate fraternal cooperation, not domination. They would form an alliance between the natural sciences and the putatively scientific elements in the social sciences, leaving the other elements out in the cold. Once that judgment is formed, a host of arguments arise to sustain it: the undesirability of fragmenting disciplines and policy offices; the value of scientists' public experience; and, of course, the protection which scientists afford against the moralistic and too nakedly political objectives of social scientists.

In an effort to learn what influential scientists thought of this problem, I asked members of the President's Science Advisory Committee, former presidential science advisers, and a few other scientists and engineers prominent in government science offices[7] whether federal policies toward the social sciences should be the responsibility of existing science policy bodies or of a new Office of the Social Sciences.

Only four favored whereas twenty-two opposed the formation of a new office for the social sciences. If, as I believe, the arguments of the four—Sidney Drell, George Kistiakowsky, George Pake, and Eric Walker—are as valid as those of the twenty-two, then the government and the disciplines can function under either arrangement, and the choice will depend on the preference of key individuals who, at the time of our inquiry, plainly wished to include the social sciences within the existing science agencies.

Broadening the sphere of these agencies, Kistiakowsky feared, would lead to a "dangerous dilution of their competence and effectiveness in the area of natural sciences and technology." As there is "a clear and identifiable gap between the natural and social sciences . . . the advisory inputs can be distinct and separate," Drell reasoned. His argument was restated by Eric Walker who, having played an active role in establishing the National Academy of Engineering to give engineers a degree of independence that they had lacked within the National Academy of Sciences, was convinced that social scientists should follow a similar course (IV, 55–56).

The overriding majority of twenty-two were satisfied with existing arrangements and did not want them disturbed by a competitive office for the social sciences. In fact, as they saw things, the social sciences had so many established channels for the presentation of advice and the defense of their interests that they did not need another. "Social scientists are scattered throughout all branches of the government, including the Cabinet itself and the White House staff," Charles Slichter wrote. "Prior to the establishment of PSAC and the OST . . . the President was much more widely separated

---

[7] The inquiry was sent to all members of the President's Science Advisory Committee, the National Academy of Sciences Committee on Science and Public Policy (COSPUP), and the National Academy of Engineering Committee on Public Engineering Policy; the presidents of the two academies, the three former presidential science advisers, two former COSPUP members, and the former deputy director of the Office of Science and Technology.

from advice in the natural sciences than in the social sciences" (IV, 52).

Harvey Brooks denied that OST and PSAC had "neglected their responsibilities" toward the social sciences. However, "there is a tremendous upsurge of interest in the social sciences, and new national goals are coming to the fore, whose achievement tends to be limited as much or more by social considerations than by technological or scientific ones. Examples are poverty, population, and pollution, as well as education" (IV, 27). In these circumstances, Brooks, James Killian, and Jerome Wiesner suggested (as had Jesse Orlansky) that it might be useful to name a second deputy director for OST with special responsibilities for, and qualifications in, the social sciences.

As matters have since developed, a social scientist, Herbert Simon, was appointed to PSAC in 1968—whereupon the Brim Commission called for "increasing the number of its social science members to at least three" (1969, p. 53). And for a while that was how things stood, James Coleman having been added to the committee in 1969 and Daniel Moynihan in 1971.

PSAC and OST have had sufficient visibility, prestige, and success to become objects of social scientists' envy, aspiration, and emulation. But it is rude to crash a party and unwise to found a strategy on one tactic. The effort to gain a firmer footing in the executive office science agencies is not incompatible with some moves in other directions. Judicious advocates of a closer rapprochement between the natural and social sciences recognize that other moves will be necessary if that rapprochement fails and, perhaps, also if it succeeds.

One such additional move, expanding the scope of the Council of Economic Advisers and the competence of its staff to embrace at least the major social aspects of economic policy, was recommended by Gerhard Colm, who later testified at length on the subject before a Senate committee (Mondale, 1968, Part 1, pp. 35–46). The National Commission on Technology, Automation, and Economic Progress had earlier recommended that the council seek to develop "a system of social accounts" which would add to prevailing measures of the national economic performance some measures of its social welfare.

The Brim Commission, of which Paul Samuelson was a member, recommended that, without adding noneconomists to the council proper, it should include among its staff and consultants "persons drawn from the relevant social sciences outside economics, and . . . from the natural sciences and engineering" who are informed about "scientific and technological trends and developments" (1969, p. 54). But, overall, economists have been cool to suggestions that it be converted into a Council of Economic and Social Advisers. "The President might as well have a Council of Political Advisers—that's the Congress and the parties," snorted one Washington economist. The CEA is reported to have declined responsibility for the panel on social indicators which was subsequently assumed by the Secretary of Health, Education, and Welfare.

A bill to establish in the Executive Office of the President a Council of Social Advisers was introduced by Senator Walter Mondale and ten liberal colleagues in 1967. Under its terms, the new council would annually submit to the President and Congress a "social report" based on improved social statistics or "indicators"[8] of social welfare, a proposal closely patterned on the Employment Act of 1946 establishing the Council of Economic Advisers and the Joint Economic Committee. The key "Declaration of Policy" of the bill stated:

> . . . the Congress declares that it is the continuing policy
> and responsibility of the Federal Government, consistent
> with the primary responsibilities of State and local govern-
> ments and the private sector, to promote and encourage such
> conditions as will give every American the opportunity to live
> in decency and dignity, and to provide a clear and precise
> picture of whether such conditions are promoted and encour-

---

[8] "A social indicator . . . may be defined to be a statistic of direct normative interest which facilitates concise, comprehensive, and balanced judgments about the condition of major aspects of a society. It is in all cases a direct measure of welfare and is subject to the interpretation that, if it changes in the 'right' direction, while other things remain equal, things have gotten better, or people are 'better off.' Thus statistics on the number of doctors or policemen could not be social indicators whereas figures on health or crime rates could be" (Department of Health, Education, and Welfare, 1969, p. 97).

aged in such areas as health, education, and training, rehabili-
tation, housing, vocational opportunities, the arts and human-
ities, and special assistance for the mentally ill and retarded,
the deprived, the abandoned, and the criminal, and by mea-
suring progress in meeting such needs.

The bill also instructed the new council to determine the extent to which existing federal programs contribute to the above policy; "to . . . develop priorities for programs designed to carry out the policy . . . and recommend . . . the most efficient way to allocate Federal resources and the level of government . . . best suited to carry out such programs." Which was quite a tall order, and it is hard to believe that a council which set itself up as such an overlord of domestic policy could long survive.

Interest in the proposal has been kept alive by a number of academic publications and *Toward a Social Report* (Department of Health, Education, and Welfare, 1969), issued by outgoing secretary Wilbur Cohen in January 1969 in response to a 1966 directive from President Johnson. The two years and ten months labor of the bureaucracy and a small horde of consultants does not enhance confidence in the ease of producing a comprehensive, reliable, and meaningful social report. In the end, we are told, the report was prepared by HEW staff "and was not reviewed by the Panel. . . . [which] bears no responsibility for the contents." Reputedly, only the staff could produce a sufficiently sanitized document.

Why is the preparation of an acceptable social report and of social indicators so much more difficult than an economic report and economic indicators? Some of the reasons were set forth in CEA chairman Gardner Ackley's testimony on the Mondale bill. Ackley was sympathetic to the humane objectives of the bill and its effort to improve social data and social policies. But, he observed, the policy objectives of the bill (quoted above) were far from clear. While the comparable declaration in the Employment Act was not "crystal clear" either, it "has been translated into a fairly unambiguous goal of promoting the maximum growth of total output that is consistent with reasonable price stability in an essentially private economy without direct controls." In contrast, "No substantial body of expert or public opinion would today agree on what it means to give 'every American the opportunity to live in decency and dignity' " or on what policies advance that goal. And the goal itself is constantly changing. A material, technological, or economic goal can be defined and measured with reasonable objectivity and reliability but not an immaterial goal such as social welfare—above all not with a single national measure comparable to the gross national product. The difficulty is not the lack of data, but the nature of man and society.

It is significant that the Brim Commission did not endorse a Council of Social Advisers. The commission stressed the importance of improving social data but opposed attempts to measure the immeasurable: "no attempt should be made to imitate an aggregate like the gross national product. If we made the mistake of producing some overall composite index of the nation's social health, it would have to be an amalgam of different and quite disparate measures, and as such probably meaningless" (1969, p. 61).[9]

The Behavioral and Social Sciences Survey Committee expressed a shade more optimism about the ultimate prospect: "the creation of a social counterpart of gross national product is not likely to be achieved in the near future" (1969, p. 102). That statement holds out hope for the longer-term future. The committee recommended a substantial effort to produce "a system of social indicators" and suggested that several trial annual reports be prepared privately; it also favored both public and private financing because a private group could explore delicate social and political issues, evaluate government programs frankly, and yet escape close administration or congressional review. The committee declined "at this time to recommend the establishment of a council of social advisers" (p. 108).

This reasoning seems cogent. Indeed, will it ever lose its cogency? Strike the rosy language from the talk of social indicators and the step from the production of social statistics, accepted as a basic function of government, to the preparation of an analytic report on those statistics is small. This step is taken constantly by

―――――――――

[9] Whereas *Toward a Social Report* defined social indicators as those statistics which provide "a direct measure of welfare," the Brim Commission usage was more neutral: "socially significant statistical descriptive data about American society, gathered in time series so as to show trends" (1969, p. 57).

many agencies, and the results are most often extraordinarily ordinary. What is special about "the" social report we have been discussing is the professional and political attention it has received and the presidential auspices sought for it. That attention may or may not give a report a superior technical quality. It can also render a report excessively politic and pragmatic, since the White House, the Kremlin, and Hell must be the three worst places in which to maintain a genuinely detached, apolitical posture. The price of White House stationery is the need loudly or quietly to support the President and his policies. Therefore there will be a need for private as well as governmental social reports. Whatever its auspices, there is something authoritarian about the idea of a single, authoritative social report.

No sooner was the BASS Committee's recommendation against an annual social report by the Executive Office at the printer when, in July 1969, President Nixon announced the establishment of a National Goals Research Staff, which would issue an annual social report from the White House. There are significant differences between a White House staff created (and since disbanded) by the President and a council set up by law and reporting to the Congress, as called for in the Mondale bill. Mondale himself was critical of the President's move.[10] But plainly his action represented a further development of the social indicator movement, with a strong tinge of futurism and of national planning which, in the present American context, must assume a voluntary or consensual character. It also represented the diminutive implementation of proposals for a national planning office advanced a year earlier by the National Planning Association (1968).

Nixon's announcement stated that the functions of the staff would include "forecasting future developments [especially in 1976,

[10] "Mondale said the National Goals Research Staff . . . would lack the prestige and visibility of a council and therefore would not attract the same caliber of professionals. He argued that because there is no provision for a legislative counterpart, the White House effort would lack the necessary communication and coordination between policy planners and lawmakers. . . . Finally, he said an institution that has earned the kind of respect paid to the Council of Economic Advisers has a 'built-in incentive to tell the truth,' because its members are subject to the criticism of their peers and the public" ("President . . . , 1969).

the nation's 200th anniversary, and 2000]. . . . measuring the probable future impact of alternative courses of action. . . . developing and monitoring social indicators that can reflect the present and future quality of American life. . . . summarizing, integrating, and correlating the results of related research activities." All of which was a heroic intellectual task for the staff of ten. "The range of subjects is, I think, as near as you can say, the range of interest of the American National Government at this point," Moynihan cheerfully told the press, with a confidence in the gift of prophecy that palm readers lack. ". . . virtually all, of the critical national problems of today could have been anticipated. . . . most of them, in fact, were anticipated . . . but there was no point at which that kind of clear sense of the future made its way into the decision processes of the American Government, and this is an effort to do so."[11]

A similar line of thought appears in the Brim Commission report, which cites a 1947 "prediction" by Robin Williams "that the nation would face riots and other violence as Negro aspirations in the United States were raised" and observes: "This prediction went unheard. . . . The events of the 1960's proved Williams correct. . . . It would be easy for the skeptic to say that we are using hindsight here. No one was listening to a lot of other suggestions by social scientists that turned out to be incorrect. But this prediction . . . was based on much empirical evidence . . . and it was generally accepted by the field of sociology" (1969, pp. 16–17).

Beard, Keynes, and, for that matter, Moynihan have developed another line of thought. "Nobody could foretell in October, 1928, whether Mr. Smith or Mr. Hoover would be elected President," Beard (1929) observed, "and yet we are asked to plot the social trajectory of the United States until the end of the century. . . . All such prognostications are hazardous intellectual adventures, with the chances, perhaps a thousand to one, against correctness." Keynes wrote, "We cannot expect to legislate for a generation or more. . . . We cannot as reasonable men do better than base our policy on the evidence we have and adapt it to the five or ten

[11] See National Goals Research Staff, Statement by the President . . . , and News Briefing by Dr. Daniel P. Moynihan on the Functions of the Staff, July 12, 1969 (*Weekly* . . . , 1969).

years over which we may suppose ourselves to have some measure of prevision" (1920, p. 204). As for Moynihan, meditating the failures of the community action program in a book published only a few months before the press conference, he wrote, "Had these developments been foreseen it may well be that wisdom in government would have dictated another course for the antipoverty program. . . . But who was to know . . . ? Exactly. It was not possible to know: it *is* not possible. Wisdom surely bespeaks moderation in projections of the future" (1969a, p. 202). Exactly.

Proposals have been advanced to attach to the Executive Office a private policy research institute based on one of three models. The first is a large, RAND-like institute with a diverse range of talent conducting confidential as well as published research. The second is patterned after the National Institutes of Health—an organization with substantial research staff of its own as well as projects conducted under contract and grant. The third, proposed by a National Academy of Sciences committee chaired by Donald Young is, an institute of decidedly academic character.[12] These proposals suffer acutely from the same difficulty as that of a staff arm of the presidency: defining their purposes in terms that are coherent, practicable, and useful. All of the large and many of the smaller problems of the nation crowd in on the presidency. Which

[12] The Young committee recommended that "the President and the Congress create and independently endow a National Institute for Advanced Research and Public Policy in Washington, D.C., to undertake continuing and long-range analyses of national policies and problems, to serve as a center for continuing interchange between government policy-makers and scientists, and to provide a forum in the nation's capital for the full exploration of the growth and application of knowledge from all the sciences to the major issues of the society." The brief discussion of the rationale for this recommendation in no way narrows or clarifies institute goals and organization; seemingly it would be an all-purpose place where all kinds of scholars, scientists as well as social scientists, in and out of government, would study all kinds of problems. In a covering letter, Harvey Brooks, chairman of the Academy Committee on Science and Public Policy, writes that his committee reviewed the recommendation and let it stand, "not because we agree with it . . . but because we believe that public and intragovernmental discussion of the institute idea is the only way by which it can be made to take practical shape and the need it seeks to fill can be more sharply defined." In short, the recommendation was advanced as a way of determining what should be recommended. Dupree (1970), a member of the Young committee, sees the institute as a device to support university research.

should be studied? This question can be answered in so many different ways that the choice of any one answer appears arbitrary; in
practice, many adventitious factors—events, personalities, opportunities—greatly influence the choice. A critical remnant of judgment remains which finally characterizes the enterprise as hard- or
soft-headed, pedestrian or insightful, successful or ineffectual.

There seems least cause to establish a purely academic institute of the type envisaged by the Young committee for, avowedly and
unabashedly, it has no focus, and even if the research done there
would be uniformly excellent, why should it be done at a new institute instead of at existing academic institutions? No harm and some
knowledge would come from it. But what practical use would it be
to the President?

A basic operating condition for any research adjunct to the
presidency is the ability to perform some work in confidence, a
condition which argues for a RAND-type unit at least for politically
sensitive work; a more widely dispersed project-type arrangement
would, however, better involve talent throughout the nation in less
urgent or sensitive research and in work which must be done outside Washington. Another basic condition is that the director of the
unit have the utmost confidence of the President as well as of intellectuals.

Beyond that, it is gratuitous to tell a president what his needs
for information are and how he should get it. If he wants to add a
touch of scholarship to the White House or try to foresee the future,
so be it. If he prefers to foster historical scholarship or string
quartets, leaving social research to existing staff, ad hoc commissions,
and the vast resources of the Executive, that would not be entirely
bad either.

A year after the Young committee recommended the establishment of a diffuse academic institute in Washington, the Brim
Commission proposed the establishment of some twenty-five applied
interdisciplinary institutes throughout the nation, each to concentrate on a large social problem such as "urban transportation systems; violence; delivery of medical services; crime." The commission contemplated institutes with from twelve to one hundred or
more professional staff members and (calculating direct and indirect costs at $50,000 per professional) an annual budget of

$600,000–$5 million or a median of perhaps $2 million, yielding a total initial annual outlay of about $50 million. Although costs would rise thereafter, it hoped that an increasing portion of their income would come from state and local governments, private foundations, industry, and other private sources. The commission called for a $10-million appropriation to enable the National Science Foundation to start establishing these institutes.

The commission would have institute staff proceed beyond the mere conduct of a study to "policy formulation" and the "development of administratively operational programs." Would such steps not constitute "action" or "administration" rather than "research"? Yes, indeed, it would. Thus, the commission recognized that an important function of a research institute can be to husband what Schon (1971) calls "gardens of competence"—specialized personnel that, free of responsibility for ongoing agency work and committed to no internal agency faction, can step in, for a period, to help introduce a new program, policy, or reorganization.

However, the institute proposal had some evident defects. One was the failure to assign priorities among the virtual infinitude of social problems and to reduce the number of projected institutes from an unrealistic twenty-five to five, three, or two, which could be initiated immediately. Though the idea of a narrowly focused institute was more realistic than the Young committee's proposal of a single diffuse national institute, the proliferation of many institutes represented another kind of diffuseness. Presumably each recommendation was another way of escaping the aggravating problems of professional and political choice; but that choice must ultimately be made by someone. If a convincing case cannot be made for starting three or five designated institutes, a better case cannot be made for starting twenty-five undesignated ones.

Doubtless, the case for new, "focused" interdisciplinary institutes was overstated. Do not many existing institutes approximate the target, and would it not be better to strengthen some of these rather than starting afresh in every case? And how feasible and fruitful is it to define and study most social problems narrowly? How narrow a problem is "violence"? Most social problems have so many causes and ramifications that, try as one may to narrow a study, each problem interlocks firmly with many others. No matter what problems an institute starts out to study, left to themselves psychologists will end up studying many other problems as well and, ultimately, much of psychology; sociologists, the nature of groups, institutions, and society; anthropologists, culture.

After all these years of effort, what great hope dare one harbor for interdisciplinary research? It bears somewhat the same relation to the world of the mind as the idea of "man" or a global society bears to the world of nations: an ideal infrequently realized. Ralph Linton once remarked that the only genuinely interdisciplinary thinking took place when two disciplines were united in one mind. Surely, interdisciplinary research should be encouraged; surely, our lives are whole while our knowledge is fractured; and surely we must try to piece it together as best we can. But to assemble under one roof scholars from many disciplines does not necessarily bind their knowledge together any more firmly than separate papers are bound together in a book. Genuine intellectual integration of different disciplines remains rare, and the more disciplines that must be integrated, the rarer it is. If there is any administrative formula for ensuring successful interdisciplinary research it has been kept remarkably secret.

The most serious weakness of the Brim Commission report was one it could do nothing about: its auspices. The National Science Foundation has had little experience, and some of that has been disastrous, at managing programs of applied research directed toward objectives defined, and products to be utilized, by government agencies. And the foundation has no responsibility for or experience at administering any substantive social program or dealing with any social problem other than that of raising and allocating money for science. To expect it suddenly to finance a number of new institutes that would become actively immersed in the study and resolution of social problems is something like expecting the Smithsonian Institution to diagnose and treat the ailments of the central city.

Summary

Of the measures that can be taken to foster the use of social research, this chapter has mainly discussed two: improving the accessibility of knowledge, and the formal arrangements for conveying social science advice to the government and for formulating government policy toward the social sciences.

In addition to the indispensable sources of knowledge in books and libraries, documentation and information services have assumed growing importance; and by facilitating public access to raw data, data centers can enable scholars throughout the nation to participate actively in the analysis of current government policy alternatives. But the widespread dissemination of research reports and data aggravates the problem of selecting that knowledge which is most pertinent to the problem at hand. Insofar as there is a large amount of redundancy in social knowledge, the problem is proportionately reduced; and in practice it is resolved by individual judgment, often exercised in private, and influenced by personal and political considerations.

Additional professional discussion of policy issues might broaden the alternatives taken into account in professional advice. The social science professions have not attained such certain knowledge or political maturity that their associations dare issue daily pronouncements on either the truth or the wisdom of government policies.

Politics is practical, not rational; it thrives on inconsistency. And so there is, in the Executive Office of the President, an Office of Science and Technology and a Council of Economic Advisers, whose few members attempt the seemingly impossible task of advising the President on all (but in fact only a few) problems of government policy toward science, technology, and the economy. I share the opinion of many that policy by and for social science is better incorporated within Executive Office agencies than in a special office. However, the government would doubtless survive such a separate office, which would either have to confine itself to a few social issues or spread itself ineffectively over a great many.

Policy research institutes are much in vogue. The Young Committee advocated the formation of one diffuse institute in Washington; the Brim Commission advised many narrower institutes throughout the nation. The wisest course does not always lie "in the middle," but in this instance I believe it does. Research institutes should be established not on the abstract ground that knowledge is needed but when a given government agency and its public constituency is genuinely interested in getting and using definable and obtainable knowledge. An effective institute is as much a political as an intellectual convenience, and its success will derive not from abstract intellectual wizardry but from the practical possibility of reconciling disparate social interests and from the political astuteness of the institute in doing so.

12

Uncertainty and Belief

The reader seeking a brief account of the contents of this book should consult the summaries at the end of each chapter. I will not repeat them here but will rather offer a few final reflections on government use of private social research.

It is fashionable among some academicians to castigate the government and to view those who work for it as one or another kind of intellectual courtesan or prostitute. That is a position which only an anarchist can consistently maintain. The hostility to government that other critics manifest can be a disguise for their opposition to a particular administration or a particular social ("capitalist") system. Disguises do not facilitate honest discourse. Political criticism is entirely legitimate—but avowedly partisan; and if an intellectual is both partisan and honest, he should not pretend to be, or expect to be treated as, nonpartisan.

A sound intellectual criticism of government service remains: that it is intellectually compromising, if not corrupting. I believe this criticism is intellectually sound and morally unsound, for it puts the truth about man above the welfare of man, as some put art above life. If public service requires some compromise with rationality and truth as the intellectual perceives them, some coarsening of the ideas whose gossamer threads can be spun unbroken in the classroom (so long as the windows are closed and the students silent), so be it. For good or bad, government remains necessary. We may seek to improve it or to change it drastically, but it is not going to disappear. No modern state has yet withered away.

So the government to which this book frequently refers could, in principle, be any government or administration—Democratic, Republican, Canadian, Swedish, socialist, or monarchist. Any scholar with political objections to that government has every right to refuse to work for it; but it would be honest for him to state that his grounds are political. The scholar has every right to political partisanship or to such political detachment as he can attain, and if some are able, by a mysterious process lesser mortals cannot fathom, to be simultaneously partisan and nonpartisan, they have every right to *that* hermaphroditic condition—but not, necessarily, a right to government support and approbation.

Schlesinger (1959) observes that "the attitude toward the intellectual is cyclical. . . . He was taken seriously in the first decade of the century and in the nineteen-thirties; he was not taken seriously in the nineteen-twenties or 'fifties. In general, when the business community is in control of the national political government, the intellectual is shut out, mocked, and rejected. When the coalition of non-business forces—a coalition of which the intellectuals ordinarily form an indispensable component—is in control of the national political government, the intellectual has a much higher status." The "intellectual" is not coterminous with "social scientist," but in view of the heavy Democratic preferences of social scientists, there is an evident danger that relations between the academic community and the government may be exacerbated, and the influence of social scientists decline, under a Republican administration.[1]

---

[1] Talking on this point to some 120 social scientists at a March 16, 1970, Washington dinner meeting of the Behavioral Science Division of the National Research Council, President Nixon's Democratic counselor Daniel

However, there are countervailing factors. Relations between many elements of the academic community and the government deteriorated so badly in the last years of President Johnson's Administration that they could hardly get much worse under a new administration. And President Nixon's long-standing interest in the social sciences[2] has been reaffirmed by his call for increased appropriations for research for the Office of Education, the Office of Economic Opportunity, and the National Science Foundation. The emphasis on program evaluation, on determining what works before large sums are expended on new programs, is obviously useful to an economy-minded administration. Should social research expenditures continue to rise in the 1970s while a large portion of the academic community remains politically alienated from the government, the research is increasingly likely to be done by the more apolitical, pragmatic sector of independent research organizations.

Applied research can be contracted to such reliable organizations and reliable reports will be delivered (but not always published), which will be utilized in reliable ways; but the results may well be pedestrian. For if research yields no intellectual surprises, if it disturbs no established notion or interest, if it tells officials only what they want to hear and never fails in the purpose they assign, it will never succeed in the larger purpose we may rightly expect: to take an independent view and provide fresh insight into public affairs. Some research that is not useful to a government agency can be very useful to the public, and the very independence which can make a professor so difficult to deal with can also make him well qualified to conduct that kind of research.

Therefore, even in its parochial interest, a government agency disregards the academy at its peril—and expense. The academy remains the heartland of every social science field, and a

---

Moynihan asked Republicans to raise their hands. Some three or four hands went up.

[2] Vice-President Nixon took the initiative in convening a group of social scientists chaired by James G. Miller that, in February 1958, issued a call for increased support for behavioral science. As Mr. Nixon informed Congressman Reuss in a December 1, 1966, letter, "the discussions I had with Dr. James Miller originated because of my personal interest in the developments in the behavioral science field." Miller has independently confirmed this account (I, 14).

research program which disregards the talent residing there will be poorer than one employing it. Good academic institutions cover the land, whereas good institutes are more localized; the services of professors and graduate students are readily available in most localities and are usually cheaper than those of research institutes. And as the academy is the breeding ground of all social scientists, its isolation from applied research programs would only perpetuate the poor preparation graduate students have received for applied work. No, attractive as that alternative may at first seem, the problem of improving the quality and usefulness of applied government research cannot be solved satisfactorily by disregarding the academy, for the academy represents the heart, not the periphery, of the problem.

I have been at pains to recognize the political element in the discord between many academic men and the government, but this source of discord is more readily recognized than resolved. If there is any way by which the fundamental disagreement between radical intellectuals and a conservative or liberal government can be resolved, I do not know what it is. Nor do I know of any way to bring the intellectual (of any political outlook) who has, in Schlesinger's phrase, vowed "unremitting hostility to power" to work peacefully, happily, and constructively for the government. I do not think he should. Schlesinger's rejoinder that "if intellectuals decided to abandon government to nonintellectuals, they would have only themselves to blame for the result" (1965, p. 744) is doubtless true; but it is also true that a constantly challenging and caustic critique of power is one invaluable function of the intellectual. We are all better off that Thoreau and Tolstoy and Bertrand Russell bowed to no temporal power. Cantankerous, eccentric, utopian, anarchistic or aristocratic, and most decidedly impractical they may have been, but shall the practical requirements of government administration circumscribe the vision of man?

With all honor to such men and regret that so few social scientists have risen to their level, they and many less enviable, embittered intellectuals of smaller human stature must be set aside for our present purpose; for, plainly, a meaningful accommodation between private intellectuals and the government can take place only among those who are prepared to reach such an accommodation within the bounds of our central political values and institutions. In the aftermath and ever-present danger of assassinations, bombs, arson, strikes, protests, hijackings, atrocities, and vituperation from all points of the compass, I have less confidence in the strength of that political center than I had in 1966, when the Reuss inquiry began. Like other social scientists, I can only draw lessons from the past in the hope that they may still have some relevance for the future.

The largest lesson that emerges from this study is the desirability of bringing academic social scientists and government officials closer together. A separation of many years cannot be ended in a few days, and as both sides are responsible for the breach, both must repair it. The academy should recognize practical research; dissertations on real social problems should be received as hospitably as scholastic exercises; new journals should be established to encourage the publication of applied research, the discussion of its special technical and ethical problems, and the evaluation of public policies and programs. Whether all of this is best accomplished by establishing new schools of applied social science, as recommended by the Behavioral and Social Sciences Survey Committee; by improving the quality of social science instruction at existing schools of business, social work, education, and public administration, as recommended by the Brim Commission; or by adding scholars interested in applied and policy research to existing graduate departments need not concern us here (although the latter two courses present fewer difficulties than does the first). Nor is this the place to elaborate a curriculum for applied social scientists, although this curriculum should, I believe, put less emphasis on the theology of science, no less on the crafts and arts of empiricism, and restore a sense of history that the disciplines have shed for the vestments of science. For to study the practical problems of the nation while disregarding their history is to blind oneself willfully, mistaking innocence for objectivity.

The most important thing government officials can do, initially, is simply to open their doors: to find time and opportunities for serious, candid, and repeated discussions with academic men. Some research will help, but, dollar for dollar, research is an expensive way to maintain contact with the academic community and must

be justified in its own right. Fellowships, internships, consultant-
ships, advisory committees, conferences on agency problems, and
invitations to examine given agency records are all cheaper ways to
start.

The notion that vast sums should be spent on social research
because we have vast social problems, because there are so many
things we do not know, or because larger sums are spent on defense,
the natural sciences, liquor, or baseball withstands little scrutiny.
The case for applied research should rest on the probable usefulness
of information ascertainable at a cost that bears a reasonable relationship to its usefulness and to the odds that the information will
be obtained in time to retain its usefulness. No doubt in some exceptional cases, such as a census, large-scale survey and operations
research, or a national educational assessment, there is no point in
starting a research program unless a great deal of money is committed to it: there are "go" and "no go" situations in research as in
rocketry. But the government probably gets more value (in information and ideas) per dollar from small programs than from very
large ones, and more from the initial millions than from those
which are added as a program grows. A better case can be made
for the value of five-, ten-, or twenty-million-dollar expenditures by
such departments as State, Justice, and Housing and Urban Development, which have had very limited extramural programs,
than, as President Nixon proposed in March 1970, for more than
doubling expenditures for educational research. Already at the
$100-million support level, this is by far the largest single program
of social research, and far from the best. It is not a coincidence that,
in the three largest social research programs at the Office of Education, the National Institute of Mental Health, and the Office of
Economic Opportunity, large sums are devoted not to research but
to the trial of new operating methods and programs. Very large-
scale research often represents a means of social change: its function
is not just to understand society but to change it.

The inexperienced and conspiracy-minded consider the government clear and calculating in its purpose. In fact, the opposite is
much closer to the truth. Most applied research programs suffer
from a lack of cogent and consistent purpose and would be improved by the formulation of narrower and more attainable goals

and by an insistence on reaching them, instead of constantly re-casting their objectives.

However, the basic trouble with social research programs lies not in the quality of their administration and research but in the difficulty of anticipating what knowledge will be needed and, then, of getting it. To know what we will later need is to be a minor prophet; and the knowledge we can get most reliably is not usually what we most need. The contingencies of social life produce the un-certainties of social science: man, not social science, is to blame. Fearing to be caught unprepared, administrators cover themselves by supporting work only tangentially related to their central ob-jectives. Attacked for narrowness, they yield on one front and another; and so the average program assumes its characteristic shape, or shapelessness, of a mop of independent projects dangling from a web of opportunity.

We cannot blame social scientists for the persistent and nagging inconclusiveness of so many of their findings, but we can blame them for failing to acknowledge it or for making pretentious claims for their accomplishments and capabilities. The syndrome of over-large claims is peculiarly widespread in contemporary social science. Probably it reflects the hope-rises-eternal spirit of man more than the promotional spirit of advertising man; but whatever the cause, the customer does not get a fair and accurate description of the wares he is offered. Accordingly, the customer—Congress, the public, and those students who still search for the truth—must learn to discount the excessive claims that are made for social science as he does those that are made for automobiles and detergents. And, while scope must always be allowed for experiment and failure, government research programs are better founded on modest expec-tations than on vain promises.

Good research administration is an art, and nowhere is that art more necessary than in managing a scattered flock of unruly scholars. The best management should be the least visible, cultivat-ing selected scholarly interests rather than imposing government requirements; the ideal is a genuine, not false, accord in which both parties learn something important and each helps the other without sacrificing any significant principle.

One important way the investigator can help is to learn to

answer the ad hoc question on the spot or by return phone. This talent is not normally acquired in graduate school but is important to government, journalism, and daily life; and it has the strictly intellectual merit of forcing early generalization while time remains to correct it and an awareness of missing data while time remains to collect them. The investigator can be more helpful if he is knowledgeable about agency affairs and knows how his work fits into the entire research program and how the program serves agency objectives. The administrator is responsible for seeing that the investigator is, in fact, accurately informed about these matters, and informed not merely about their formal status but about the underlying issues that concern agency staff.

If an investigator is to work seriously at an agency problem and not merely regard it as a convenient way to pursue his own interests, agency officials have a return obligation to take his work seriously. An investigator has no right to have his recommendations adopted but every right to a fair hearing. To ensure this consideration, one Washington institute wrote into its contract a provision requiring two assistant secretaries to devote several hours to a briefing on its report. It would also be useful for agency officials and the investigator to meet six months or a year after the submission of a report to discuss its impact and what has happened to the recommendations and why.

Publication is the method by which the academy asserts, and the research institute often obscures, its scholarly reputation and independence. Yet the conventional academic doctrine of full publication is founded on the public character of its data—Ziman (1968) defines science as public knowledge—or the generalized, anonymous way that they are used. Applied research into the problems of identifiable individuals and groups cannot fruitfully and ethically be conducted by the same rules that govern academic research. The investigator who publishes whatever he knows will breach confidences that were assumed if not asserted; he will confirm the academician's reputation for irresponsibility and make it more difficult for others to work the territory he has despoiled.

Nonetheless, honest and accurate publication is vital to the public interest. An important function of applied research is to ensure that the interests of unorganized, unvocal, and poorly informed citizens are taken into account by government. The honest investigator serves to represent the unrepresented, and while part of that function can be performed in an unpublished report, the larger part requires publication, which informs the uninformed and can generate the kind of political pressure the government cannot ignore as readily as it can an unpublished report.

To get beneath the surface of formal facts to more significant truths, the social scientist must obtain access to information not yet on public record; and he can ethically do so only with the voluntary consent of informants and under such terms as they may set. If he rejects unacceptable terms, he may also have to dispense with the accompanying information. Only when he holds some power over his informants is this situation basically altered—and, often enough, the middle-class investigator does enjoy a position of personal authority, if not power, over his informants. However, he has less authority over senior government officials, who can exact the right to review a research plan and the final report as a condition for providing access to confidential information or the funds with which such information can be obtained. The conflict between the tendency of government and private sources to conceal information whose disclosure might harm their interests and the investigator's effort to obtain and publish precisely that kind of information is inherent in policy research. No ethical or administrative rules can overcome the conflict, though hopefully such rules and an understanding of the practical alternatives can ameliorate it.

Charity and the golden rule remain good guides, too often neglected by investigators whose cold pursuit of cold truth can mask political and personal hostilities. It would also be only fair and would help to promote trust between social scientists and their oft-suffering subjects if some of the latter (and, in studies of government programs, these include the responsible government administrators) had an opportunity to comment on the report and these comments were appended to any publication.

None of the foregoing is intended to suppress wrongdoing or to condone the restrictive practices I have documented. The intent is to promote conditions under which applied research on public problems can be conducted not just once but continually, constructively, and honestly. The alternatives can only be the withholding of information by officials and their efforts to repel investigators' hostile forays or to render them superficial, uninformed, and outdated.

If research is to be frank, it must be independent; and if it is to be truly independent, the investigator should not fear the loss of future contracts from the commissioning agency. Therefore research which might hurt the sponsoring agency should be conducted by an investigator who has no interest in continued agency financing or be sponsored by a higher governmental level not directly implicated in any adverse findings and yet able to act on them. Thus, bureau officials can effectively sponsor research to improve their own management; research that might strip a bureau of important powers should be financed by the office of the secretary; research that might reflect adversely on the secretary's performance should be contracted by the Executive Office of the President; and research critical of the President should be financed by a private foundation or by bipartisan or opposition forces in the Congress and the nation.

As most of the social science associations have failed to prepare or enforce meaningful codes of professional conduct, is it too unreasonable for a simple code to be incorporated in the terms of government-sponsored research? The code might include a few provisions about fairness, honesty, the protection of confidences, and the avoidance of conflicts of interest; and an ethics committee of the Social Science Research Council or the National Academy of Sciences could be appointed to investigate cases seriously affecting the public interest.

In conclusion, what can be said about the value of social research to the government and the nation? And let us here disregard the oppressive volume of uninsightful research and speak only of good empirical and theoretical work. Assuredly, it is helpful, even necessary, in many public affairs;[3] but it is insufficient, of itself, to dictate public policy.

[3] See Beard: "If it is true . . . that there is a great deal of rubbish in this mass of knowledge, it is also true that within the accumulated knowledge of the social sciences is knowledge absolutely indispensable to the conduct of government, economy, and society in general. It is not always easy to say when this or that bit of knowledge is useful, but it may be declared with confidence that, deprived of the knowledge embraced in the social sciences, society in general, American society in particular, would dissolve in

The present dimensions of the social sciences are, to a surprising extent, a development of the period since the end of World War II, during which there has been a fourfold expansion in the membership of the five major social science associations. (In 1947, there were 20,700 and in 1967, 81,400 members of the psychological, economic, political science, sociological, and anthropological associations.) This growth reflects genuine national needs for information and services that social scientists can provide, but it reflects other needs as well. To some, social science represents a highbrow kind of social work; to others, an instrument of social reform; to still others, a tool of scientific management. One of its most important functions is simply to serve as a mode of education and a language of discourse, replacing for our secular society the functions which the humanities earlier served.

And the social sciences constitute a kind of secular religion[4] which offers metropolitan man an empirical world view, a sense of order and meaning, a means by which he may make his way through life's incalculable complexities. As Waldo observes:

. . . social science has and will have, to the extent that

---

ruinous chaos, with results of terrific, though not entirely predictable, consequence to mankind" (1934, p. 14). Exaggerated, perhaps, but we may accept the statement all the more readily when we think how close American society is to dissolving "in ruinous chaos" without being deprived of the knowledge of the social sciences. To be sure, other societies—Tibet, France, colonial America—prosper without that knowledge, employing literate men to collect whatever social data are really needed. Social data are no monopoly of social scientists.

4 "Social scientists do not hold any special privilege over philosophers, essayists, novelists, poets, the clergy, or the leaders of political parties or social movements in substantive issues concerning the definition, the choice, or the hierarchy of values or national goals. Whenever they contribute to the definition of some great ends likely to shape the future of mankind, the social sciences turn from a technical knowledge into a kind of secular religion; it is not altogether clear how far they can claim any 'scientific' superiority over the more traditional forms of religious activity when this transformation occurs.

"New values, new goals, new perspectives have been created by such great minds as Marx, Darwin, or Freud whose inventive capacities and boldness in vision far exceed the potentialities of the average social scientist, engaged in the regular exercise of his profession. It may well be true that a new religion might come from the established social sciences" (Lécuyer, 1969).

*it explains and justifies our policy choices, not just a clinical
and a rejective function, but a symbolic, a legitimatizing, and
an ideological function. I argue, in other words, that in the
sociological-anthropological perspective social scientists will
have religious and political functions. We may protest in all
honesty and with deep conviction that this is not our intent or
desire, that we wish to function as scientists, pure and simple—
but if the old legitimacies crumble in the modern "crisis of authority," does not science itself raise a claim to legitimatize
decision? I believe there is no denying that the social scientist
will exercise much the same social role and function as the
Roman temple priest who read the future from the entrails
of oxen—though the social scientist reads it from graph, from
report, from computer [1961, p. 28].*

Perhaps this statement explains better than anything else
the seemingly low level of use of most social research, because the
only use that can be designated as legitimate is that in which identifiable action follows from verified knowledge. But if that were the
only type of permissible action, life would cease. Social science has
more uses than its scientific devotees will attest. For they would
have to acknowledge its unscientific uses: its effects on our beliefs
and values, and its subjective—personal, political, ideological, and,
in a very real sense, religious—uses. Thus man subjectivizes objectivity, turning his feeble knowledge into reeds of belief.

Bibliography

ABERLE, D. "Letter." *American Anthropological Association Fellow Newsletter.* May 1967, 7.

ACKLEY, G. "The Contribution of Economists to Policy Formation." *Journal of Finance,* May 1966, 169–177.

ADAMS, R. D. "Ethics and the Social Anthropologist in Latin America." *American Behavioral Scientist,* June 1967, 16–21.

AGGER, R. E., and others. "Proposed Statement on Professional Ethics." *Public Administration Review,* Sept. 1967, 285–286.

American Anthropological Association. "Resolution on Freedom of Publication." *American Anthropologist,* 1949, *51,* 370.

American Anthropological Association. "Executive Board Statement on Government Involvement in Research." *American Anthropological Association Fellow Newsletter,* Oct. 1966, 2.

American Anthropological Association. "Statement on Problems of Anthropological Research and Ethics by the Fellows of the American Anthropological Association." Washington, D.C., April 1967 (2 pp.).

American Anthropological Association, Ethics Committee. "Report." *Newsletter of the American Anthropological Association,* April 1969, 3–6.

American Psychological Association. *Ethical Standards of Psychologists*. Washington, D.C., 1953.

American Psychological Association. *Casebook on Ethical Standards of Psychologists*. Washington, D.C. 1967.

American Psychological Association, Committee on Scientific and Professional Ethics and Conduct. "Rules and Procedures." *American Psychologist,* 1961, 829–832: 1968, 362–366.

American Sociological Association, Committee on Standards and Ethics in Research Practice. "Report." *American Sociological Review,* Dec. 1953, 683–684.

American Sociological Association, Section on Social Psychology. "Certification Requirements and Procedures for Social Psychologists." *American Sociological Review,* Dec. 1960, 931–932.

ANGELL, R. C. "The Ethical Problems of Applied Sociology." In P. L. Lazarsfeld and others (Eds.), *The Uses of Sociology*. New York: Basic Books, 1967.

"APA Board of Directors Expresses 'Profound Distress' with Vietnam War." *APA Monitor,* July 1972, 1.

BACH, G. L. "Economics in the High Schools: The Responsibility of the Profession." *American Economic Review,* May 1961, 579–586.

BACH, G. L. "Report of the Committee on Economic Education." *American Economic Review,* May 1967, 709–710.

BALTZELL, E. D. *The Protestant Establishment*. New York: Vintage, 1966.

BAY, C. "Letter." *American Political Science Review,* Dec. 1967, 1096.

BEALS, R. L. *Politics of Social Research*. Chicago: Aldine, 1969.

BEALS, R. L., and EXECUTIVE BOARD. "Background Information on Problems of Anthropological Research and Ethics." *American Anthropological Association Fellow Newsletter,* Jan. 1967, 2–13.

BEARD, C. A. "Political Science." In W. Gee (Ed.), *Research in the Social Sciences*. New York: Macmillan, 1929, 269–291.

BEARD, C. A. *The Nature of the Social Sciences*. New York: Scribner's, 1934.

BECKER, H. S. "Against the Code of Ethics." *American Sociological Review,* June 1964, 409–410.

BEECHER, H. K. "Ethics and Clinical Research." *New England Journal of Medicine,* June 16, 1966, 1354–1360.

Behavioral and Social Sciences Survey Committee (BASS). *The Behavioral and Social Sciences: Outlook and Needs*. Washington, D.C.: National Academy of Sciences, 1969.

BELL, D. (Chairman) *Report to the President on Government Contracting for Research and Development.* Washington, D.C.: Bureau of the Budget, 1962.

BELL, J. E. "Minutes of the Executive Committee Meeting." *American Economic Review,* May 1950, 592.

BERNARD, J. "Report of the Committee on Ethical Principles in Research." *American Sociological Review,* Dec. 1955, 753–758.

BERNSTEIN, M. (Chairman) *Ethical Problems of Political Scientists.* Interim report. Committee on Professional Standards and Responsibilities. Washington, D.C.: American Political Science Association, Sept. 1967. Multilithed.

BERNSTEIN, M. (Chairman) *Ethical Problems of Academic Political Scientists.* Final report. Committee on Professional Standards and Responsibilities. Washington, D.C.: American Political Science Association, 1968.

BERREMAN, G. D. "Speech to Council." *Newsletter of the American Anthropological Association,* Jan. 1971, 18–20.

BIDERMAN, A. D. "Report of the Committee on Government Sponsorship and Freedom in Research." *American Sociologist,* Nov. 1967, 240–241.

BIDERMAN, A. D. "Report of the Committee on Government Sponsorship and Freedom of Research." *American Sociologist,* Nov. 1968, 339–341.

BLOUGH, R. "Political and Administrative Requisites for Achieving Economic Stability." *American Economic Review,* May 1950, 165–178.

BORDIN, E. S. "Our BPA Chairman Speaks Out." *American Psychologist,* Aug. 1965, 692–693.

BOULDING, K. E. *The Skills of the Economist.* Cleveland: Howard Allen, 1958.

BOULDING, K. E. *The Impact of the Social Sciences.* New Brunswick, N.J.: Rutgers University Press, 1966.

BOULDING, K. E. "Dare We Take the Social Sciences Seriously?" *American Behavioral Scientist,* June 1967, 12–16.

BRAYBROOKE, D., and LINDBLOM, C. E. *A Strategy of Decision.* New York: Free Press, 1963.

BRIM, O. G., JR. (Chairman) *Knowledge into Action: Improving the Nation's Use of the Social Sciences.* Report of the Special Commission on the Social Sciences of the National Science Board. Washington, D.C.: National Science Foundation, 1969.

BUGENTAL, F. T. "What the 'Professional' Complains About." *American Psychologist,* Jan. 1967, 51.

BURCHARD, W. W. "Lawyers, Political Scientists, Sociologists—and Concealed Microphones." *American Sociological Review,* Dec. 1958, 686–691.

BURNS, A. F., and SAMUELSON, P. A. *Full Employment, Guideposts and Economic Stability.* Washington, D.C.: American Enterprise Institute for Public Policy Research, 1967.

CALKINS, R. "The Production and Use of Economic Knowledge." *American Economic Review,* May 1966, 530–537.

CARTTER, A. *An Assessment of Quality in Graduate Education.* Washington, D.C.: American Council on Education, 1966.

"Caucus for a New Political Science." Letter by twelve members. *P.S.,* Winter 1968, 38–40.

CLARK, J. M. "Recent Developments in Economics." In E. C. Hayes (Ed.), *Recent Developments in the Social Sciences.* Philadelphia: Lippincott, 1927.

CLOWER, R. W., and others. *Growth Without Development.* Evanston, Ill.: Northwestern University Press, 1966.

COLEMAN, J. S. *The Evaluation of Equality of Educational Opportunity.* Baltimore: Center for the Study of Social Organization of Schools, Johns Hopkins University, 1968.

Comptroller General of the United States. *Need for Improved Guidelines in Contracting for Research with Government-Sponsored Nonprofit Contractors.* Washington, D.C.: General Accounting Office, 1969.

COMTE, A. *The Positive Philosophy.* Vol. 2. Translated by H. Martineau. London: George Bell, 1896.

COOK, S. W. (Chairman) "Ethical Standards for Psychological Research." Committee on Ethical Standards in Psychological Research. *APA Monitor,* July 1971, 9–28.

COOK, S. W. (Chairman) "Ethical Standards for Research with Human Subjects." Committee on Ethical Standards in Psychological Research. *APA Monitor,* May 1972, i–xix.

COSER, L. A. "Report of the Committee on Professional Relations." *American Sociologist,* Nov. 1967, 244–245.

COTTRELL, L. S., JR. "Strengthening the Social Sciences in the Universities." In *The Social Sciences at Mid-century.* Minneapolis: University of Minnesota Press, 1952.

CRICK, B. "The Science of Politics in the United States. *Canadian*

Journal of Economics and Political Science, Aug. 1954, 308–320.

CRONBACH, L. J. "The Role of the University in Improving Education." *Phi Delta Kappan,* June 1966, 539–545.

DAHL, R., and others. "Report of the Executive Committee." *American Political Science Review,* June 1967, 565–568.

DAVIS, K. "The Perilous Promise of Behavioral Science." In *Research in the Service of Man.* Committee on Government Operations, U.S. Senate, 90th Congress, 1st Sess., 1967, 23–32.

Department of State, U.S. "Government-Sponsored Foreign Affairs Research, Procedures for Review." *Federal Register,* Jan. 12, 1966, 358–360.

Department of State, U.S. *A Report on the First Three Years.* Foreign Affairs Research Council. Washington, D.C., Aug. 1968. Multilithed.

DUPREE, A. H. "A New Rationale for Science." *Saturday Review,* Feb. 7, 1970, 55–57.

"Economists Go for the Money—and Get It." *Business Week,* Jan. 29, 1972, 62.

EHRICH, R. W. "Letter." *Newsletter of the American Anthropological Association,* Nov. 1970, 2.

EICHORN, D. "Background Paper: Commission on the Composition of Council." *American Psychologist,* Jan. 1968, 59–63.

ERIKSON, K. T. "Report of the Committee on Professional Ethics." *American Sociologist,* Aug. 1972, 28.

FASCELL, D. (Chairman) *Behavioral Sciences and the National Security.* Hearings, Subcommittee on International Organizations and Movements, Committee on Foreign Affairs, U.S. House of Representatives, 89th Congress, 1st Sess., Part IX, July 8, 13, 14, and Aug. 4, 1965.

FASCELL, D. (Chairman) *Behavioral Sciences and the National Security.* Report No. 4. Subcommittee on International Organizations and Movements, Committee on Foreign Affairs, U.S. House of Representatives, 89th Congress, 2d Sess., Jan. 25, 1966.

Federal Statistics. Vol. I. Report of the President's Commission. Washington, D.C.: The White House, 1971.

FEDOR, W. "Politics and Economics." *Chemical and Engineering News,* Oct. 21, 1968, 28.

FEINBERG, L. "Allen Reorganizing Office of Education." *Washington Post,* July 18, 1969, p. A4.

Foreign Area Research Coordination Group. "Foreign Area Research Guidelines." *FAR Horizons,* Jan. 1968, 3–6.

FOSTER, G. M. "Report of the President," *Annual Report 1970.* Washington, D.C.: American Anthropological Association, 1971a, 2–6.

FOSTER, G. M. "Letter." *New York Review of Books,* April 8, 1971b, 43–44.

FOX, C. J. "Democratic Elitism Close to Home." *P.S.,* Spring 1971, 126–129.

FOX, D. J. "Issues in Evaluating Programs for Disadvantaged Children." *Urban Review,* Dec. 1967, 5–9.

FRIEDMAN, N. *The Social Nature of Psychological Research.* New York: Basic Books, 1967.

FULBRIGHT, J. W. *Congressional Record,* daily edition, April 18, 1968, pp. S4240, S4243.

FULBRIGHT, J. W. *Congressional Record,* daily edition, May 1, 1969, p. S4418.

GAMSON, W. A. "Sociology's Children of Affluence." *American Sociologist,* Nov. 1968, 286–289.

GARDNER, J. W. *"A.I.D. and the Universities."* Washington, D.C.: Agency for International Development, 1964.

GARVEY, W. D. and GRIFFITH, B. C. "Scientific Information Exchange in Psychology." *Science,* Dec. 25, 1964, 1655–1659.

GLAZER, N. "The Ideological Uses of Sociology." In P. F. Lazarsfeld and others (Eds.), *The Uses of Sociology.* New York: Basic Books, 1967.

GORDON, K. "Advance Knowledge or Perish." In C. Dobbins and C. Lee (Eds.), *Whose Goals for American Higher Education?* Washington, D.C.: American Council on Education, 1968.

GOUGH, K. "World Revolution and the Science of Man." In T. Roszak (Ed.), *The Dissenting Academy.* New York: Vintage, 1968.

GOULDNER, A. W., and SPREHE, J. T. "Sociologists Look at Themselves." *Trans-Action,* May/June 1965, 42–44.

GREENBERG, D. S. "The National Academy of Sciences: Profile of an Institution (III)." *Science,* April 28, 1967, 488–493.

GRIMSHAW, A. D. "Report of the Committee on Public Policy." *American Sociologist,* Nov. 1970, 414–416.

HANDLER, P. "Scientific Choice and Scientific Priorities in Biomedical Research." A paper presented at the Second NIH [National

Institutes of Health] International Symposium. Williamsburg, Va,. March 1, 1965.

HARRIS, F. (Chairman) *Federal Support of International Social Science and Behavioral Research.* Hearings, Subcommittee on Government Research, Committee on Government Operations, U.S. Senate, 89th Congress, 2d Sess., June 27, 28; July 19 and 20, 1966; 1967a.

HARRIS, F. (Chairman) *National Foundation for Social Sciences.* Hearings, Subcommittee on Government Research, Committee on Government Operations, U.S. Senate, 90th Congress, 1st Sess., on S. 836. Feb. 7, 8, and 16; June 2, 6, 7, 20, and 21; June 27, 28; July 12 and 13, 1967. Parts 1–3. 1967b.

HELLER, W. *New Dimensions of Political Economy.* Cambridge, Mass.: Harvard University Press, 1966.

HELWEG, G. C. *Ethics: An Area of Growing Concern.* Unpublished Paper, 1967.

HEXTER, J. H. "Some American Observations." *Journal of Contemporary History,* Jan. 1967.

HORN, S. "Ideas in Action: The Relations Between the Academic Community and Elected Representatives." *Congressional Record,* Senate, Jan. 17, 1966, 379–382.

HOWTON, L. "Evaluating Juvenile Delinquency Research." In B. Rosenberg and others (Eds.), *Mass Society in Crisis.* New York: Macmillan.

HUGHES, E. C. "Report of the Committee on Training and Professional Standards." *American Sociological Review,* Dec. 1956, 763–764.

HUGHES, T. L. Letter of July 10, 1967. *Newsletter of the American Anthropological Association,* June 1968, 9–10.

HUMPHREY, H. H. "A Magna Carta for the Social and Behavioral Sciences." *American Behavioral Scientist,* Feb. 1962, 11–14.

HUNTER, M. "Birth Control Research Report is Quashed by Surgeon General." *New York Times,* Sept. 7, 1962, p. 25.

Interstate and Foreign Commerce Committee. *Impact of Public Health Grant Programs on Medical Research and Education.* U.S. House of Representatives, 1964.

ISAACS, S. "Asia Anthropology: Science or Spying?" *Washington Post,* Nov. 22, 1971, pp. A1, 10.

JOHNSON, L. B. "My Political Philosophy." *Texas Quarterly,* Winter 1958.

JOHNSON, L. B. *Public Papers of the Presidents of the United States.* Vol. 2. Washington, D.C.: 1965.

JOHNSON, L. B. *Public Papers of the President of the United States.* Vol. 2. Washington, D.C.: Government Printing Office, 1966.

KEYNES, J. M. *The Economic Consequences of the Peace.* New York: Harcourt, Brace, 1920.

KEYNES, J. M. *The General Theory of Employment, Interest, and Money.* New York: Harcourt, Brace, 1936.

LADD, E. C., JR. *Professors and Political Petitions.* Paper prepared for annual meeting of American Political Science Association, Washington, D.C., 1968.

LADD, E. C., JR. "American University Teachers and Opposition to the Vietnam War." *Minerva,* 1970, 542–556.

LADD, E. C., JR. and LIPSET, S. M. "American Social Scientists and the Growth of Campus Political Activism in the 1960's." *Social Science Information,* 1971, *10*(2), 105–120.

LADD, E. C., JR., and LIPSET, S. M. "Politics of Academic Natural Scientists and Engineers." *Science,* June 9, 1972, 1091–1099.

LANGER, E. "Crisis at Berkeley." *Science,* April 9, 1965, 198–202.

LANGER, E. "Human Experimentation: New York Verdict Affirms Patient's Rights." *Science,* Feb. 11, 1966, 663–666.

LAZARSFELD, P. F., and THIELENS, W., JR. *The Academic Mind.* Glencoe, Ill.: Free Press, 1958.

LAZARSFELD, P. F., and others (Eds.) *The Uses of Sociology.* New York: Basic Books, 1967.

LECUYER, B-P. (Rapporteur) *The Role of the Social Sciences in Setting National Goals.* Copenhagen: UNESCO Round Table on Social Research Policy and Organization, 1969. Mimeographed.

LEVINE, R. A. "Evaluation of Office of Economic Opportunity Programs—A Progress Report." *American Statistical Association, Proceedings of the Social Statistics Section 1966,* 342–351.

LIPPMANN, W. *Public Opinion.* New York: Penguin Books, 1946 (first published in 1922).

LIPPMANN, W. *Conversations with Walter Lippmann.* Boston: Little, Brown, 1965.

LIPSFT, S. M. "American Intellectuals: Their Politics and Status." *Daedalus,* Summer 1959, 460–486.

LIPSET, S. M., and DOBSON, R. B. "The Intellectual as Critic and Rebel." *Daedalus,* Summer 1972, 137–198.

LIPSET, S. M., and LADD, E. C., JR. "The Politics of American Sociologists." *American Journal of Sociology,* July 1972, 67–104.

LOVEJOY, A. "Academic Freedom." In *Encyclopedia of the Social Sciences.* Vol. 1. New York: Macmillan, 1930.

LYONS, G. M. *The Uneasy Partnership, Social Science and the Federal Government in the Twentieth Century.* New York: Russell Sage, 1969.

MC CLINTOCK, C. G., and others. Political Orientations of Academically Affiliated Psychologists." *American Psychologist,* March 1965, 211–221.

MAC EWAN, A. "Statement." *American Economic Review,* May 1970, 488–489.

MACHIAVELLI, N. *The Prince.* Translated by W. A. Marriott. London: Everyman's Library, 1938.

MACKIE, R., and CHRISTENSEN, P. *Translation and Application of Psychological Research.* Goleta, Calif.: Human Factors Research, 1967.

MANN, J. "Evaluating Educational Programs." *Urban Review,* Feb. 1969, 12–13.

MARRIS, P., and REIN, M. *Dilemmas of Social Reform.* New York: Atherton, 1967.

MEAD, M. (Chairman) "Report of the Committee on Ethics." *Human Organization,* Spring 1949.

MEAD, M. (Chairman) *Report of the Ad Hoc Committee to Evaluate the Controvery Concerning Anthropological Activities in Relation to Thailand to the Executive Board of the American Anthropological Association.* Washington, D.C., Sept. 27, 1971.

MILLETT, J. D. (Chairman) "Political Science as a Discipline," Committee on Standards of Instruction. *American Political Science Review,* June 1962, 417–421.

MONDALE, W. *Full Opportunity and Social Accounting Act.* Hearings, Subcommittee on Government Research, Committee on Government Operations, U.S. Senate, 90th Congress, 1st Sess., on S. 843, 1967, Parts 1–3, 1968.

MONSEN, R. J., JR., and CANNON, M. W. *The Makers of Public Policy.* New York: McGraw-Hill, 1965.

MOORE, W. E. "Letter." *American Sociologist,* Nov. 1965, 4.

MOORE, W. E. "Letter." *American Sociologist,* Nov. 1967, 221.

MORGENSTERN, O. *On the Accuracy of Economic Observations.* Second edition. Princeton, N.J.: Princeton University Press, 1963.

MORIARTY, J. "Proposed Ethical Guidelines Spark Diverse Reactions by Psychologists." *APA Monitor,* April 1972, 1, 9.

MORRIS, N. "Prisons in Evolution." *Federal Probation,* Dec. 1965, 20–32.

MOSAK, J. L. "Discussion." *American Economic Review,* May 1966, 556–558.

MOYNIHAN, D. P. "What is 'Community Action'?" *The Public Interest,* Fall 1966a, 3–8.

MOYNIHAN, D. P. "The Crisis of Confidence." Statement presented to the Subcommittee on Executive Reorganization of the Senate Committee on Government Operations, Dec. 13, 1966b. (Reproduced in Reuss, II, 575–583).

MOYNIHAN, D. P. *Maximum Feasible Misunderstanding.* New York: Free Press, 1969a.

MOYNIHAN, D. P. "Toward a National Urban Policy." *The Public Interest,* Fall 1969b, 3–20.

MYRDAL, G. *An American Dilemma.* New York: Harper, 1944.

MYRDAL, G. *Objectivity in Social Research.* New York: Pantheon, 1969.

National Academy of Sciences. *Basic Research and National Goals.* Committee on Science and Astronautics, U.S. House of Representatives, 1965.

National Academy of Sciences. *Doctorate Recipients from United States Universities 1958–1966.* Washington, D.C., 1967.

National Academy of Sciences. *Careers of Ph.D's, Academic Versus Nonacademic.* Washington, D.C., 1968.

National Planning Association. *Program Planning for National Goals.* Washington, D.C., 1968.

National Science Foundation. *Federal Funds for Research, Development, and Other Scientific Activities.* Vol. XVI, Washington, D.C., 1967.

National Science Foundation. *Reviews of Data on Science Resources,* April 1968a, No. 14.

National Science Foundation. *Federal Funds for Research, Development, and Other Scientific Activities.* Vol. XVII. Washington, D.C., 1968b.

National Science Foundation. *American Science Manpower 1968.* Washington, D.C., 1969.

National Science Foundation. *National Patterns of R&D Resources, 1953–1971.* Washington, D.C., 1970.

National Science Foundation. *American Science Manpower 1970.* Washington, D.C., 1971.

NELSON, B. "Philip Handler: National Academy of Sciences Nominates a Worldly 'High Priest.' " *Science,* Nov. 29, 1968, 981–984.

NICOLAUS, M. "Remarks at ASA Convention." *American Sociologist,* May 1969, 154–156.

NOURSE, E. G. "Discussion on Council of Economic Advisers." *American Economic Review,* May 1950, 180–190.

NOURSE, E. G. *Economics in the Public Service.* New York: Harcourt, Brace, 1953.

NOURSE, E. G. "The Employment Act and the 'New Economics.' " *Virginia Quarterly Review,* Autumn 1969, 595–612.

ODEGARD, P. H. *Political Power and Social Change.* New Brunswick, N.J.: Rutgers University Press, 1966.

Office of Education, U.S. *Educational Research and Development in the United States.* Washington, D.C., 1969.

Office of Science and Technology, U.S. *Privacy and Behavioral Research.* Washington, D.C., 1967.

OGG, F. A. "The American Political Science Review." *American Political Science Review,* Supplement, Feb. 1930, 187–197.

Organisation for Economic Co-operation and Development (OECD). *The Social Sciences and the Policies of Governments.* Paris, 1966.

Organisation for Economic Co-operation and Development. *Reviews of National Policies for Education. United States.* Paris, 1971.

ORLANS, H. "The Uses of Sociology" (review). *American Sociological Review,* Aug. 1968a, 625–630.

ORLANS, H. "Making Social Research More Useful to Government." *Social Science Information,* Dec. 1968b, 151–158.

ORLANS, H. *The Nonprofit Research Institute.* New York: McGraw-Hills, 1972.

ORLANS, H. "D&R Allocations in the United States." *Science Studies,* in press.

PARSONS, T. "Comment." *Daedalus,* Summer 1959, 493–495.

PARSONS, T. "The Editor's Column." *American Sociologist,* Feb. 1966, 68–70.

PIFER, A. "The Nongovernmental Organization at Bay." *Annual Report.* New York: Carnegie Corporation, 1966.

PIFER, A. "The Quasi Nongovernmental Organization." *Annual Report.* New York: Carnegie Corporation, 1967.

Policy and Planning Board, American Psychological Association. "Structure and Function of APA: Guidelines for the Future." *American Psychologist,* Jan. 1972, 1–10.

"President Establishes Social Research Staff," *The Washington Report,* Aug.-Sept. 1969, p. A4.

RAYMONT, H. "Anthropologists to Clarify Ethics." *New York Times,* Nov. 21, 1966, p. 11.

"Results of ASA Ballot on American Government Policy in Vietnam." *American Sociologist,* May 1968, 164.

REUSS, H. S. (Chairman) *The Use of Social Research in Federal Domestic Programs. Part I—Federally Financed Social Research —Expenditures, Status, and Objectives. Part II—The Adequacy and Usefulness of Federally Financed Research on Major National Social Problems. Part III—The Relations of Private Social Scientists to Federal Programs on National Social Problems. Part IV—Current Issues in the Administration of Federal Social Research.* A staff study for the Research and Technical Programs Subcommittee of the Committee on Government Operations. Washington, D.C., 1967.

RIVLIN, A. M. *Systematic Thinking for Social Action.* Washington, D.C.: Brookings Institution, 1971.

ROSENFELD, E. "Social Research and Social Action in Prevention of Juvenile Deliquency." In A. Gouldner and S. M. Miller, (Eds.), *Applied Sociology.* New York: Free Press, 1965.

ROSE, A. "Letter." *American Sociologist,* 1965, 29.

ROSENTHAL, R. *Experimenter Effects in Behavioral Research.* New York: Appleton-Century-Crofts, 1966.

ROSSANT, M. J. "Ethics in the Age of the Economist." *Business Economics,* Fall 1967, 20–21.

ROSSI, P. H. "Boobytraps and Pitfalls in the Evaluation of Social Action Programs." *American Statistical Association, Proceedings of the Social Statistical Section 1966,* 127–332.

ROSSI, P. H. "Minutes." *American Sociologist,* Feb. 1970, 57–71.

ROSSI, P. H. "Minutes." *American Sociologist,* Feb. 1971, 63–76.

ROUSE, I. "Education of a President." *Newsletter of the American Anthropological Association,* Jan. 1969, 6–10.

RUDERMAN, F. A. "Sociological Research and the Field of Social Work." New York, 1968. Multilithed.

SACKREY, C. M., JR. "Economics and Black Poverty." *Review of Black Political Economy,* Winter/Spring 1971, 47–64.

SAMUELSON, P. A. "Economists and the History of Ideas." *American Economic Review,* March 1962, 1–18.

SAULNIER, R. "An appraisal of Federal Fiscal Policies: 1961–1967." *Annals of the American Academy of Political and Social Science,* Sept. 1968, 63–71.

SAYRE, W. "Scientists and American Science Policy." *Science,* March 24, 1961, 359–364.

SCHEFF, T. "For an Academic Lobby." *American Sociologist,* August 1968, 249–250.

SCHLESINGER, A. M., JR. "Comment." *Daedalus,* Summer 1959, 487–488.

SCHLESINGER, A. M., JR. *A Thousand Days.* Boston: Houghton Mifflin, 1965.

SCHON, D. A. "Maintaining an Adaptive National Government." In H. S. Perloff (Ed.), *The Future of the U.S. Government.* New York: Braziller, 1971.

SCHULER, E. A. "Letter." *American Sociologist,* August 1967, 162–163.

SCHULTZ, S. D. "Inadequate Support Seen for Professional Psych." *APA Monitor,* August 1972, 2.

SCHULTZE, C. L. *"The Politics and Economics of Public Spending."* Washington, D.C.: Brookings Institution, 1968.

SCULLY, M. "Faculty Members, Liberal on Politics, Found Conservative on Academic Issues." *Chronicle of Higher Education,* April 6, 1970, 1, 4–5.

SHERWIN, C. W. "The Coupling of the Scientific and Engineering Communities to Public Goals." Address at University of Illinois, Oct. 13, 1967.

SHILS, E. A. "Social Science and Social Policy." *Philosophy of Science,* July 1949, 219–242.

SILK, L. S. *The Business Economist and the Academic Economist.* Paper given at 39th annual conference of Southern Economic Association. St. Louis, Nov. 13, 1969.

SILK, L. S. "Economists Developing Trend Toward Modesty." *New York Times,* March 9, 1970, p. 53.

SILVERMAN, C. *The President's Economic Advisers.* University, Ala.: University of Alabama Press, 1959.

SILVERT, K. H. "American Academic Ethics and Social Research Abroad." In I. L. Horowitz (Ed.), *The Rise and Fall of Project Camelot.* Cambridge, Mass.: MIT Press, 1967.

SMITH, B. L. R. *The RAND Corporation.* Cambridge, Mass.: Harvard University Press, 1966.

Society for Applied Anthropology. "Statement on Ethics." *Human Organization,* Winter 1963–1964, 237.

SOMERS, R. H. The Mainsprings of the Rebellion: A Survey of Berkeley Students in November 1964. In S. M. Lipset and S. S.

Wolin (Eds.), *The Berkeley Student Revolt.* New York: Anchor, 1965.

SOMIT, A., and TANENHAUS, J. *American Political Science, A Profile of a Discipline.* New York: Atherton, 1964.

SOROKIN, P. A. "Report of the President." *American Sociologist,* Nov. 1965, 34.

SPAULDING, C. B., and TURNER, H. A. Political Orientation and Field of Specialization among College Professors. *Sociology of Education,* Summer 1968, 245–262.

SPENCER, H. *The Study of Sociology.* New York: Appleton, 1896.

SPENGLER, J. J. "Social Science and the Collectivization of *Hubris.*" *Political Science Quarterly,* March 1972, 1–21.

"Statement of Concern of the ASA Council: Involvement of ASA in Issues of Public Policy. *American Sociologist,* Aug. 1969, 261–262.

STEWART, A. C. (Chairman) "Report of Committee on Publications Policy." Submitted and approved by the board of trustees March 29, 1968. New York: Center for Urban Education, 1968.

SUCHMAN, E. A. *Evaluative Research.* New York: Russell Sage, 1967a.

SUCHMAN, E. A. "Public Health." In P. F. Lazarsfeld and others (Eds.), *The Uses of Sociology.* New York: Basic Books, 1967b.

TERBORGH, G. "Ethics of Advocacy." *Business Economics,* Fall 1967, 18–19.

TOLCHIN, M. "City Paid $75 million in 1969 in Fees to Private Consultants." *New York Times,* July 1, 1970, 41.

TURNER, H. A., and HETRICK, C. C. "Political Activities and Party Affiliations of American Political Scientists." *Western Political Quarterly,* Sept. 1972, 361–374.

TURNER, H. A., and others. "Political Orientations of Academically Affiliated Sociologists." *Sociology and Social Research,* 1963a, 273–289.

TURNER, H. A., and others. "The Political Party Affiliation of American Political Scientists. *Western Political Quarterly,* Sept. 1963b, 650–665.

VAUGHAN, T. R. "Governmental Intervention in Social Research." In G. Sjoberg (Ed.), *Ethics, Politics, and Social Research.* Cambridge, Mass.: Schenkman, 1967.

VOLKART, E. H. "Report of the Executive Officer." *American Sociologist,* Nov. 1967, 232–234.

WALDO, D. "Comments." In *Research for Public Policy.* Washington, D.C.: Brookings Institution, 1961.

WALSH, J. "Stanford Research Institute: Campus Turmoil Spurs Transition." *Science,* May 23, 1969, 933–936.

WANDT, E., and others. *An Evaluation of Educational Research Published in Journals.* Washington, D.C.: American Educational Research Association, 1967. Multilithed.

WARD, L. F. *Applied Sociology.* New York: Ginn, 1906.

WARNER, W. L. and LUNT, P. S. *The Social Life of a Modern Community.* New Haven: Yale University Press, 1941.

Weekly Compilation of Presidential Documents, July 21, 1969, pp. 982–988.

WEINBERG, A. "The New Estate." *Bulletin of the Atomic Scientists,* Feb. 1964, 16–19.

WILDAVSKY, A. "Rescuing Policy Analysis from PPBS." *Public Administration Review,* March/April 1969, 189–202.

WILENSKY, H. *Organizational Intelligence.* New York: Basic Books, 1967.

WILLIAMS, R. M. "Minutes of the Second 1967 Council Meeting." *American Sociologist,* Nov. 1967, 224–225.

WILSON, L. "A President's Perspective." In F. C. Abbott (Ed.), *Faculty-Administration Relationships.* Washington, D.C.: American Council on Education, 1958.

WOLF, E. R., and JORGENSEN, J. G. "Anthropology on the Warpath in Thailand." *New York Review of Books,* Nov. 19, 1970, 26–35.

WOLFLE, D. "Social Science Research and International Relations." *Science,* Jan. 14, 1966, 155.

WOLFLE, D. "Social Science Research on Foreign Areas." *Science,* Dec. 20, 1968, 1335.

WOOLDRIDGE, D. E. (Chairman) *Biomedical Science and Its Administration.* Washington, D.C.: The White House, 1965.

WRIGHTSTONE, J. W. "Evaluating Educational Programs." *Urban Review,* Feb. 1969, 5–6.

YOUNG, D. (Chairman) *The Behavioral Sciences and the Federal Government.* Advisory Committee on Government Programs in the Behavioral Sciences. Washington, D.C.: National Research Council, National Academy of Sciences, 1968.

YOUNG, W. M., JR. *Remarks Prepared for Delivery at the American Sociological Association.* Boston, August 27, 1968. Xeroxed.

ZIMAN, J. M. *Public Knowledge.* Cambridge, England: Cambridge University Press, 1968.

ZIMMERMAN, F. L. "Attacking the SST." *Wall Street Journal,* Jan. 9, 1967.

Index